W0115077

Lecture Notes in Computer Science

Vol. 1: GI-Gesellschaft für Informatik e.V. 3. Jahrestagung, Hamburg, 8.–10. Oktober 1973. Herausgegeben im Auftrag der Gesellschaft für Informatik von W. Brauer. XI, 508 Seiten. 1973.

Vol. 2: GI-Gesellschaft für Informatik e.V. 1. Fachtagung über Automatentheorie und Formale Sprachen, Bonn, 9.–12. Juli 1973. Herausgegeben im Auftrag der Gesellschaft für Informatik von K.-H. Böhling und K. Indermark. VII, 322 Seiten. 1973.

Vol. 3: 5th Conference on Optimization Techniques, Part I. (Series: I.F.I.P. TC7 Optimization Conferences.) Edited by R. Conti and A. Ruberti. XIII, 565 pages. 1973.

Vol. 4: 5th Conference on Optimization Techniques, Part II. (Series: I.F.I.P. TC7 Optimization Conferences.) Edited by R. Conti and A. Ruberti. XIII, 389 pages. 1973.

Vol. 5: International Symposium on Theoretical Programming. Edited by A. Ershov and V. A. Nepomniaschy. VI, 407 pages. 1974.

Vol. 6: B. T. Smith, J. M. Boyle, J. J. Dongarra, B. S. Garbow, Y. Ikebe, V. C. Klema, and C. B. Moler, Matrix Eigensystem Routines – EISPACK Guide. XI, 551 pages. 2nd Edition 1974. 1976.

Vol. 7: 3. Fachtagung über Programmiersprachen, Kiel, 5.–7. März 1974. Herausgegeben von B. Schlender und W. Frielinghaus. VI, 225 Seiten. 1974.

Vol. 8: GI-NTG Fachtagung über Struktur und Betrieb von Rechensystemen, Braunschweig, 20.–22. März 1974. Herausgegeben im Auftrag der GI und der NTG von H.-O. Leilich. VI, 340 Seiten. 1974.

Vol. 9: GI-BIFOA Internationale Fachtagung: Informationszentren in Wirtschaft und Verwaltung. Köln, 17./18. Sept. 1973. Herausgegeben im Auftrag der GI und dem BIFOA von P. Schmitz. VI, 259 Seiten. 1974.

Vol. 10: Computing Methods in Applied Sciences and Engineering, Part 1. International Symposium, Versailles, December 17–21, 1973. Edited by R. Glowinski and J. L. Lions. X, 497 pages. 1974.

Vol. 11: Computing Methods in Applied Sciences and Engineering, Part 2. International Symposium, Versailles, December 17–21, 1973. Edited by R. Glowinski and J. L. Lions. X, 434 pages. 1974.

Vol. 12: GFK-GI-GMR Fachtagung Prozessrechner 1974. Karlsruhe, 10.–11. Juni 1974. Herausgegeben von G. Krüger und R. Friehmelt. XI, 620 Seiten. 1974.

Vol. 13: Rechnerstrukturen und Betriebsprogrammierung, Erlangen, 1970. (GI-Gesellschaft für Informatik e.V.) Herausgegeben von W. Händler und P. P. Spies. VII, 333 Seiten. 1974.

Vol. 14: Automata, Languages and Programming – 2nd Colloquium, University of Saarbrücken, July 29–August 2, 1974. Edited by J. Loeckx. VIII, 611 pages. 1974.

Vol. 15: L Systems. Edited by A. Salomaa and G. Rozenberg. VI, 338 pages. 1974.

Vol. 16: Operating Systems, International Symposium, Rocquencourt 1974. Edited by E. Gelenbe and C. Kaiser. VIII, 310 pages. 1974.

Vol. 17: Rechner-Gestützter Unterricht RGU '74, Fachtagung, Hamburg, 12.–14. August 1974, ACU-Arbeitskreis Computer-Unterstützter Unterricht. Herausgegeben im Auftrag der GI von K. Brunnstein, K. Haefner und W. Händler. X, 417 Seiten. 1974.

Vol. 18: K. Jensen and N. E. Wirth, PASCAL – User Manual and Report. VII, 170 pages. Corrected Reprint of the 2nd Edition 1976.

Vol. 19: Programming Symposium. Proceedings 1974. V, 425 pages. 1974.

Vol. 20: J. Engelfriet, Simple Program Schemes and Formal Languages. VII, 254 pages. 1974.

Vol. 21: Compiler Construction, An Advanced Course. Edited by F. L. Bauer and J. Eickel. XIV. 621 pages. 1974.

Vol. 22: Formal Aspects of Cognitive Processes. Proceedings 1972. Edited by T. Storer and D. Winter. V, 214 pages. 1975.

Vol. 23: Programming Methodology. 4th Informatik Symposium IBM Germany Wildbad, September 25–27, 1974. Edited by C. E Hackl. VI, 501 pages. 1975.

Vol. 24: Parallel Processing. Proceedings 1974. Edited by T. Fen VI, 433 pages. 1975.

Vol. 25: Category Theory Applied to Computation and Control. Pr ceedings 1974. Edited by E. G. Manes. X, 245 pages. 1975.

Vol. 26: GI-4. Jahrestagung, Berlin, 9.–12. Oktober 1974. Her ausgegeben im Auftrag der GI von D. Siefkes. IX, 748 Seiten 1975.

Vol. 27: Optimization Techniques. IFIP Technical Conference Novosibirsk, July 1–7, 1974. (Series: I.F.I.P. TC7 Optimizatio Conferences.) Edited by G. I. Marchuk. VIII, 507 pages. 1975

Vol. 28: Mathematical Foundations of Computer Science. 3r Symposium at Jadwisin near Warsaw, June 17–22, 1974. Edite by A. Blikle. VII, 484 pages. 1975.

Vol. 29: Interval Mathematics. Procedings 1975. Edited by K. Nick VI, 331 pages. 1975.

Vol. 30: Software Engineering. An Advanced Course. Edited b F. L. Bauer. (Formerly published 1973 as Lecture Notes in Eco nomics and Mathematical Systems, Vol. 81) XII, 545 pages. 1975

Vol. 31: S. H. Fuller, Analysis of Drum and Disk Storage Units. I 283 pages. 1975.

Vol. 32: Mathematical Foundations of Computer Science 1975 Proceedings 1975. Edited by J. Bečvář. X, 476 pages. 1975.

Vol. 33: Automata Theory and Formal Languages, Kaiserslauter May 20–23, 1975. Edited by H. Brakhage on behalf of GI. V 292 Seiten. 1975.

Vol. 34: GI – 5. Jahrestagung, Dortmund 8.–10. Oktober 1975 Herausgegeben im Auftrag der GI von J. Mühlbacher. X, 755 Seite 1975.

Vol. 35: W. Everling, Exercises in Computer Systems Analysi (Formerly published 1972 as Lecture Notes in Economics an Mathematical Systems, Vol. 65) VIII, 184 pages. 1975.

Vol. 36: S. A. Greibach, Theory of Program Structures: Scheme Semantics, Verification. XV, 364 pages. 1975.

Vol. 37: C. Böhm, λ-Calculus and Computer Science Theory. Pr ceedings 1975. XII, 370 pages. 1975.

Vol. 38: P. Branquart, J.-P. Cardinael, J. Lewi, J.-P. Delescaill M. Vanbegin. An Optimized Translation Process and Its Applicatic to ALGOL 68. IX, 334 pages. 1976.

Vol. 39: Data Base Systems. Proceedings 1975. Edited by H. Hasse meier and W. Spruth. VI, 386 pages. 1976.

Vol. 40: Optimization Techniques. Modeling and Optimization in t Service of Man. Part 1. Proceedings 1975. Edited by J. Cea. X 854 pages. 1976.

Vol. 41: Optimization Techniques. Modeling and Optimization in th Service of Man. Part 2. Proceedings 1975. Edited by J. Cea. XI 852 pages. 1976.

Vol. 42: James E. Donahue, Complementary Definitions of Pr gramming Language Semantics. VII, 172 pages. 1976.

Vol. 43: E. Specker und V. Strassen, Komplexität von Entscheidung problemen. Ein Seminar. V, 217 Seiten. 1976.

Vol. 44: ECI Conference 1976. Proceedings 1976. Edited by Samelson. VIII, 322 pages. 1976.

Vol. 45: Mathematical Foundations of Computer Science 197 Proceedings 1976. Edited by A. Mazurkiewicz. XI, 601 pages. 197

Vol. 46: Language Hierarchies and Interfaces. Edited by F. L. Baue and K. Samelson. X, 428 pages. 1976.

Vol. 47: Methods of Algorithmic Language Implementation. Edite by A. Ershov and C. H. A. Koster. VIII, 351 pages. 1977.

Vol. 48: Theoretical Computer Science, Darmstadt, March 197 Edited by H. Tzschach, H. Waldschmidt and H. K.-G. Walter o behalf of GI. VIII, 418 pages. 1977.

Lecture Notes in Computer Science

Edited by G. Goos and J. Hartmanis

63

Natural Language Communication with Computers

Edited by Leonard Bolc

Springer-Verlag Berlin Heidelberg GmbH 1978

Editor
Leonard Bolc
Institute of Informatics
Warsaw University
PKiN, pok. 850
00-901 Warszawa/Poland

Library of Congress Cataloging in Publication Data
Main entry under title:

Natural language communication with computers.

(Lecture notes in computer science ; 63)
Bibliography: p.
Includes index.
1. Interactive computer systems--Addresses, essays, lectures. 2. Question-answering systems--Addresses, essays, lectures. 3. Language data processing--Addresses, essays, lectures. I. Bolc, Leonard, 1934- II. Series.
QA76.9.I58N37 001.6'4 78-15393

AMS Subject Classifications (1970): 68-02, 68A30, 68A45
CR Subject Classifications (1974):

Additional material to this book can be downloaded from http://extras.springer.com.

ISBN 978-3-540-08911-7 ISBN 978-3-540-35765-0 (eBook)
DOI 10.1007/978-3-540-35765-0

Originally published by Springer-Verlag Berlin Heidelberg New York in 1978.

2145/3140-543210

PREFACE

In recent years in numerous countries, attempts have been made to develop natural language systems of communication with computers.

This research has been initiated by well-known research institutes sponsored often by government research programs.

This publication should facilitate an exchange of information, concerning the present state of research in this area.

The authors would like to express their thanks to Springer-Verlag for publishing this volume.

Warsaw, May 1978 Leonard Bolc

CONTENTS

A FORMALISM FOR THE DESCRIPTION OF QUESTION ANSWERING SYSTEMS

Camilla Schwind
Technische Universität München

ABSTRACT

The following article presents a formalism for the description of a natural language based intelligent system. The meaning of natural language texts is to be represented by a *state logic*. This is an extension of predicate logic by special operators, which are applied to formulae and make their truth value dependent on the state of the world in which the formula is evaluated. The extension of the non-logical symbols depends also on the state of the world and it may change when a state changes. Natural language texts are described syntactically by a formal grammar, which is an extension of a CHOMSKY-grammar. The alphabet consists of complex symbols and the structure of these symbols is given by special rules. The derivation rules of our grammar are applied to symbols in different way which constitutes an extension of the usual method. The application of a rule is governed by the structure of the symbols and on applying one rule, we can derive a set of sentences. Natural language texts are translated into state logic formulae by special functions which are associated with the production rules. These functions depend on the syntactic structure of the sentences and on the world in which the sentences are evaluated. We will give a detailed example for the application of the whole formalism.

INTRODUCTION

Since the early 60's intelligent systems have been developed which are capable of understanding natural language sentences, of answering questions according to their knowledge bases, or of carrying out commands. Most of these systems have been designed in regard to their special problem areas which are very different from each other (eg. [1], [2], [3], [4], [5], [6]). But all such systems are confronted with the same main problems:

(1) The representation of the knowledge which is formulated in a system and which is manipulated by the natural language sentences.
(2) The handling of the natural language input sentences, that is, the

syntactic analysis of texts and the translation of them into a semantic representation.

We intend to propose a formalism that describes these two problem areas in a very general manner so that existing natural language based intelligent systems fit into this formalism. The heart of the knowledge representation system is a state logic containing special operators for immediately following and preceding states (+,-) as well as for all future states (F) and all past states (P). Similar systems have also been mentioned in [7]. But the crucial point is: In usual tense logic systems, the structure of tense has been studied only as to its "pure logical" properties; we could only prove theorems like "If p is true from today on then it will be true from tomorrow on" ($Fp \rightarrow +Fp$). In intelligent systems however, we need theorems about the nonlogical properties of state changes. The tense structure of a world is determined by changes within the world which affect the nonlogical symbols of the world, i.e. the functions or predicates: If a robot takes a block *a* lying on a block *b*, then this causes a change of the world (i.e. a state transition) with the meaning of the predicate symbol ON changing. If a flower grows, this causes a change of the world, with the meaning of the function symbol SIZE changing. If we incorporate such nonlogical change descriptions into a formal system, we will be able to prove theorems like: "If only *a* lies on the table and John takes it, then the table will be empty at the following instant".

Taking into account these considerations, a model for the formal system can be given by a set of classical structures M and a binary relation R_0 on M, with $(\alpha,\beta) \in R_0$ iff there are objects in α which can be subject to some change and the resulting structure is β. Such Kripke-type semantics has been used for the semantic characterization of modal logic ([8],[9]). Truth values are assigned to formulae depending on the state of the world in which the formula is evaluated. And the state operators take into account the truth value of a formula in some other states which can be "reached" from the actual state.

Let us consider as an example a world consisting of three blocks *a*,*b*, c and two hands h and h' (Figure 1). The possible changes, i.e. the possible actions which can be executed next, are that h takes *b* or h' takes *b*. After that the hand can put *b* on the floor or can put it back on *a*. So the model turns out to be a general state transition network that contains all "possible" changes of the world or we may also say contains descriptions of all actions which can be executed by some of the objects of the world.

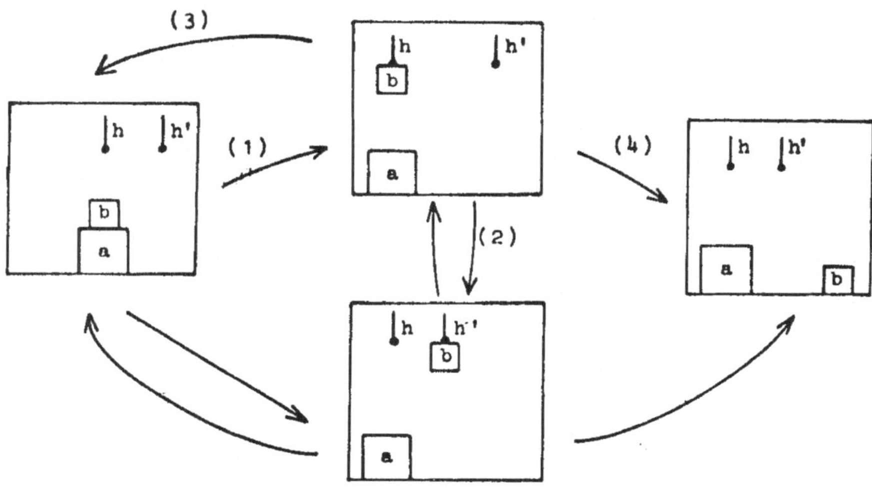

(1) h takes b . (2) h gives b to h' . (3) h puts b on a . (4) h puts b on the floor.

Figure 1

The language of the state logic is formalized by a set of axioms and inference rules for which completeness has been proven.

Natural language texts are analysed syntactically by a formal grammar which is an extension of a CHOMSKY-grammar. The alphabet consists of symbols which are in their turn composed of pairs (feature, value). The algebraic properties of these structured symbols have been studied in [10]. Their structure is defined by insertion rules which specify what features with what values can be contained in one structured symbol. The set of the structured symbols is ordered by inclusion and this ordering gives rise to a modified definition of derivability. If $(P_1 \dots P_m, Q_1 \dots Q_n)$ is a production rule, we can replace each occurrence of $P'_1 \dots P'_m$ within a string by $Q'_1 \dots Q'_n$ provided $P_i \subseteq P'_i$ and $Q_j \subseteq Q'_j$ for $1 \leq i \leq m$ and $1 \leq j \leq n$. Structured symbols are used in a formal grammar describing natural language sentences in the following way: There is one "starting feature", cat, the value set of which are the categories usually appearing in natural language grammars: NP (noun phrase), VP (verb phrase), N (noun), DET (determiner), etc. Further features characterize properties according to which categories are subclassified; e.g. v is a feature whose values are it (intransitive), t (transitive), p (prepositional) and these values subclassify verbs; t is a feature with the properties perf (perfect), pres (present) and fut (future) and specifies the time of a verb. Semantic features are incorporated into the grammar in the same formal way; e.g. "animate" is a semantic feature whose values are + and - belonging to nouns. It is clear that not just any features can be combined together and that values of cat cannot appear indiscriminately in a structured symbol with any feature. The insertion rules determine the possible combinations.

The natural language sentences are transduced into state logic formulae. This translation is performed by functions which are associated with the production rules. This concept of assigning a semantic representation to sentences depending on their syntactic structure has been introduced by Knuth [11] and Koster [12] for the semantic description of programming languages. So we propose an attributed feature grammar for the syntactic description of natural language sentences and the transduction of sentences into state logic formulae.

We pursued two aims with this proposal:

(1) Natural language syntax should be described by a context free language without transformation rules introduced in [13]. Transformation rules are a very cumbersome means of analysing sentences. The real motivation for introducing them has been to associate the same "deep" structure to sentences which have the same meaning but a different "surface" structure. And this has been claimed because one would get the same semantic representation for sentences which had the same meaning but were syntactically different. In our system the semantic representation of a sentence is generated with the help of applications. We have no "surface" and "deep" structure and different sentences have different syntactic structures; but the system generates logically equivalent formulae for them.

(2) The use of structured symbols as alphabetic elements allows us to formulate production rules which are rule classes. Derivability is defined in such a way that production rules can be formulated incompletely, that is to say not all features of an alphabetic element have to be specified in all production rules. The "missing"

features can be calculated by application of an insertion rule, which adds features to alphabetic symbols according to the features belonging already to that symbol. It is possible to add such features during sentence analysis when they are needed for the analysis and it is possible to neglect them when they are not needed. This is advantageous in natural language analysis, because there are many features of categories or words which are sometimes redundant in sentence analysis and sometimes are not. See for example the sentence "The woman is sitting in the café". The feature value + for the feature "animate" of the noun "woman" is not needed for the analysis of this sentence.

THE FORMAL SYSTEM Z FOR THE REPRESENTATION OF THE MEANING OF NATURAL LANGUAGE SENTENCES

The language of Z, L, is an extension of classical predicate logic. It has its predessessors in modal logic [8] and in tense logic [7]. We have however avoided the concept of tense logic here, the proposed system being neither antisymmetric nor linear.

L consists of the following symbols:
Individual variables $x, y, z, \ldots x_1, \ldots y_1, \ldots z_1, \ldots$; s_i-place function symbols F_i, where $s_i \in \omega$; r_j-place predicate symbols R_j, where $r_j \in \omega$; $\wedge, \neg, \vee, +, -, F, P$. Terms and formulae are formed in the usual way and if A is a formula, then $+A$, $-A$, FA, PA is. We now want to select a certain subset of the set of all formulae to be the set of *valid* formulae. In classical predicate logic, this is done by introducing the concept of a structure which consists of a set of objects and functions and relations between the objects. For our extension of predicate logic we use a set of classical structures, together with a binary relation that reflects the meaning of the state operators. Truth values are assigned to formulae depending on the given structure and the actual state of the structure.

A structure for Z is given by the pair $\mathcal{A} = \langle \{A_\alpha : \alpha \in M\}, R_0 \rangle$ where

(1) $M \neq \phi$ is called the set of states of $\mathcal{A}$.
(2) $R_0 \subseteq M \times M$ is a binary relation on M.
(3) For every $\alpha \in M$ $A_\alpha = \langle OB, (f_i^\alpha)_{i \in I}, (p_j^\alpha)_{j \in J} \rangle$ is a classical structure:
(3.1) $OB \neq \phi$ is the set of the objects of the system.
(3.2) $f_i^\alpha : OB^{s_i} \to OB$ is a partial mapping which assigns s_i-tuples of elements of OB to elements of OB for $s_i \in \omega$.
(3.3) $p_j^\alpha \subseteq A^{r_j}$, $r_j \in \omega$ is a r_j-place relation on OB.

The transitive, reflexive closure of R_0 is denoted by R.

We consider $\mathcal{A}$ as a mapping assigning an element of OB to every term of L and a truth value to every variable-free formula of L and every state $\alpha \in M$.
Let t be a term and $\alpha \in M$:
(1) If t is the name of an object a of OB, then $\mathcal{A}(\alpha, t) = a$
(2) If t is not a name, then $t = F_i\, t_0 \ldots t_{s_i-1}$, since t is

variablefree for some s_i-place function symbol F_i. Then
$A(\alpha, F_i t_o \dots t_{s_i-1}) = f_i^{(\alpha)}(A(\alpha,t_o),\dots A(\alpha,t_{p_i-1}))$

Let now be A a closed formula of L:

(3) If $A \equiv [t_1 = t_2]$, then
$A(\alpha,A) = T$ iff $A(\alpha,t_1) = A(\alpha,t_2)$

(4) If $A \equiv p_j t_o \dots t_{r_j-1}$, then
$A(\alpha,A) = T$ iff $(A(\alpha,t_o), \dots, A(\alpha,t_{r_j-1})) \in p_j^{(\alpha)}$

(5) If $A \equiv \neg B$, then
$A(\alpha,A) = T$ iff $A(\alpha,B) = F$

(6) If $A = B \wedge C$, then
$A(\alpha,A) = T$ iff $A(\alpha,B) = A(\alpha,C) = T$

(7) If $A = \forall x B$, then
$A(\alpha,A) = T$ iff $A(\alpha,B_x[c]) = T$ for all $c \in OB$.

(8) $A(\alpha,+A) = t$ iff for all β such that $\alpha\ R_o\ \beta$
$A(\beta,A) = T$

(9) $A(\alpha,-A) = t$ iff for all β such that $\beta\ R_o\ \alpha$
$A(\beta,A) = T$

(10) $A(\alpha,FA) = t$ iff for all β such that $\alpha\ R\ \beta$
$A(\beta,A) = T$

(11) $A(\alpha,PA) = t$ iff for all β such that $\beta\ R\ \alpha$
$A(\beta,A) = T$.

A formula A is *valid in a state* α *of a structure* A iff $A(\alpha,A) = T$ and a formula A is *valid in a structure* A iff $A(\alpha,A) = T$ for all $\alpha \in M$.
A formula A is *valid* iff it is valid in every structure A.

We have given a set of logical axioms and inference rules for which completeness has been proven.

The existence of functions and predicates within each A_α for the appropriate symbols of $L(S)$ allows us to describe nonlogical changes within the world in a very general way. For an example, think of a child piling up sand. This "action" causes a change of the world in that the size of the pile will increase. If we choose the unary function symbol SIZE to mean the size of an object we can formalize this in the following way: Let c be the name of the child, h be the name of the pile, its size at state α being 5 and at state β being 10 :

$$SIZE^{\alpha}(h) = 5; \quad SIZE^{\beta}(h) = 10 ; \quad \alpha \, R_o \, \beta$$

and we can verify the formula

$$SIZE(h) = 5 \ \wedge \ PILE(c,h) \ \wedge \ \neg + \neg \, SIZE(h) = 10 \, .$$

A FORMAL LANGUAGE FOR THE SYNTACTIC ANALYSIS OF NATURAL LANGUAGE TEXTS

Texts are analysed syntactically with the help of a formal grammar, which is an extension of a CHOMSKY-grammar. The alphabet consists of finite sets, which are generated by "insertion rules". The insertion rules are applied to "start symbols". These start symbols correspond to the alphabetic elements which one founds usually in phrase structure grammars for natural languages: S (sentence), NP (noun phrase), VP (verbal phrase), N (noun), V (verb), etc. Insertion rules subclassify the categories in such a way that for every category there is a set of alphabetic elements. E.g.: for NP we get:
[NP,(e,+)],[NP,(e,-)] (noun phrase with embedding "the child who is playing the piano" and without embedding "the green ball"),
[NP,(c,+)],[NP,(c,-)] (composed noun phrase "the teacher and all his pupils" and not composed "my father"); for V we get: [V,(vk,trans)], [V,(vk,itrans)] (transitive and intransitive verb), [V,(t,perf)] (verb in perfect form), [V,part f] (verb in participle form).
Our grammar has rule classes instead of rules according to the structure of the alphabetic elements. Our grammar is a special van Wijnjaarden grammar [14].

Structured symbols

The following definitions are from [10]:

Definition 1
Let M be a finite set, $(B_m)_{m \in M}$ a family of finite sets, where $B_m \neq \emptyset$. Then every partial mapping $a\colon M \to \cup\{B_m | m \in M\}$ where $a(m) \in B_m$ is called a *structured symbol* over M. The elements of M are called *features*, the domain of a is called *feature set of* a and is noted $d(a)$; the elements of B_m are called *values of* m and $a(m)$ *value of* m *in* a.

Let C be the set of all structured symbols over M. The following relations are defined over C:

$$a \subseteq b \leftrightarrow d(a) \subseteq d(b) \text{ and } \forall m \in d(a)\quad a(m) \subseteq b(m)$$

$$a \tau b \leftrightarrow \forall m \in d(a) \wedge d(b)\quad a(m) = b(m)$$

If $a \tau b$, the a and b are also called *compatible*.

$a \rho b \leftrightarrow d(a) = d(b)$

ρ is an equivalence relation. Equivalence classes for $S \subseteq M$ are denoted by $<S>$. We write also $<m>$ instead of $<\{m\}>$.
The greatest lower bound belonging to $\subseteq$ is denoted by $\sqcap$, the least upper bound by $\sqcup$, the latter being defined only for compatible a and b.
Notation: A structured symbol a with the domain $\{m_1,\ldots m_k\}$ and values $\{\alpha_1,\ldots,\alpha_k\}$, such that $a(m_i) = \alpha_i$ is written $[\alpha_1 m_1,\ldots,\alpha_k m_k]$. The unusual notation is used in phonology where structured symbols characterize phonemes.

We use structured symbols in our formal grammar for natural languages in the following way:

(1) There is one feature, cat (category), that plays a special part and whose values are the categories usually needed in a natural language grammar: S (sentence), NP (noun phrase), VP (verbal phrase) etc.
(2) There are further features whose values stand for properties according to which these categories are subclassified. The features turn out to be ordering principles according to which a category can be subclassified. E.g. the feature p subclassifies verbs and its possible values are numbers 1, 2, 3 which stand for the number of complements to the verb.
(3) Semantic criteria are also characterized by features and these "semantic" features are not distinguished from "syntactical" features.

Insertion rules

The features are ordering principles for the grammatical categories. Therefore they always refer to certain categories and the alphabet of the grammar is a strict subset of the set of all structured symbols. [N cat, itrans v] for example is not a meaningful alphabetic element because nouns are not subclassified according to transitiveness.

Definition 2

An *insertion rule* for C is a pair $p = (a,A)$, where $a \in C$ and $A \subseteq <S>$ for $S \subseteq M$ and $d(a) \cap S = \emptyset$.
p is called *applicable* to $x \in C$ iff
(A1) $a \subseteq x$ and

(A2) $d(x) \cap S = \emptyset$

Let $R \subseteq C \times \{A | A \subseteq \langle S \rangle, S \subseteq M\}$ a set of insertion rules. Let $u, v \in C$.

Then $u \; imp_o \; v$ iff $\exists p \in R$, $p = (a,A)$ and p is applicable to u and $\exists b \notin A$: $v = u \sqcup b$. As a result of (A2) u is compatible with b and the least upper bound is defined. We write also $u \; imp_o \; v$. The reflexive, transitive closure of imp_o is denoted by imp.^{p} We write also $u \; {}_{p_1 \ldots p_n}imp \; v$ if $u \; imp_{p_1 o} \; u_1 \ldots imp_{p_n o} v$.

Insertion rules generate subsets of C in an analogous way as production rules generate languages.

If R is a set of insertion rules and $a \in C$, then we denote the set of structured symbols generated from a by R by

$$L(R,a) = \{x \in C \mid a \; {}_{p_1 \ldots p_n}imp \; x \; ; p_i \in R\}$$

and we set

$$_T L(R,a) = L(R,a) \cap \{x \in C \mid \neg \exists y \in C : x \; imp_o \; y\} .$$

Insertion rules for structured symbols are applied to symbols of the form [X cat], which figure as "start symbols" for the alphabetic elements and $_T L$ (R, [X cat]) is the set of alphabetic elements belonging to the category X .

Feature grammars

Feature grammars are defined in the same way as CHOMSKY-grammars, but the derivability concept is modified according to the alphabet structure. The alphabet of a feature grammar is to be the set of all structured symbols which can be derived from a set of feature values of the feature cat of a set of features M by some given insertion rules R. Now it is often the case that production rules are independent of the subclassification of the alphabetic elements and that they should be applied to all subclassifications. Let us consider for an example the rule [NP cat] → [DET cat, indef d][NG cat] replacing "noun phrase" by "indefinite article" "noun group". The rule which replaces "noun phrase" by "definite article" "noun group" has the same structure. For that reason we intend to write a rule [NP cat] → [DET cat][NG cat] generating all chains [DET cat,...][NG cat,...], that is to say all chains having the same length as the chains occurring within the rule and containing the chains elementwise. The feature grammars defined here provide us with this possibility.

Definition 3

A feature grammar is a tupel

$G = (M, (B_m)_{m \in M}, R, cat, S, \Sigma, \Pi)$, where

$M \neq \emptyset$ finite set of features

$(B_m)_{m \in M}$ family of finite value sets for the features

R set of insertion rules for the set C of structured symbols over M

$cat \in M$ starting feature

$S \in B_{cat}$ starting value of cat

$\Sigma \subseteq B_{cat}$ set of terminal values of cat

$\Pi \subseteq C^+ \times C^*$ †) set of production rules, where for every $a \in C$ occurring within a production $p \in \Pi$: $cat \in d(a)$: Let $p = (X_1 \ldots X_n, Y_1 \ldots Y_m) \in \Pi$, then $cat \in d(X_i)$ and $cat \in d(Y_j)$ for all i,j : $1 \leq i \leq n$ and $1 \leq j \leq m$.

Let B be a value of cat. Then we set

$C_B = L(R, [B\ cat])$

${}_TC_B = {}_TL(R, [B\ cat])$

$C_{B'} = \cup\{C_B | B \in B'\}$ for $B' \subseteq B_{cat}$

${}_TC_{B'} = \cup\{{}_TC_B | B \in B'\}$

These definitions are extendable over strings over B_{cat}. Let $b = B_1 \ldots B_n \in B_{cat}^*$. Then we set

$C_b = \{a | a = a_1 \ldots a_n;\ a_i \in L_{B_i}\}$

${}_TC_b = \{a | a = a_1 \ldots a_n;\ a_i \in {}_TL_{B_i}\}$

$C_B = \cup\{C_b | b \in B\}$ for $B \subseteq B_{cat}^*$

${}_TC_B = \cup\{{}_TC_b | b \in B\}$ for $B \subseteq B_{cat}^*$

After what we said at the beginning, it is natural that the definition of derivability for feature grammars must be extended in such a way that, given a production rule (p,q), we can apply all production rules (p',q') provided $p \subseteq p'$ and $q \subseteq q'$. We only have to pay attention to the fact that we generate only such q' which are contained in the alphabet specified by the insertion rules.

---

†) C^* is the free word semi-group over C and $C^+ = C^* \setminus \{\varepsilon\}$ where ε is the empty string.

<u>Definition 4</u> *Derivability*

Let $x,y \in C^*$. Then y *is derivable from* x in Π, $x \underset{o}{\longrightarrow} y$ iff $x = x'p'x''$ and $y = x'q'x''$ and $\exists(p,q) \in \Pi$ and $\exists p'',q'' \in C_{B_{cat}}^*$ such that $p \subseteq p' \subseteq p''$ and $q \subseteq q' \subseteq q''$.

We write also $x \underset{o\ (p,q)}{\longrightarrow} y$ or $x \underset{o\ \Pi}{\longrightarrow} y$.

As usual $\longrightarrow$ is the transitive, reflexive closure of $\underset{o}{\longrightarrow}$.

The set of sentences derivable by a feature grammar G is $L(G) = \{x | x \in C$ and $[S\ cat] \longrightarrow x\}$ and ${}_TL(G) = L(G) \cap ({}_TC_\Sigma)^*$ is the *language* generated by G.

The set of production rules of a feature grammar G is not limited according to $C_{B_{cat}}$, i.e. there can be productions (p,q), where p (or q) $\not\subseteq x$ for all $x \in C_{B_{cat}}^*$. However, as can easily be seen in the definition of derivability, such production rules can never be applied. So we can eliminate such production rules in Π without changing the set of derivable sentences.

The type of a feature grammar is defined in exactly the same way as the type of a CHOMSKY-language.

C and therefore ${}_TC_{B_{cat}}$ being finite, it is possible to replace every production rule (p,q) of a feature grammar, which is a rule class, by all production rules (p',q') where $p \subseteq p'$ and $q \subseteq q'$, provided p' and q' are contained in elements p'' and q'' of ${}_TC_{B_{cat}}^*$ The CHOMSKY-grammar obtained in this way is equivalent to the appropriate feature grammar.

So we have proved the following theorem.

<u>Theorem</u>

For every feature grammar G of type i there is an equivalent CHOMSKY-grammar of the same type.

<u>Semantic attributes</u>

Every natural language sentence generated by a feature grammar must be translated into a state logic formula. This transduction is a mapping from the set of sentences together with their derivations into the set of state logic formulae. It is calculated by semantic attributes and attribute functions. This formalism has been introduced in [11] for the description of the semantics of programming languages. To every alphabetic element we associate a set of *attributes* and to every attribute a set of values. For every production rule a set of *attribute functions* is given for each attribute belonging to an alphabetic element occuring within the rule. The attribute functions define all of the attribute values of an alphabetic element they belong to in terms of the attributes belonging to other alphabetic elements occuring within the same production rule. So, attribute functions are many-place and have as arguments tupels of attribute values of those attributes belonging to alphabetic elements which occur in the appropriate definition. The values of the attribute functions are again attribute values. So, if we think of a phrase structure tree reflecting the derivational structure of a sentence, attribute functions transport attribute values within the tree from node to node. This is done in two directions, from the root to the leaves and from the leaves to the root. Therefore, two kinds of attributes are used: *derived* which carry values from the leaves to the root and *inherited* which carry values from the root to the leaves. Therefore, for every production rule and for every derived attribute belonging to an alphabetic element on the left side of the production rule there is an attribute function mapping values of other attributes belonging to alphabetic elements on the right side of the production rule to a value from the value set of this derived attribute. This value is the value of that attribute for the node labelled with the alphabetic element on the left side of the production rule to which the attribute in question belongs. Likewise there is an attribute function for every inherited attribute belonging to an alphabetic element on the right side of a production rule. This function takes attribute values of other attributes belonging to other alphabetic elements occuring within the same production rule and maps them into a value of the value set of that inherited attribute. This value is the value of that attribute for that node.

Additionally, we need one special derived attribute, w , that belongs to the starting elements of the feature grammar and whose value is the expression designed to represent the *meaning* of the whole sentence. This special attribute, also called the *main* attribute, is used to define what is a semantically correct sentence: The attributes are partial functions which map phrase structure trees to logical formulae. So we can define that a sentence, s , is *semantically correct*, if it is syntactically correct, i.e. it can be analysed by the feature grammar, and if w is defined for its phrase structure tree.

We will not give a formal definition of attributed grammars here; the working of the mechanism will be demonstrated by a detailed example.

TRANSLATION OF NATURAL LANGUAGE DIALOGS INTO STATE LOGIC FORMULAE

An attributed English grammar fragment is given and discussed in detail. The grammar analyses natural language dialogs and maps them to state logic formulae.

The alphabet

Here we describe what features and what insertion rules are used for a natural language grammar.

Features:

a Kind of adjective.
We distinguish between two kinds of adjectives:
(i) relational adjectives (value r) which describe a property of a noun in comparison with other nouns; e.g. *big, old.*
(ii) adjectives that select a subset of the set of all objects they can refer to, i.e. these objects that have the property described by the adjectiv; e.g. *round, black.*

cat Starting feature category.
The values of cat correspond to alphabetic elements usually needed in transformational grammars for natural languages: S for sentence; NP for noun phrase (e.g. *the worm eating green snails*); V for verb; NG for noun group (NP without embeddings and without article, e.g. *large yellow teeth*); A for adjectives; DET for determiner (e.g. *the, all, any, some*); PN for proper name; PRON for pronoun; PP for prepositional phrase (e.g. *on the table*); ADV for adverbial (e.g. *today, always*).

cp Composition of nouns, noun phrases, noun groups, or prepositional groups.
The possible values of cp are + and - according as the corresponding noun or group is compound (e.g. *the teacher and all his pupils* is a compound noun phrase and generated by [NP,+ cp]).

d Type of determiner.
d has the values def (definite article), indef (indefinite article), all (for pronouns like *all, every*), and ex (for pronouns like *some*).

dc Degree of comparison.
The values of dc can be abs, comp, sup according as the corresponding adjective is in absolute, comparative, or superlative

form (e.g. *good, better, best*).

eb Embedding.
The values of eb are + or - according as the corresponding noun phrase has a sentence or a noun phrase embedded.

f Form of a verb.
The values of f are part for verbs in participle form (e.g. *eating*) and prop for verbs in "propositional" form (e.g. *eats*).

kc Kind of conjunction.
This feature subclassifies sentence conjunctions. Its values are: cond for conditional (e.g. *if ... then*); caus for causal (e.g. *because*); temp for temporal (e.g. *after*); conc for concessive (*although*); fin for final (*in order to*).

m Negation.
The possible values are + resp. - according as the corresponding verb is negated.

n Number.
The values are plur for plural and sing for singular.

pl Number of "supplements" of a verb or a noun.
The possible values of pl are 1,2,3 : Intransitive verbs are one-place (e.g. *work*); two-place verbs have one object (e.g. *know, John knows Mary*); three-place verbs have two objects (e.g. *give, John gives Mary a book*). Nouns are one-place (e.g. *table*) or two-place (e.g. *father, John is the father of Mary*).

rel Subclassification of relative clauses.
The values of rel are subj,obj1,obj2 according as the relative pronoun is the subject, the first or the second object of the corresponding relative clause.

t Tense of a verb.
The values of t are past,pres,fut.

Insertion rules

(NP,<{eb,cp}>)
Noun phrases can have embeddings and can be compound.

([NP,- cp],<{n,pl}>)
(NG,<{n,pl}>)
(N,<{n,pl}>)
Noun phrases that are not compound and noun groups and nouns are in singular or plural form and are specified according to their number of places.

(A,<a>)
An adjective is relational or not.

([r a],<dc>)
Relational adjectives can be compared.

(V,<{pl,m,n,t,f}>)
Verbs are specified according to their number of possible supplements, to negation, number, and tense and they are in participle form or not.

Derived attributes

ag is defined for noun groups, NG, noun phrases, NP, and for imperative sentences, [S,imp s] . The value of ag is a constant or a variable of L(Z) which is the name of the object described by the noun group or phrase. For an imperative sentence, the value of ag is the name of the "person" to whom the command is addressed.

con is defined for determiners, DET, and elementary noun phrases, [NP,- cp, - eb], and for verbs. For every noun phrase, there is a connector which links the noun phrase formula with the other sentence formula fragments. This connector depends on the kind of determiner belonging to the noun phrase. It is the empty word, ε, if there is no determiner, i.e. the noun phrase is expanded to "pronoun" or "proper name".
Example: The sentence *all men work* is represented by $\forall x[\text{MAN } x \rightarrow \text{WORK } x]$, the sentence *some men work* by $\exists x[\text{MAN } x \wedge \text{WORK } x]$. Depending on the determiner *all* resp. *some* the connector is $\rightarrow$ resp. $\wedge$.
The value of con for a verb is $\neg$ if the verb is negated and ε if it is not.

gm belongs to NP . It is used for the generation of questions if an ambiguity arises.
Example: Let *the green ball* be a noun phrase. If there is more than one green ball in the structure a question is generated *what ball do you mean?*

h is defined for conjunctions, CONJ, and has as its value the connector of L(Z) belonging to the conjunction.
Example: h(*or*) = $\vee$.

log is the main attribute and its value is the formula belonging to the sentence. log is also defined for other categories and then its value is a formula or a formula followed by a connector or a quadrupel (quantifier, formula, term, connective). log is defined for

(1) Adjectives; e.g. RED x for "*x is read*"

(2) Adjective groups as conjunction of the formulae for the adjectives

(3) Noun groups as conjunction of the formulae of the nouns and the adjectives the noun group is composed of; e.g. "a green parrot" is represented by $\exists x[\text{PARROT } x \wedge \text{GREEN } x]$.

(4) Noun phrases as conjunctions of the formulae of the noun groups and supplements the noun phrase is composed of; e.g. *the green parrot, which ...* is represented by $\exists x[\text{PARROT } x \wedge \text{GREEN } x \wedge l]$ where $l = \log(S)$ and S is the relative clause *which ...* .

(5) Prepositional phrases PP; e.g. *on the table* is represented by ON x t where x is the name of the object of the noun phrase the prepositional phrase is embedded in and t the name of the object described by *table*.

op is defined for sentence adverbs, ADV, and its value is the appropriate operator.

q is defined for determiners, DET, and its value is the quantifier for the appropriate noun phrase. In the example given below for con this quantifier is $\forall$ resp. $\exists$ for *all* resp. for *some*.

sy is defined for verbs, V, nouns, N, prepositions, PREP and its value is the predicate symbol representing that concept.

top is defined for verbs, V, and has as its value the tense operator of L(Z) depending on the tense of the verb.

w is a "global" attribute belonging to every non-terminal element. The value of w is the state of the structure in which the dialog is evaluated. We need this information for the assignment of object nouns to noun phrases that describe that object.

Inherited attributes

agr is defined for adjectives, adjective groups and sentences embedded into a noun phrase. The value of agr is the name of the object the adjective refers to. For a sentence it is the name of the object described by the noun phrase the sentence is embedded in.

agcr is defined for adjectives in comparative form and its value is the name of the object that is compared with the object the adjective refers to.

ix is defined for nouns, noun groups and noun phrases. The attribute functions generate bounded variables for noun phrases like *all children*. These variables have the form x_1, x_2, ... x_i and their indexes are generated by the attribute ix.

syr is defined for relational adjectives and its value is the predicate symbol that represents the noun the adjective belongs to.

Attribute functions for lexical rules

In the following, we describe how the most important word categories are represented in state logic. We shall explain in detail the attribute functions for the lexical rules.

(1) Verbs are represented by predicate symbols of the appropriate number of places. We are aware of the manifold difficulties which can arise whenever this number is not uniquely determinable. Problems connected with this have often been described and discussed (e.g. [15]). We have not resolved this problem but we think it should be possible to come to terms with it with the help of the following practical device. For every verb the number of supplements is fixed and part of the lexical information for that verb. Whenever the verb occurs in a text with one or more supplements missing the empty variable places are filled up by dummy elements. When it occurs with supplements not provided in the lexicon the additional formula fragments must be connected with the rest of the sentence formula by $\wedge$.

[V,x t, y m, z pl] :: v
sy(V) = $\bar{v}$

$\bar{v} = \bar{v}^{(z)}$ is the z-place predicate symbol representing the meaning of the verb.

The connector of V is ϵ or $\neg$ depending on the value y of the feature m :
con([+ m]) = ϵ
con([- m]) = $\neg$

The tense operator of V depends on the value x of the feature t :
top([pres t]) = ϵ
top([past t]) = $\neg P \neg$
top([fut t]) = $\neg F \neg$

$\neg P \neg$ means "there is an instant in the past such that ..."; and $\neg F \neg$ means "there is an instant in the future such that...".

The values of the attributes con and top are operators which are placed at the head of the whole sentence the verb occurs in. They operate on the whole sentence.

(2) Nouns are represented by one- or two-place predicate symbols or by one-place function symbols. One-place nouns are all nouns describing objects, e.g. *table, house, block*, and nouns describing animals or humans, e.g. *mouse, baby*. Two-place nouns also describe things or persons but they express at the same time a relationship to other things or persons; examples are all nouns expressing congeniality relations as *father, mother, aunt*.

N1 [N,x pl] ::= a
sy([N,x pl]) = $\bar{a}$

$\bar{a} = \bar{a}^{(x)}$ is the x-place predicate symbol representing the meaning of the noun.

Function nouns always correspond to adjectives expressing the same type of measure function. For each of these adjectives a measure function is introduced mapping the objects the adjective can refer to into the set of natural numbers. This will be described in detail below. The same function is needed for the representation of the function noun.

N2 [N,r a] ::= b
sy([N,r a]) = φ_b

$\varphi_b = \varphi_b^{(1)}$ is the one-place function symbol belonging to b .

Example: φ_{length} = LENGTH
φ_{size} = SIZE

We have not treated "abstract" nouns such as *eternity, love, malice* because these kinds of nouns have hardly been dealt with in existing question-answering-systems. Such concepts appear in [2], but there they are treated in a very "material" manner. They are measurable and they operate exactly like concrete nouns. The degree of *malice* or *health* of somebody is expressed by numbers and these numbers increase or decrease depending on the things that happen in the world. We think that for a better treatment of such nouns it would be necessary to use higher order predicate symbols but we would need predicates that can operate on other predicates of different types and this possibility is not provided in type logic.

"Mass" nouns (see [16]) have not been treated semantically. They cannot be treated like concepts, i.e. represented by predicate symbols. Sometimes they have the same properties as constants, sometimes they act like predicates.

(3) Adjectives

The state logic formula representing the meaning of the proposition contained in the adjective is built up on the lexical level of the grammar. Therefore, log belongs to A .

As mentioned above, we distinguish between two kinds of adjectives

(3.1) Adjectives that select a subset of the set of all objects they can refer to. All adjectives describing colors belong to this group; the noun phrase *the red balls* designs a subset of the set of all balls, the balls being red. Other adjectives selecting a subset are *round, open*. These adjectives cannot be compared. They are represented by one-place predicate symbols.

A1 [A,s a] ::= u
log(A) = $\bar{u}$ agr(A)

$\bar{u} = \bar{u}^{(1)}$ is the one-place predicate symbol representing the adjective u . The inherited attribute agr has as its value the name of the object the adjective refers to within the appropriate sentence and this value is assigned to agr within the rule AG1, or AU2 when A is generated.

Example: *the red table*. log(red) = RED t , where t is the name of the object the noun phrase is describing.

(3.2) Adjectives that express a relation between the objects they refer to. These adjectives describe the property of an object in comparison with other objects belonging to the same conceptual category; i.e. being comprehended by the same predicate. For example, if we are speaking of *a big dog*, we mean a dog whose size exceeds a certain number of centimeters characteristic for dogs. And the size that is meant if we speak of *a small elephant* is another absolute size. A sentence like *this big dog is much smaller than that small elephant* must be verifyable. Such "relational" adjectives are paired: (*young,old*),(*small,big*),(*thin,fat*),(*soft, hard*). A pair of relational adjectives orders the set of the objects it refers to according to the measurable property expressed by the adjective. So the pair (*young,old*) orders all things that have an age according to that age. Relational adjectives are comparable.

For every pair (a_1,a_2) of relational adjectives there are the following functions, relations, and constants:

(i) φ_a is a function symbol whose extension takes as its domain a subset of the universe of the structure the logic is characterized in, namely the subset of all objects the adjectives a_1,a_2 can refer to. The range of the extension of φ_a is $\mathbb{N}^{\{i_a\}}$, i.e. natural numbers indexed by an index typical for the adjectives a_1 and a_2. For example i_a = meter for a_1 = *small* and a_2 = *big*. Let $A = (\{A_s : s \in M\}, R_0)$ be a structure of Z .

$$\varphi_a^{(s)} : T \to \mathbb{N}^{\{i_a\}}, T \subseteq OB$$

T is the subset of the set of objects OB of A a_1 and a_2 refer to.

(ii) OP_{a_1} and OP_{a_2} are two-place predicate symbols, describing the "indexed" ordering of the objects referred to by a_1 and a_2 according to the property expressed by a_1 and a_2. The extensions of OP_{a_1} and OP_{a_2} are totally ordered binary relations on $\mathbb{N}^{\{i_a\}}$ one inverse to the other. Their extensions do not differ with different states of A .

So we set for all $s \in M$ and $n,m \in \mathbb{N}$
$(i_a,n)OP_{a_1}(i_a,m) \leftrightarrow n \le m$
and
$(i_a,n)OP_{a_2}(i_a,m) \leftrightarrow n \ge m$

Example: $OP_{young} = \le_{jears}$ and
$OP_{old} = \ge_{jears}$

(iii) For every predicate P such that a_1 and a_2 refer to objects of the extension of P, there are two constants $CS_{a_1,P}$ and $CS_{a_2,P}$ belonging to $\mathbb{N}$ and limiting the scale for values of φ_a for objects "of type P". We wish to express by this that an object of the conceptual category P can reach a minimal size of about $CS_{a_1,P}$ and a maximal size of about $CS_{a_2,P}$ according to the properties a_1 and a_2.

So we can fix for every predicate symbol P comprehending objects a_1 and a_2 can refer to:
$CS_{a_1,P} \in \mathbb{N}$
and
$CS_{a_2,P} \in \mathbb{N}$

Example: $CS_{old,dog} = 20$
$CS_{young,man} = 20$

(iv) CS_{a_1} and CS_{a_2} are absolute measure numbers for all objects a_1 and a_2 can refer to independently of a predicate P.

So, we can set
$CS_{a_1} = \min\{CS_{a_1,X}$: X predicate symbol of L(Z) such that $CS_{a_1,X}$ is defined$\}$
and
$CS_{a_2} = \max\{CS_{a_2,X}$: X predicate symbol of L(Z) such that $CS_{a_2,X}$ is defined$\}$

The state logic expression, log([A,r a]), representing the meaning of a relational adjective is composed of the symbols introduced above. log([A,r a]) depends on the degree of comparison of the adjective, i.e. of the value of the feature dc within the structured symbol the lexical rule is applied to.

(3.2.1) Absolute

A2 [A, abs dc] ::= u

$$\log(A) = \varphi_u \; agr(A) \; OP_u \; CS_{u,syr(A)}$$

agr(A) is the name of the object u refers to within the appropriate text; its value is assigned in NGP, see later. syr(A) is the predicate symbol belonging to the object u refers to. If u occurs within a nounphrase of the form "determiner" u "noun", syr(A) is the lexical entry for the noun. If agr(A) is a proper name, e.g. in the sentence *John is tall*, syr(A) cannot be found directly in the same sentence and not always within the same text. It must be searched for within the structure in which the text or the dialog is evaluated.

Example: *all small dogs*

φ_{small} = SIZE

$CS_{small,dog}$ = 0.3

$OP_{small} = \leq_{meter}$

The lexical rule is [A,pos dc] := *small* and we get

$\log(A)$ = SIZE $x_1 \leq_{meter}$ 0.3

x is the bound variable being the name of the object.

(3.2.2) Comparative

A3 [A,comp dc] ::= u

$$\log(A) = \varphi_u \; agr(A) \; OP_u \; \varphi_u \; agcr(A)$$

The value of agcr is the name of the object agr(A) is compared with. It is not always possible to find agcr(A) within the same sentence; as in these other cases this value must be found in the dialog or text structure.

Example: *John is older than Mary*. We have the lexical rule [A,comp dc] ::= *older* for the generation of the adjective and we get:

φ_{old} = AGE

$OP_{old} = \geq_{jears}$

agr (A) = *John*

agcr(A) = *Mary*

log (A) = AGE *John* $\geq_{jears}$ AGE *Mary*

In the sentence *the elder brother* ... we must find in the dialog structure the object "brother" is compared with, i.e. the name of the person whose elder brother is being spoken about.

(3.2.3) Superlative

A4 [A, sup dc] ::= u

$log(A) = \forall x[syr(A)x \rightarrow \varphi_u\ agr(A)\ OP_u\ \varphi_u x]$

Example: *the biggest dog*

Let [A,sup dc] ::= *biggest* be the appropriate lexical rule.

Then we get

syr(A) = DOG

agr(A) = d

$OP_{big} = \geq_{meter}$

φ_{big} = SIZE

$log(A) = \forall x[DOG\ x \rightarrow SIZE\ d \geq_{meter} SIZE\ x]$

(4) Prepositions

P1 [PREP,n pl] ::= p

$sy(PREP) = \bar{p}$

$\bar{p} = \bar{p}^{(n)}$ is an n-place predicate symbol describing the meaning of the preposition p .

(5) Predicate symbols are also used for the description of such relations between nouns that are not expressed by a fixed word category. We have for an example the OWN-relation which can be expressed by pronouns, by verbs, by prepositions; or by cases; e.g. *his dog, John has a dog, John owns a dog, the dog of John, John's dog*. In all these examples the relationship OWN between *John* and *the dog* is expressed.

(6) Determiner

As mentioned above, there are four types of determiners. Depending on the type a quantifier and a connector are assigned to DET which are needed for the construction of the formula describing the meaning of the appropriate noun phrase. The quantifier becomes the quantifier for the whole noun phrase and the connector is the connector with which the formula is attached to the other formula fragments belonging to the other sentence fragments.

DET ::= u

D1 con([DET,indef d]) = $\wedge$
q([DET,indef d]) = $\exists$

Here, u is an indefinite article like *a* , or is the empty string if DET is in plural form, i.e. the value of the feature n for the structured symbol [DET,...] is plur.

Example: "a dog ..." is represented by $\exists x_1$[DOG $x_1 \wedge$ ..., $\exists$ and $\wedge$ are the values of con and q respectively.

D2 con([DET,def d]) = $\wedge$
q([DET,def d]) = ϵ

Noun phrases with definite article like "the ball" design always a certain, fixed object of the world which is already known in the context and so has already a name. Therefore we do not generate an expression like $\exists x$[BALL x ...] , but the name of the object mentioned is searched for in the structure. We will discuss the problems of this representation below, when we discuss the rules generating the noun phrase.

D3 con([DET,ex d]) = $\wedge$
q([DET,ex d]) = $\exists$

The lexical entries for determiners specified by [ex d] are pronouns like *some*.

Example: *Some children are working* is represented by $\exists x_1$[CHILD $x_1 \wedge$ WORK x_1] . $\exists$ and $\wedge$ in this formula are generated depending on the pronoun *some*.

D4 con([DET,all d]) = $\rightarrow$
q([DET,all d]) = $\forall$

Pronouns like *every* and *each* are generated by a determiner specified by [all d] and the appropriate quantifier is $\forall$ and the connective is $\rightarrow$.

Example: *all children play* ... is represented by
$\forall x_1$[CHILD $x_1 \rightarrow$ PLAY x_1] .

(7) Temporal adverbs

Naturally, it is possible to describe any time refinement with the help of the time operators +, -, F, P. We demonstrate here the one-place time operators of Z for some time adverbial groups. In the following, A is always the formula representing the natural language sentence the temporal adverb belongs to.

ADV1 ADV ::= *always*
op(ADV) = (a)

(a) is a defined operator of Z

$$(a)\,A \leftrightarrow FPA \wedge PFA$$

This means that from every state from now on we can go to every state into the past and from every state from now on into the past we can go into the future and A is true in all states we can "reach" on this way. We would like to stress that what is meant by a temporal adverb depends on the structure in which sentences are evaluated. If we consider a linear time structure, it would be sufficient to represent *always* by FPA. Our representation demands a totally connected time structure; otherwise isolated points cannot be "reached" by means of F and P. This consideration is important because we require that time adverbs have non-logical meanings, i.e. what they are represented by depends on a given structure and not only on a given logic, that is to say it does not depend on the logic but on the interpretation of the logic. We conceive of time as a non-logical concept.

ADV2 ADV ::= *almost always*
op(ADV) = (aa)

$$(aa)\,A \leftrightarrow (a)\,[\neg + \neg A \ \vee \ \neg - \neg A]$$

A is almost always true if for every state ((a)) there is an immediately preceding or following state in which A is true. Intuitively speaking, A is almost always true if it can be "reach-ed" starting from every state.

ADV3 ADV ::= *sometimes*
op(ADV) = (m)

$\textcircled{m} A \leftrightarrow \neg FP \neg A \vee \neg PF \neg A$

sometimes A means that there are states in the future from which we can find states in the past such that A holds, or there are states in the past starting from which states in the future are reachable where A is true.

ADV4 ADV ::= *almost never*
op(ADV) = (an)

$\text{(an)} A \leftrightarrow \textcircled{a} [\neg +A \vee \neg -A]$

This means that in every state ((i)) we can reach another immediately preceding or following state where A is false.

ADV5 ADV ::= *never*
op(ADV) = (n)

$\textcircled{n} A \leftrightarrow FP \neg A \wedge PF \neg A$

In every state reachable by first going into the future and then into the past or by first going into the past and then into the future A is false.

Naturally, we can derive the following furmulae:

$\textcircled{n} A \leftrightarrow \textcircled{a} \neg A$

$\text{(an)} A \leftrightarrow \text{(aa)} \neg A$

It is clear how we can refine the time even more by applying the operators + and - more often. So we can describe adverbial groups like *seldom, very seldom, very,very seldom, rather often, very often* and so on.

Attributed production rules

Here we present a part of the production rules together with their attribute functions. English sentences are mapped to state logic formulae and the formula representing a text is the conjunction of the formulae of the single sentences.

Noun groups

NG1 NG ::= N
log([NG,1 pl]) = sy(N) ag(NG)
log([NG,2 pl]) = sy(N) ag(NG) ags(NG)
ag(NG) = $x_{ix(NG)}$
sy(NG) = sy(N)

NG2 NG_1 ::= A NG_2[†)]
log(NG_1) = log(A) $\wedge$ log(NG_1)
ag(NG_1) = ag(NG_2)
sy(NG_1) = sy(NG_2)
agr(A) = ag(NG_2)
syr(A) = sy(NG_2)
ix(NG_2) = ix(NG_1)

In NG1, the state logic expression representing the noun group is constructed. It has the form Px or Pxy, where P is the one- or two-place predicate symbol representing the noun. P is the value of sy for N , x resp. y of ag resp. ags for N resp. NG , these values having been assigned to on the lexical level described above. ag(NG) is the name of the object described by the noun phrase. It is generated within this production rule and has the form x_i where i = ix(NG) is a subscript. This subscript is generated on sentence level, i.e. within a production rule S ::= ··· , because it must be guaranteed that different variables are generated for different noun phrases occuring within one sentence. For these variables occur as terms within one single predicate, the verb predicate of the verb of the sentence. NG2 generates noun phrases such as *the beautiful flower*. The formula representing the meaning of the adjective has been generated on the lexical level. It is linked with the formula representing the noun group which has been constructed in NG1 by the connector $\wedge$. All the other attribute values are submitted identically.

---

†) Subscripts are used to distinguish between identical non-terminals occuring within the same rule.

Noun phrases

NP1 [NP,- cp, - eb] ::= DET NG

log(NP) = (q(DET),log(NG),ag(NG),con(DET))

ag(NP) = ag(NG) if con(DET) $\neq \epsilon$

ag(NP) = c if con(DET) = ϵ and M = {c}

where M = {z : w(NP)(s(NP),log(NG)$_{ag(NG)}$[z]) = T}

ag(NP) = $y_{ix(NG)}$ else

gm(NP) = $\emptyset$ if ag(NP) $\neq$ $y_{ix(NG)}$

gm(NP) = <*what* sy(NG)> if card M > 0

gm(NP) = <*there is no* sy(NG)> if M = $\emptyset$

The value of log for an elementary noun phrase is a quadrupel (quantifier, state logic expression, object name, connector); the state logic expression consists of the proposition the noun group contains; the quantifier which depends on the type of the determiner quantifies this expression; the value of ag is the name of the object the noun phrase describes and the value of con is the connector with which the noun phrase is linked to the other sentence formulae fragments. These values, q, log, ag, con, are the constituents of the state logic expression representing the noun phrase. This expression is only formed on sentence level. E.g. For the noun phrase *all men* within the sentence *all men work* we get log = ($\forall$,MAN x_1,x_1,$\rightarrow$) . The definite logical expression representing the noun phrase is $\forall x_1$MAN x_1 and the definite expression for the sentence is $\forall x_1$[MAN x_1 $\rightarrow$ WORK x_1]; $\rightarrow$ is the connector linking the noun phrase formula to the verb phrase formula. The reason for this is that the constituents of compound noun phrases such as *the teacher and all his pupils* or *neither John nor Mary* must be still available on sentence level because they are arranged within the logical expression in another order than within the natural language sentence. In fact we have transposed the problem otherwise resolved by a transformation to the semantic level, and attribute functions perform the task of transformational rules in transformational grammars. Noun phrases with definite article are not represented by the logical expression but only by an object name. The name of the object described by the noun phrase is either a bounded variable or a constant. This depends on the type of the determiner. If it is subclassified by [all d] or by [ex d] or by [indef a], i.e. it is *all* or *some* or *a* etc., then the noun phrase expression is quantified and the object name is the variable x_i which has been generated within NG1. Otherwise, i.e. if the determiner is subclassified by [def d], the noun phrase is definite, i.e. it has the form *the u* and we must find the object c that is spoken of. The search condition is that c has the properties described by the noun phrase and that c is the only object of the world having these properties. The sentence *Take the big green ball!* is unambiguous only if it is clear what ball is meant, i.e. if there is only one ball that is green. This search condition is formulated by the attribute function for ag. w(NG) is the structure the dialog is evaluated in, s(NP) is the actual state of the dialog. The search condition requires that c is the only constant of the structure, w(NP), such that log(NG)[c] is true in w(NP) at state s(NP). If the search condition cannot be verified a following up sentence must be generated. It is a question of the form *what* sy(NG) if the noun phrase is ambigues, i.e. there is more than one z such that log(NG)[z] is true. It is a sentence *there is no* sy(NG) if there is no such z. This following up sentence is generated by the attribute function gm. The logical expression representing a noun phrase *the u* is $\bar{u}[c]$ where $\bar{u}$ is the logical erpression representing the noun group u and c is the constant designated by the noun phrase. We could also generate $\exists x[\bar{u}[x] \wedge \forall y[\bar{u}[y] \rightarrow x = y]$. The first expression $\bar{u}[c]$ can be derived from the second semantically by searching for an object c such that $\bar{u}[c]$ holds. Together with the requirement that the set of x such that $\bar{u}\,x$ holds contains only one element we have exactly the search condition of NP1. In NP1 we have formulated it in terms of structure and truth condition, i.e. on the semantic level of the logic. In the alternative approach it is formulated on the syntactical level of the logic only. In our solution we must verify the expression of the second solution, $\exists x[\bar{u}x \wedge \forall y[\bar{u}y \rightarrow x = y]]$ when analysing the sentence and transducing it, namely when generating ag(NP). If we take the second solution we first generate the expression and evaluate it when the parsing of the sentence is already finished. In each of the two cases the search condition is the same. The difference is only when, i.e. on what level, we execute the necessary deductions. The advantage of our solution is that an ambiguity is discovered during sentence analysis and a following up question for resolving such an ambiguity can be generated and answered immediately.

```
NP2  [NP,- z,- ob] ::= PN
     log(NP) = (ε,ε,ag(NP),ε)
     ag(NP)  = sy(PN)
     con(NP) = ε
```

If a noun phrase consists only of a proper name it does not contain a logical proposition. The only "information" contained in such a noun phrase is the object name, i.e. the proper name.

```
NP3  [NP,- z,- e] ::= PRON
     log(NP)  = (ε,ε,ag(NP),ε)
     ag(NP)   = ag(PRON)
     con(NP)  = ε
```

As in the case of proper names a pronoun only refers to an object and does not contain a logical expression. ag(PRON), i.e. the name of the object the pronoun refers to must be found in the structure the sentence is evaluated in. There is no general rule for finding this object. One can compare the objects mentioned in the text and take the nearest one that fits morphologically and semantically, i.e. has the same number and gender and the semantic features the appropriate verb demands. Questions such as *What is meant by he?* are generated for ambiguities that are not resolvable in this way.

NP4 [NP,- z,- e,x pl] ::= POSSPRON[NG,x pl]

log([NP,1 pl]) = (ε,beg,ag(NG),ε)

where beg = $\log(NG) \wedge REL_{NG} ag(POSSPRON) ag(NG)$

log([NG,2 pl]) = (∃,log(NG),ag(NG),∧)

agr([NG,2 pl]) = ag(POSSPRON)

ag(NP) = ag(NG)

con(NP) = ∧

If a possessive pronoun precedes a one-place noun there is a binary relation between the object the possessive pronoun refers to and the object the noun refers to. This relation is not explicitly mentioned. What relation is meant must be concluded from the semantic descriptions of the two objects. If the possessive pronoun refers to an animate object and the noun to a thing REL_{NG} is most probably the ownership relation. If the noun refers to a part of the body REL_{NG} is more probably the PART-OF-relation, if the two refer to things REL_{NG} is probably the PART-OF-relation too.

For a two-place noun the relation between the two objects is already expressed by the predicate symbol representing the noun. Finding ag(POSS PRON) meets the same difficulties as for ag(PRON).

Noun phrases with embedded sentences

NP5 $[NP_1, - z, + e] ::= [NP_2, - z]\ [s,\ rl\ ks]$

$\log(NP_1) = (\pi_1(\log(NP_2)), l, \pi_3(\log(NP_2)), \pi_4(\log(NP_2)))$

$$l = \begin{cases} \log(S) \wedge & \text{if } \pi_1(\log(NP_2)) = \varepsilon \\ \pi_2(\log(NP_2)) \wedge \log(S) & \text{else} \end{cases}$$

$ag(NP_1) = ag(NP_2)$

$agr(NP_2) = ag(NP_1)$

The state-logic-formula representing the relative clause is linked by $\wedge$ with the noun phrase formula. ks is a feature (kind of sentence) subclassifying sentences into relative clauses (value rl) and assertive sentences (value as). π_i is the i-the projection. We need this mapping here because log(NP) has already been generated as a quadrupel (q,log,ag,con) (rules NP1 to NP4) and log(S) must be connected with the logical expression representing NP_2 which is the second constituent of the quadrupel $\log(NP_2)$. The quantifier $q(NP_2)$ is not generated until a rule S ::= NP V ... is applied, i.e. at sentence level Thus, log(S) is always in the domain of the quantifier. The sentence *All the children who are playing here are eleven years old* is represented by $\forall x[\text{CHILD } x \wedge \text{PLAY } x\ p \rightarrow \text{AGE } x = (\text{jears},11)]$. This case distinction is needed for relative clauses referring to proper names, i.e for sentences like *John, who is working in London,...* . Here the NP *John* is represented by $(\varepsilon,\varepsilon,$*John*$,\varepsilon)$. The proposition log(S) for the relative clause *who is working in London* must be linked by $\wedge$ with the other formula fragments of the sentence. The object being described by the noun phrase NP_2 is the same as is described by the relative pronoun of the embedded sentence. Its name must be made accessible to the sentence by agr_0 .

Prepositional complements are treated in the same way as embedded sentences, i.e. the expression representing the prepositional phrase is linked by $\wedge$ with the noun phrase.

Compound noun phrases

NP6 $[NP_1, + z]$ ::= NP_2 CONJ NP_3
$log(NP_1)$ = $(log(NP_2), log(NP_3), h(CONJ))$
$ix(NP_2)$ = $ix(NP_1)$
$ix(NP_3)$ = $ix(NP_1)$

This rule is for noun phrases such as *John and Mary, the teacher or the children, neither my father nor I*. The value of h is the logical connector corresponding to the conjunction: e.g. h(*neither* ... *nor*) = $\downarrow$ and h(*either* ... *or* ...) = $\nleftrightarrow$. $log(NP_1)$ is generated as such a triplet because the conjunction has such an effect to the noun phrase that the sentence the noun phrase is contained in is a compound sentence linked by this conjunct. E.g. the sentence *I know John and Mary* has the same meaning as *I know John and I know Mary*.

Sentences

We have production rules for types of sentences differing as to the kind and the number of verb complements. We will give here as an example the rule for a sentence with three verb complements. All the other sentence generation rules have the same form.

S1 [S,as ks] ::= NP_1[V,x t,y m, z f,3 pl] NP_2 NP_3

log(S) = top([x t]) con([y m]) $\alpha(sy(V), log(NP_1), log(NP_2), log(NP_3))$
$ix(NP_1)$ = 1
$ix(NP_2)$ = 2
$ix(NP_3)$ = 3

α is a partial function. Its arguments are the expressions log(NP) generated within the NP-rules. α constructs a well-formed logical expression from the formula fragments which are the constituents of the $log(NP_i)$. sy(V) is the predicate symbol for the verb U. $log(NP_i)$ is either a quadrupel (quantifier, formula fragment, object name, connector) or a triplet (l_1, l_2, h) where l_1 and l_2 are again expressions log(NP) (i.e. triplets or quadrupels) and h is a connector of L(Z). In the first case $log(NP_i)$ is called elementary.

Now we are able to define α for an n-place verb predicate.

Definition scheme of $\alpha(sy,l_1,\ldots l_n)$

I. Let all l_i be elementary, i.e. $l_i = (q_i,F_i,ag_i,con_i)$.
$\alpha(sy,l_1,\ldots l_n) =$
$q_1 ag_1'[F_1 \text{ con}_1\ q_2\ ag_2'[F_2 \ldots q_n ag_n'[F_n\ \text{con}_n\ sy\ ag_1 \ldots ag_n\underbrace{]\ldots]}_{n}$

$ag_i' = \varepsilon$ if $q_i = \varepsilon$ and $ag_i' = ag_i$ else
Example for the two-place verb *know*:
From the sentence *Every boy knows a girl* we get:
$\log(NP_1) = (\forall, \text{Boy } x_1, x_1, \rightarrow)$
$\log(NP_2) = (\exists, \text{GIRL } x_2, x_2, \wedge)$
$sy(V) = \text{KNOW}$
$\alpha(\text{KNOW},(\forall,\text{BOY } x_1,x_1,\rightarrow),(\exists,\text{GIRL } x_2,x_2,\wedge))$
$= \forall x_1[\text{BOY } x_1 \rightarrow \exists x_2[\text{GIRL } x_2 \wedge \text{KNOW } x_1\ x_2]]$

II. Let i_o be the least i such that l_{i_o} is not elementary.
$l_{i_o} = (k_1,k_2,h)$.
$\alpha(sy,l_1,\ldots l_{i_o-1},(k_1,k_2,h),l_{i_o+1},\ldots l_n) =$
$\alpha(sy,l_1,\ldots l_{i_o-1},k_1,l_{i_o+1},\ldots l_n)\ h$
$\alpha(sy,l_1,\ldots l_{i_o-1},k_2,l_{i_o+1},\ldots l_n)$

If there is more than one non-elementary noun phrase argument of α α is only defined when the two corresponding connectors h_i and h_j are compatible. Let $l_i = (k_1,k_2,h_i)$ and $l_j = (m_1,m_2,h_j)$. Then α is only defined if
$(\alpha(sy,l_1,\ldots k_1,\ldots m_1,\ldots l_n)\quad h_j\quad \alpha(sy,l_1,\ldots k_1,\ldots m_2,\ldots l_n))$
$h_i(\alpha(sy,l_1,k_2,\ldots m_1,\ldots l_n)\ h_j\ \alpha(sy,l_1,\ldots k_1,\ldots m_2,\ldots l_n))$
$\equiv (\alpha(sy,l_1,\ldots k_1,\ldots m_1,\ldots l_n)\ h_i\ \alpha(sy,l_1,\ldots k_2,\ldots m_1,\ldots l_n))\ h_j$
$\quad(\alpha(sy,l_1,\ldots k_1,\ldots m_2,\ldots l_n)\ h_i\ \alpha(sy,l_1,\ldots k_2,\ldots m_2,\ldots l_n))$
This holds iff
$(x_1\ h_j\ x_2)\ h_i(y_1\ h_j\ y_2) \equiv (x_1\ h_i\ y_1)\ h_j(x_2\ h_i\ y_2)$

Examples: $\downarrow$ is not compatible with itself.
$(a \downarrow b) \downarrow (c \downarrow d) \neq (a \downarrow c) \downarrow (b \downarrow d)$
For this α is not defined for a sentence like *Neither the teacher nor his pupil know neither the alphabet nor multiplication tables*. Such a sentence is refused semantically. The sentence is incorrect because it allows more than one analysis.

$\nleftrightarrow$ is selfcompatible:
a $\nleftrightarrow$ (b $\nleftrightarrow$ c) ≡ (a $\nleftrightarrow$ b) $\nleftrightarrow$ c and therefore
(a $\nleftrightarrow$ b) $\nleftrightarrow$ (c $\nleftrightarrow$ d) ≡ (a $\nleftrightarrow$ c) $\nleftrightarrow$ (b $\nleftrightarrow$ d)
The two analyses of the sentence *Either John or Mary drink either champagne or beer* have the same meaning representation.

It is obvious that α acts like a transformation rule analysing a sentence like *a and b do c and d* into *a does c and a does d and b does c and b does d.*

The value of top is the sentence's tense operator determined by the value x of the feature t . con is ¬ or ε according to whether the verb is negated or not. The subscripts of the object variables of the NP are generated on sentence level, within an S-rule since NP that are different on this level must receive different object names because they are within the scope of one verb predicate, the verb predicate of the verb of the sentence, sy(V) .

Relative clauses

For relative clauses the relative pronoun is generated directly and it is not the result of the application of a transformation rule to a noun phrase once generated. As before we have a sentence rule for every type of relative clause, corresponding to the kind and the number of verb complements and to the grammatical function of the relative pronoun in the sentence. We give an example rule for a verb with three complements and the relative pronoun as its first object.

S2 [S,obj1 rel] ::= RP NP_1 [V,x t,y m,z f,3 pl] NP_2
log(S) = top([x t]) con ([y m])
$\alpha(sy(V), log(NP_1), (\varepsilon, \varepsilon, agr(S), \varepsilon), log(NP_2))$
$ix(NP_1) = 1$
$ix(NP_2) = 2$

The argument of α corresponding to the relative pronoun RP is elementary and refers to another NP within the sentence. The name of its object is agr(S) and has been assigned within NP5 . log, q, and con are empty because the object does not contain any statement (any concept).

Compound sentences

C1 $S ::= S_1[\mathrm{CONJ}, x\ kc]\ S_2$
$\log(S) = \log(S_2)\ \ h([x\ kc])\ \log(S_1)$

This rule describes compound sentences as *John works in the garden if it does not rain* or also *John works in London and Mary studies at Essex.* $h([x\ kc])$ is the connector of $L(Z)$ representing the conjunction. It depends on the value of kc .

C1.1 $x = \mathrm{cond}$
$h([\mathrm{cond}\ kc]) = \rightarrow$

Conditional links between sentences are expressed by $\rightarrow$.

Example: *I will take the umbrella if it rains. It rains* is S_2 ; *if* is $[\mathrm{CONJ},\mathrm{cond}\ kc]$ and *I will take the umbrella* is S_1 . The sentence is represented by $S_2 \rightarrow S_1$.

C1.2 $x = \mathrm{temp}$
S_1 *after* S_2 is represented by
$\log(S_2) \wedge \neg + \neg \log(S_1)$

i.e. $\log(S_2)$ and there is an immediately following state where $\log(S_1)$.

Example: *I went to bed after I had eaten. I had eaten* is S_2 and *I went to bed* is S_1 . The sentence is represented by $\log(S_2) \wedge \neg + \neg \log(S_1)$; i.e. *I had eaten* and then *I went to bed.*

C1.3 $x = \mathrm{caus}$
S_1 because S_2 is represented by
$\boxed{m}[\log(S_2) \rightarrow \log(S_1)] \wedge \log(S_1) \wedge \log(S_2)$

i.e. sometimes S_2 implies S_1 and S_1 and S_2 both hold.

Example: *I am wet because it is raining.* S_1 is *I am wet* and S_2 is *it is raining.* The representation is
$\boxed{m}[\log(S_2) \rightarrow \log(S_1)] \wedge \log(S_1) \wedge \log(S_2)$; i.e. sometimes ($\boxed{m}$) if *it is raining I am wet* and *I am wet* and *it is raining.*
We are aware of the problems arising in connection with causality. Our

formalization does not prevent that things which are sometimes true at the same time are causally related. But we think that humans intend to relate causally things in this way.

C1.4 $x = \text{conc}$

S_1 *although* S_2 *is represented by*

$\text{(aa)}[\log(S_2) \rightarrow \neg \log(S_1)] \wedge \log(S_1) \wedge \log(S_2)$

i.e. almost always $\log(S_2)$ implies $\neg\log(S_1)$ and the both hold.

Example: *I do not take the umbrella although it is raining;* this means almost always *I take the umbrella* if *it is raining* and *it is raining* and *I do not take the umbrella;* i.e. $\text{(aa)}[\log(S_2) \rightarrow \neg\log(S_1)] \wedge \log(S_2) \wedge \log(S_1)$ where S_1 is *I do not take the umbrella* and S_2 is *it is raining.*

Sample sentence generation

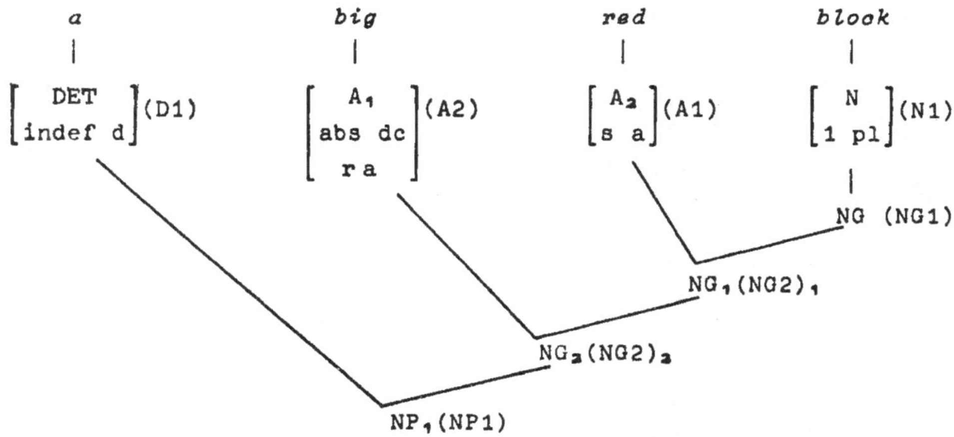

(D1) $\text{con(DET)} = \wedge$

$\quad\ \text{q(DET)} = \exists$

(A2) $\log(A_1) = \text{SIZE agr}(A_1) \geq_{\{\text{meter}\}} CP_{big,\text{syr}(A_1)}$

$\quad\ $ where $\text{SIZE} = \varphi_{big}$ and $\geq_{\{\text{meter}\}} = OP_{big}$

(A1) $\log(A_2) = \text{RED agr}(A_2)$

(N1) $\text{sy(N)} = \text{BL}$

$\quad\ \text{BL} = \text{BL}^{(1)} = \overline{block}$

(NG1) $\log(\text{NG}) = \text{BL ag(NG)} = \text{BL } x_{ix(\text{NG})}$

$\quad\ \text{ag(NG)} = x_{ix(\text{NG})}$

$sy(NG) \quad = BL$

$(NG2)_1 \quad log(NG_1) = RED\ agr(A_2) \wedge BL\ x_{ix(NG)}$

$= RED\ x_{ix(NG)} \wedge BL\ x_{ix(NG)}$

$ag(NG_1) \quad = ag(NG)$

$sy(NG_1) \quad = sy(NG)$

$agr(A) \quad = ag(NG) = x_{ix(NG)}$

$syr(A) \quad = sy(NG) = BL$

$ix(NG) \quad = ix(NG_1)$

$(NG2)_2 \quad log(NG_2) = SIZE\ x_{ix(NG_1)} \geq_{\{meter\}} (meter,1) \wedge RED\ x_{ix(NG_1)} \wedge BL\ x_{ix(NG_1)}$

The values of the other attributes ag, sy,agr,syr and ix are submitted identically.

(NP1) $log(NP_1) = (\exists,1,x_{ix(NP_1)},\wedge)$ where

$1 = size\ x_{ix(NP_1)} \geq_{\{meter\}} (meter,1) \wedge RED\ x_{ix(NP_1)} \wedge BL\ x_{ix(NP_1)}$

Let $log(NP_1) = l_1$

If the noun phrase NP_1 is the part of a compound noun phrase

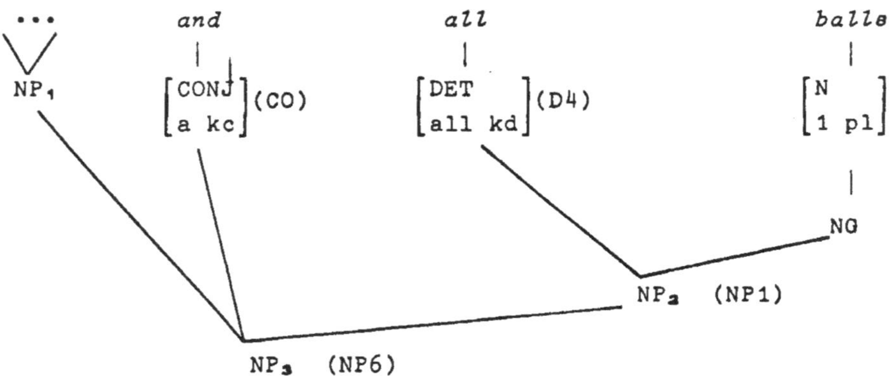

we get

(D4) $con(DET) = \rightarrow$

$q(DET) \quad = \forall$

(CO) $h(CONJ) \quad = \wedge$

(NP1) NP_2 is derived like NP_1 :

$log(NP_2) = (\forall,BALL\ x_{ix(NP_2)},x_{ix(NP_2)},\rightarrow) = l_2$

(NP6) $log(NP_3) = (l_1,l_2,\wedge)$

Let now be NP_3 the object of a sentence

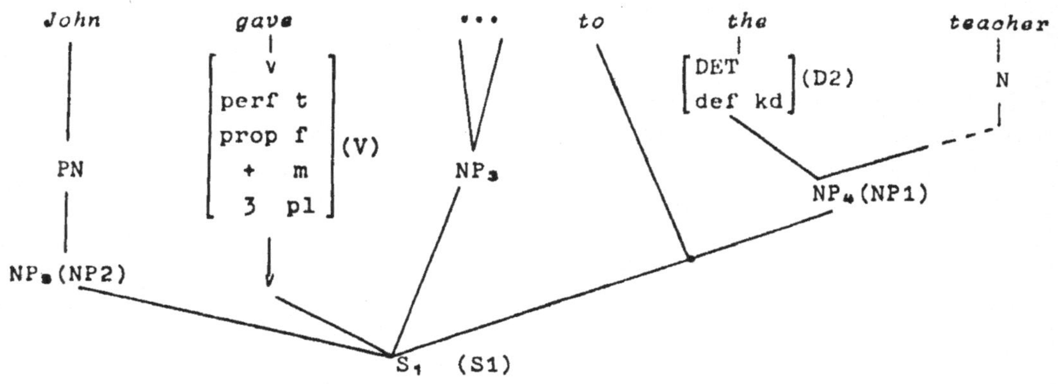

(NP2) $log(NP_8) = (\varepsilon,\varepsilon,John,\varepsilon)$
$ag(NP_8) = John$
$con(NP_8) = \varepsilon$

(D2) $con(DET) = \wedge$
$q(DET) = \varepsilon$

Let the appropriate structure, $w(NP)$, contain more than one object which is a teacher; i.e. Tc_1 and Tc_2 for c_1,c_2 objects of $w(NP)$.

(NP1) $log(NP_4) = (\varepsilon,Tx_{ix(NP_4)},y_{ix(NP_4)},\wedge)$
$ag(NP_4) = y_{ix(NP_4)}$
$gm(NP_4) = $ <*what teacher*>

The sentence analysis is interrupted here and the following up question *what teacher?* is generated. When it is answered, say by c, or by a more detailed description, e.g. *who is working in Munich*, this answering noun phrase is evaluated in the same way and if necessary another following up question is generated. When the answer is satisfying the object found, c, is inserted into $log(NP_4)$ and we then get

$$log(NP_4) = (\varepsilon,Tc,c,\wedge)$$

(S1) $log(S_1) =$
$$\neg P\neg\ \alpha(GIVE,(\varepsilon,\varepsilon,John,\varepsilon),(l_1,l_2,\wedge),(\varepsilon,Tc,c,\wedge))$$
$$= \neg P\neg[\alpha(GIVE,(\varepsilon,\varepsilon,John,\varepsilon),l_1,(\varepsilon,Tc,c,\wedge)) \wedge \alpha(GIVE,(\varepsilon,\varepsilon,John,\varepsilon),l_2,(\varepsilon,Tc,c,\wedge))]$$

$$= \neg P \neg [[\exists x_2 [SIZE\ x_2 \geq_{\{m\}} (m,1) \wedge RED\ x_2 \wedge BLx_2 \wedge [Tc \wedge GIVE\ \textit{John}\ x_2\ c]]] \wedge [\forall x_2 [BALL\ x_2 \rightarrow [Tc \wedge GIVE\ \textit{John}\ x_2]]]]$$

Let now S_2 be a relative clause embedded into a noun phrase, where S_2 is S_1 with *John* replaced by *who*:

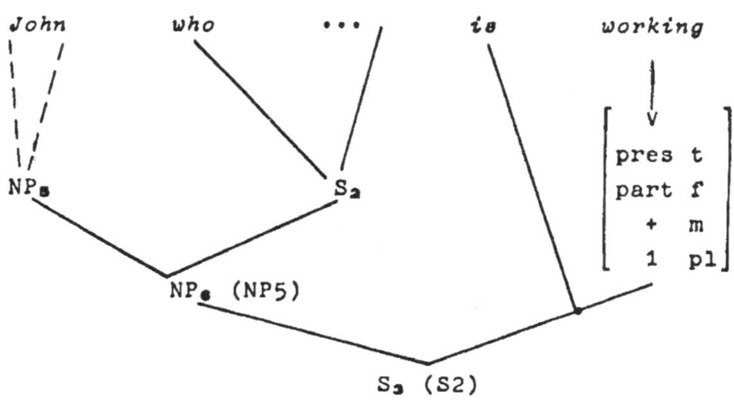

(NP5) $log(NP_6) = (\epsilon, log(S_1)\wedge, \textit{John}, \epsilon)$
$ag(NP_6) = \textit{John}$
$agr(S_2) = \textit{John}$

(S3) is a sentence generation rule not explicitely mentioned here.
$log(S_3) = \alpha(WORK, (\epsilon, \epsilon, \textit{John}, \epsilon))$
$= log(S_1) \wedge WORK\ \textit{John}$

Let this sentence be embedded into a causal sentence

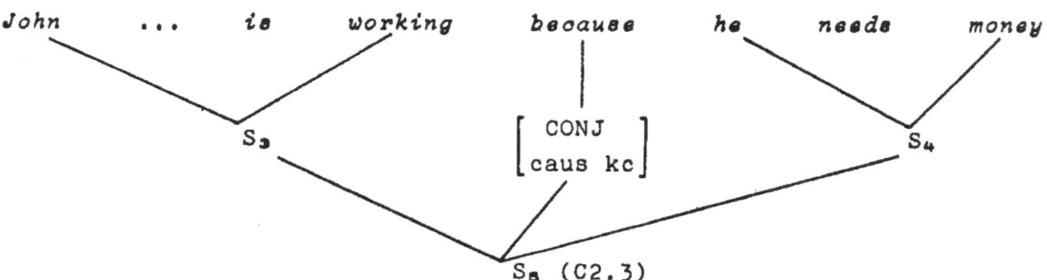

(C2.3) is not explicitely mentioned here. This rule generates compound sentences where the superordinated sentence precedes the subordinated one.

$$\log(S_8) = \text{(m)}[\log(S_4) \rightarrow \log(S_3)] \wedge \log(S_4) \wedge \log(S_3)$$

Dialogs

A dialog is a sequence of sentences of L(G) where a question is followed by an assertive sentence, the answer, or by another question, the following up question. A command or a statement is followed by another statement *I carried it out* or *I understand* or by a following up question. Following up questions are generated whenever the sentence contains an ambiguity; i.e. a definite noun phrase whose object cannot be determined or a pronoun the reference of which cannot be determined.

Definition

1. A *dialog cycle* on a structure $A = (\{A_s : s \in M\}, R_0)$ in a state s is a sequence S QC A where
   S is a sentence of L(G)
   QC is empty or a sequence of pairs QB where Q is a following up question of the form *what u* and B is an answer of the form *c* or *the v*. QC is empty if there is no following up question to S, i.e. gm = ∅. $QC = Q_1 B_1 Q_2 B_2 \ldots Q_n B_n$ if $gm = \{Q_1, Q_2, \ldots Q_n\}$.
   A is the answer to S. If S is a question A is *yes* or *no* or of the form *the u* or c. If S is a wh-question A is of the form *the v* resp. c and $A(s,l) = T$ where l is log(S) with the variable generated for the question word replaced by the name of the object described by *the v* resp. by c. If S is an alternative question A = yes iff $A(s,\log(S)) = T$. If S is a command A is *I carried it out* or *I cannot do it*. If S is an assertive sentence A is *I understand*.

2. A *dialog* on a structure $A = (\{A_s : s \in M\}, R_0)$ is a sequence of dialog cycles $D_1\ D_2 \ldots D_n$ on A in $s_1\ s_2 \ldots s_n$ such that for $1 \le i < n$ $s_i\ R\ s_{i+1}$ and $s_i \neq s_{i+1}$ iff $D_i = S_i Q Z_i A_i$ and S_i is a command and A_i = *I carried it out*.

This means a dialog is evaluated in a Z-structure. It constitutes a path through the structure along R_0 and it makes a step forward whenever a command is carried out. We will see in the following paragraph what is the effect of a command in a structure.

CHARACTERIZATION OF QUESTION-ANSWERING-SYSTEMS BY Z-STRUCTURES

Here we shall describe how a structure for the state logic can characterize a natural language understanding system. The knowledge that is formulated in such a system is represented by a Kripke-structure. In connection with this the non-logical interpretation of state transitions is very important. The very general model of Kripke-structures is used in such a way that the relation R_0 bears a non-logical meaning. For two structures A_s and $A_{s'}$, $s\ R_0\ s'$ holds iff the "world" $A_{s'}$ is obtained from the world A_s as the result of an action which can be executed within A_s. What actions can be executed within a world depend on the extensions of the non-logical symbols. On natural language level actions are verbs. We characterize all these dependencies by non-logical axioms.

Worlds, state changes and their dependence on action verbs

A world is a set of objects that have certain properties, i.e. a color, a size, etc. They are subclassified by conceptualizations like MAN, TREE, TABLE, HUMAN, etc. There are relations which can hold between objects, i.e. position relations such as ON, BESIDE-OF, etc., or "abstract" relations such as the ownership relation OWN. All these elements of a world are represented by the language of the state logic as it can be concluded from the description of the last paragraph. Objects are constants, properties are predicate or function symbols, relations are predicates of the appropriate number of places. Verbs are relations between objects too and they are represented by predicate symbols of the appropriate number of places. We can distinguish two types of verbs, called *static verbs* and *dynamic verbs*. An n-place verb is called *static* if it does not describe an action that changes relations or functions of objects of the world; i.e. if the formula representating the assertion of the verb holds within a structure this does not effect any change on objects of the structure. Examples of static verbs are *believe, want, know*. An n-place verb is called *dynamic* if a structure is subject to some change whenever the action described by the verb is executed in it. Examples are *take, give, grow, put*. If somebody takes a thing the position of that thing changes, i.e. the extension of the predicate symbols ON, BEHIND etc., and the extension of the static verb predicate symbol HOLD changes, because the person holds the thing now. Constructive verbs are always dynamic, e.g.

build, paint. She builds a house. He paints a picture. The appropriate thing comes into existence by execution of the action. Further, there are conditions for the execution of an action. a *takes* b is only possible if a does not yet hold anything and if b has a position such that it can be taken, i.e. there is nothing on b. We describe both the conditions and the consequences of an action by non-logical axioms. And the appropriate structure must have the property that in whatever state all the conditions of an action hold there must be some following state in which its consequences are realized. We would like to point out a peculiarity which arises when logical expressions containing dynamic verbs are evaluated: If an expression $\bar{v}x_1 \ldots x_n$ holds within a state of a structure for a dynamic verb v this does not mean that the appropriate action is really executed but that it is possible to execute it; i.e. all the conditions are true and there is a following state where all the consequences are true. It is always possible that within a state more than one action can be executed but not all at the same time and so there are several following states which do not depend on each other. What actions are "really" executed is described by a text or a dialog which constitutes something like a path through a structure.

Characterization of action verbs by non-logical axioms

Definition

For every n-place action verb v there are two non-logical axioms defining v

(1) Condition axiom (CA)

$\bar{v}x_1 \ldots x_n \leftrightarrow C[x_1,\ldots x_n]$

(2) Execution axiom (EA)

$\bar{v}x_1 \ldots x_n \rightarrow E[x_1,\ldots x_n]$

C is called the *condition of* v and

E is called the *execution of* v

(CA) and (EA) are called *action axioms of* v.

Naturally $C[x_1,\ldots x_n] \rightarrow E[x_1,\ldots x_n]$ holds.

(CA) describes what requirements must be complied with by the objects involved in an action in order that the action can be executed.

Example: *take*

(CA) TAKE xy $\leftrightarrow$ HAND x $\wedge$ THING y $\wedge$ $\neg$HOLD x z $\wedge$ $\neg$ON z y
This means: x can take y iff x is a hand and y is a thing and x does not hold any other object and there is nothing on y .

(EA) describes the consequences of the execution of an action. E in (EA) has the form $\neg + \neg x$ and x does not contain F,P,+,- as substring.

Example: *take*
(EA) TAKE x y $\rightarrow$ $\neg + \neg$[HOLD x y $\wedge$ $\neg$ON y z]
This means: if x takes y then there is an immediately following state such that x holds y and y is not lying on anything.

Since C $\rightarrow$ E holds always we have:
For every action verb v and every state s there is a state s' immediately following s , ($s \; R_0 \; s'$), where the results of the execution of the action described by v hold whenever its conditions hold.

So, we can define a model for action verbs:

Definition
Let $A = (\{A_s : s \in M\}, R_0)$ be a Z-structure and V a set of action verbs and N a set of non-logical axioms; i.e. condition and execution axioms for all $v \in V$ and all the other non-logical axioms. Then A is a *model* for Z and N iff $A(s,A) = T$ for all $A \in N$ and all $s \in M$.

Because of the correctness of Z the following theorem holds:
Let $A = (\{A_s : s \in M\}, R_0)$ be a model for Z and N and V a set of action verbs. Then for every $s \in M$ and every $v \in V$ such that C is the condition of v and $E = \neg + \neg E'$ is the execution of v we have
$A(s,C) = T \Rightarrow$ there is s' such that $s \; R \; s'$ and $s \neq s'$ and $A(s,E') = T$

The differentiation between (CA) and (EA) is important too for the use of the axioms when deriving answers to questions or executing commands Then a system must first verify (CA), if this is not possible a state of the world must be found where (CA) holds. This is done by the use of other axioms. When (CA) is verified (EA) can be carried out and the dialog can pursue its path within the structure. So (CA) and (EA) constitute "heuristic" aids for the execution of commands.

CONCLUSION

We have given a device to describe how natural language sentences can be translated into a semantic representation and how one can represent an underlying knowledge system. The proposed formalism only constitutes a first attempt in formalizing "what is understanding of natural language text". Among the most important problems is a better and more refined subclassification of adjectives, a satisfactory description of mass nouns and a revision of the logic to allow the appearence and disappearence of objects of the world. As to the latter we have either to revise the substitution rule or allow only closed formulae to be manipulated by inference rules. Both restrictions are not very satisfactory solutions (see also [17], [18], [19]).

REFERENCES

[1] Winograd, T., Understanding Natural Language. Academic Press 1972.

[2] Schank, R.C. and Abelson, R.P., Scripts, Plans, and Knowledge. Advance Papers of the IJCAI 4, Sept. 1975.

[3] Bobrow, D., Natural Language Input for a Computer Problem Solving System. In Minsky, M., Ed., Semantic Information Processing. Cambridge: The MIT Press, 1968.

[4] Kellogg, C., A. Natural Language Compiler for on-line Data management. Proceedings of the Fall Joint Computer Conference. New York: Spartan, 1968.

[5] Woods, W.A., Transition Network Grammars for Natural Language Analysis. Comm. of the ACM vol.13, Nr.10, Oct.1974.

[6] Ershov, A.P., Mel'chuk, I.A., Nariniany, A.S., RITA - An Experimental Man-Computer System on a Natural Language Basis. Advance Papers of the IJCAI 4, Sept.1975.

[7] Rescher, N. and Urquhart, A., Temporal Logic. Springer Verlag, Wien 1971.

[8] Kripke, S.A., Semantical Analysis of Modal Logic I Normal Modal Propositional Calculi. Zeitschr. f. math. Logik und Grundlagen d. Math. Bd.9, 1963.

[9] Schütte, K., Vollständige Systeme modaler und intuitionistischer Logik. Springer Verlag 1968.

[10] Braun, S., Eigenschaften strukturierter Symbole in formalen Sprachen. Habilitationsschrift, München 1971.

[11] Knuth, D.E., Semantics of Context-Free Languages. Math. Syst. Theory 2, 1969.

[12] Koster, C.H.A., Affix-Grammars. In Peck, J.E.L., ALGOL 68 Implementation, North Holland Publ. Comp. 1971.

[13] Chomsky, N., Aspects of the Theory of Syntax. Cambridge, MIT 1965.

[14] van Wijngaarden, A., Ed., et al., Report on the Algorithmic Language ALGOL 68.

[15] Bruce, B., Case Systems for Natural Language. Artificial Intelligence 6, 1975.

[16] Moravcsik, J., Mass Terms in English. In Hintikka et al. Ed., Approaches to Natural Language, D. Reidel Publ. Comp. 1973.

[17] Hintikka, J., Modality and Quantification. Theoria 1961.

[18] Kripke, S.A., Semantical Considerations on Modal Logic. Acta Philosophica Fennica 1963.

[19] Montague, R., Universal Grammar. Theoria 36, 1970.

ACCESS TO DATA BASE SYSTEMS VIA NATURAL LANGUAGE

Klaus-Dieter Krägeloh

Peter C. Lockemann

Fakultät für Informatik
Universität Karlsruhe

Abstract

Communication with computer via natural language is one of the major concerns of artificial intelligence. Modern approaches try to achieve this goal by simulating human language perception. The resulting models are highly complex, because the semantics of natural language statements must remain largely unrestricted. The communication with a commercially available data base system, on the other hand, deals with a heavily restricted formal model of the subject matter in the form of a data base. This is mainly due to the large amount of data that must be inspected and manipulated within reasonably short time. The semantics of any dialogue with the machine are such that all statements can be related to the formal model.

In light of this difference the definition of a natural query language for data base systems and the mapping of natural language statements to a modelling system will have to be approached in a manner different from artificial intelligence. In general one will try to make use of the results of linguistic research in artificial intelligence to the extent that they can take the simpler requirements of data base systems into account. In other cases different and perhaps more pragmatic solutions will be required.

The intent of this paper is to illustrate such an approach to natural language access to a data base system. In doing so a number of premises for natural language analysis in data base systems are developed concerning the syntactic model, morphemic analysis, semantic validity tests etc. These premises underly the work on a data base system that provides for a set-theoretic modelling system and a German language interface.

I Goals of natural language processing for data base systems

1.1 Simulation of natural language understanding

Natural language communication with the computer has a relatively long tradition in informatics. Depending on their objectives, these activities fall into one of two disciplines, artificial intelligence (AI) or data base technology (DT).

In AI the conception of language understanding systems is part of the more comprehensive aim to simulate cognitive processes on the computer [1,2]. The basic concern of AI in this connection is the linguistic component of cognition, i.e. the assignment of meaning to language entities. Characteristic for man is his capability of producing a cognitive image of his environment. This image (called a model) is always an abstraction from the real world, chosen with respect to the purpose it is to serve. In language understanding, the statements about the real world are related to the cognitive model (assignment of meaning), and thus cause reactions such as modifications of the model, evaluation of the model, or answers.

The simulation of this process above all requires specification of a modelling system (MS), by means of which any environment or part of it can be described as a model (representation problem). A language understanding system is always based on a model formulated in some MS. Further, there is a need for mechanisms which put natural-language expressions in relation to that model (fitting problem [1]).

Characteristic for human language understanding is the fact that meaning cannot directly be constructed from some basic units of meaning [1]. Instead, complex relations between the model objects enter as well into the meaning of language units such as words. Winograd mentions words like "virtue" or "democracy" as examples. In order to account for the aspect of relations, special modelling systems are usually developed for language processing. This, however, leads to very complex MS and, consequently, to extensive models even in those cases where only small sections of the environment are considered (e.g. semantic memories [3], dependency networks [4], demons [5]).

Obviously the complexity and the size of the model affects the fitting problem and, if of concern, the rules for deriving the system reactions.

Take as an example the task to find in an extensive semantic net all those subnets corresponding in their structure to a given net.

Both in human cognition and in the case of its simulation, models must be physically represented, and operators for manipulating them must be realized. In the first case we assume a practically unlimited memory (brain, neurons, etc.). This provides a fully associative solution of the fitting problem even for highly complex model structures, such as recollection of impressions, moods, etc.. In computer simulation, however, we have to deal with physical devices and processes of limited capacity and duration. Given a complex MS and its corresponding extensive models, this merely allows for the description and representation of a drastically limited portion of the environment. Likewise, no manipulation of models on an associative basis is directly possible on a computer as yet. Instead, the associative behaviour must be simulated thus causing considerable costs and process times, e.g. long response times in an interactive mode.

This problem will certainly become less troublesome as new hardware technologies become commercially available (use of micro processors, new storage devices, LISP-machines, etc.). Still, it is by no means clear from current discussions, whether human cognition and its simulation on computer really differ just quantitatively and not qualitatively [6].

If one approaches the same problem from data base technology, however, one must take into account the necessity of administrating and processing very large volumes of data. Consequently, even though a data base is usually again regarded as the model of some real world [7,8], the modelling system cannot be chosen completely at will but must meet a number of conditions:

1) At justifiable costs, the MS must allow for the description of even such worlds whose number of objects and facts to be modelled is very large (i.e. model representation should take up as little storage space as possible).
2) The rules for manipulating the models should be kept simple, since the time for evaluating even extensive models is very limited (acceptable response times in a data base system).

Under these conditions, data base systems must restrict their MS to those that can be formalized and are simple compared to those in AI. Models in data base technology will abstract from the real world far more than the usual AI models.

Consequently, the range of situations to which they are applicable will be much smaller than in AI, since they are much more likely to reject details that one may wish to include in them. Thus, models in DT are generally oriented towards a comparatively narrow purpose. Since in DT the operators defined on models are few, they are usually included in the MS which is then called a data model [9,10,11,12,13].

Natural language access to data base systems has frequently been discussed, by providing easy access to users not familiar with formal models one hopes the system to become more widely available [14,15,16, 17].

Because of the differences in MS, it is obvious that language understanding systems for large data bases have to be based on something other than the simulation of cognitive processes. In DT the MS are rigorously defined by the interfaces of existing data base systems. Consequently, the language can be restricted to an extent necessary and reasonable for the usage of the system. Under these conditions natural language in data base systems, although much more divers than programming languages, is still a formal language.

For practical use, these restrictions are quite acceptable. For instance, tests of the user behaviour in case of data base systems that provided (simulated) access by unrestricted English language have shown, that the wealth of natural language expressions is never utilized [18]. Even more, certain query structures were used almost all of the time, thus indicating that a natural language interface for data base systems becomes highly stylized from the user's point of view, too. This might be due to a certain lethargy of the user, to whom it is difficult to conceptualize complex statements [19].

The objective of this paper is to examine the consequences for natural language processing subject to the conditions imposed by data base system interfaces. This will include discussion of the question which results from AI may be incorporated in the development of natural languages for data base access, and to which extent, without violating the aspect of practicability. In addition to AI, text analysis techniques in documentation (automatic indexing, morphemic analysis [20,21,22]) are another large area that may contribute their results. The conclusions of these considerations will be illustrated in this paper by means of natural language access to a particular data base system.

As mentioned above, the differences in MS have a clear effect on the linguistic approach. We shall explore this further by giving a rough outline of the development of language processing in AI and DT.

1.2 Approaches to natural language processing in AI

The early language processing systems in AI concerned themselves with the problem of translating a natural language into another [23]. These systems posessed a certain knowledge of the external structure of the languages (grammar), and of the correspondences between words of the languages (dictionary of synonyms). These approaches failed, since grammar and dictionary by themselves proved insufficient to deal with the different meaning of sentences like [1]:

(1) The fish was bought by the cook.

(2) The fish was bought by the river.

The system would have something to know about the real world to which the sentence is applied in order to recognize the difference in the meaning of "by the cook" (person) and "by the river" (place).

Due to the failure in the early sixties of these approaches in translation one turned to the broader question of how to simulate language understanding on the computer in general. One indication of a computer system's capability to comprehend natural language would be, e.g. whether in man-machine communication the machine responds in a manner that seems "plausible" to its human partner. A system would be perfect if it passed the Turing test [24].

In order to enable the simulation of human language understanding, at least knowledge about the meaning of words relative to a specific environment must be provided (as we pointed out earlier). For this purpose the environment or part of it has to be modelled (MS). A certain portion of the model is assigned to the word as its meaning. The examples below, however, show that this approach is still not sufficient [25]:

(3) John jumps higher than Peter.

(4) John jumps higher than the Eiffel tower.

In order to recognize that (4) is meaningless, the system requires a more extensive knowledge of the environment than the (complex) meaning of individual words. The model must contain the fact that no living being can jump higher than the Eiffel tower, in general, it must establish relations between model parts.

Some of the MS used in the past cannot meet this condition or, at best, only if applied to sections of an environment too small to be of any interest. In particular, this applies to the earliest language understanding systems such as STUDENT [26], SIR [27], BASEBALL [28], ELIZA [29]. For example, the STUDENT system used equations as MS, i.e. it was restricted to a small mathematical world; ELIZA used patterns that were suitable only for very specific situations of a dialogue.

Many MS have the characteristics of a formal language; best-known among these is predicate logic (applied to a language understanding system by Coles [30]).

In a formal-language MS the environment is ultimately modelled by means of certain basic units (axioms). Strictly speaking, they already belong to the class of MS which do not meet the demand for deriving the meaning of words from complex structures with diverse dependencies between model parts. Winograd [31] or Woods [32], therefore, preferred to construct more complex MS from programmes which provide both the description of environment situations and operational changes.

Other authors (e.g. Shank [4]) argue that language understanding could only be simulated on the basis of cognitive relations, and correspondingly developed as MS complex data structures such as semantic memories [3] or dependency networks [4]. The representation problem is solved by demonstrating the capabilities of the MS on severely restricted worlds (blockworld [31], Airline guide [32], lunar geology [33], industrial enterprise [34]).

1.3 Approaches to natural language processing in DT

The application of computers to the processing of large data sets in industry and public administration lead to the development of a class of special-purpose program systems known under the name of "data base systems". A data base system provides for mechanisms for the description management and processing of large sets of data.

Modern data base systems [11,35,36,37,38] are based on MS (designated as "data models") which make feasible the modelling of extensive environments. The structure of most MS is such that it is possible to formalize the description of models according to comparatively simple rules and to express their processing by means of algorithms. The formal languages developed for that purpose are called the interfaces of data base systems. Well known MS in use are the Relational Model [9], the Hierarchical Model [13], the Network Model [10], and the Binary Relation Model [12].

As soon as one attempted to make data base systems available to the casual user unfamiliar with EPD, even simple formalization rules and their corresponding formal languages proved to be a severe handicap to many users. Natural language as an end user language offers some hope of overcoming these problems, since the user need not learn a new and artificial language, but will only have to observe restrictions on a language already well-known to him. Natural language access to data base systems could be the particular advantage in areas like industrial management, medicine, pharmacy, engineering or public administration where even in data retrieval - as part of a problem solving process - the user may employ the very language in which he generally formulates his problem and solution (also see [17, 33]).

The scope of meanings of natural language queries to a data base system is determined by the MS (data model). Generally, such an MS is not oriented towards cognitive theories as it is in AI. The interface of the data base system is maintained no matter what language is chosen for accessing it, i.e. in the case of natural language access, too. In these systems the aim of language processing is to translate natural language queries into expressions of the formal language at the system interface.

Kellog was one of the first to advance this approach. He chose as the MS of his CONVERSE system [39] a formal language dedicated to information retrieval and hence containing operators typical for this purpose. Likewise, Woods put his procedural semantics into the form of an interface, in which predicate and function symbols were defined for the underlying procedures. Both these approaches fall into an area between the AI- und DT-methodology. Also to be included at this is the work by Thompson [40], whose ring structures may be interpreted both as the representation of cognitive relations and as the realization of a binary relational model [12]. While Thompson did not develop a formal interface, he - just like Woods - was heavily concerned with the integration of large data bases into his REL system.

The expressiveness of natural language goes far beyond the power of the interfaces of available data base systems. In order to make some use of this expressiveness the formal MS must at least allow for lengthy expressions based on a small number of operators (such as the definition of algorithms, nesting of functions). In general, this capability is only found in so-called navigating systems [41]. In these a complex problem is described by a single expression which is divided into a large number of successive or parallel steps during processing. The results of steps serve to the following steps as a guide to further search in the data base. A classic example is the relational model; suggestions exist for a natural language access to it [17,42]. Counter examples seem to be the Network Model, the Hierarchical Model, or simply file management. Correspondingly, no approaches have been published for use of natural-language access to them.

Other data models that might provide a basis for navigating systems are binary relations [12], LEAP-structures [43] or mathematical sets and relations [16]. The latter will serve as our starting point for demonstrating natural-language access to a data base system.

2 A set-theoretic modelling system (set language)

The set-theoretic modelling system of KAIFAS is a formal language MS based on set and relation algebra. In order to express algorithms in the language, the language elements must be classified into operators, operands and the control structure [38,44]. The operand (object) types of the set language together with their symbols are listed in fig. 2-1 together with examples from a pharmaceutical application. The symbols for the instances of types are generated by indexing the symbols of the corresponding object types. The language includes the standard set-theoretic operators (fig. 2-2). Special operators map relations to sets. Further, some logical and relational operators are defined.

The control structure of the language determines the sequential order in which the operators are executed. This is indicated in the language by expressions in functional notation, e.g.:

$$\in (I_{\text{Steicardin}}, M\cap (M_{\text{prescription drug}}, Vg(R_{\text{drug}}, I_{\text{heart neurosis}})))$$

(Interpretation: Is Steicardin a prescription drug for heart neurosis?)
The operators were applied in the sequence: Vg, M$\cap$, $\in$.

Loops are introduced by the use of bounded quantifiers. They offer the (only) possibility to formulate queries of any degree of complexity:

(1) Are all drugs for glaucoma prescription drugs?
(2) Which antibiotics are incompatible with cytostatic drugs?

In both examples the flow of control is identical:
For each element of a given set (i.e. "drugs for glaucoma" or "antibiotics") a certain condition (e.g.: to be a prescription drug, to be incompatible with cytostatic drugs) is subject to a test. In (2) only those elements are listed for which the test yields "true". (1) corresponds to the following formulation in the set-theoretic machine:

$$AL(x_1, Vg(R_{\text{drug}}, I_{\text{glaucoma}}), \in (x_1, M_{\text{prescription drug}}))$$

Important quantifiers are:

AL: all, every	EI: some
DB: which	ZB: how many

Bounded quantifiers contain three arguments:

(a) The name of a bound variable, each of its substitutions defining an invocation of the loop: x_1
(b) An expression resulting in a set of objects (range): $Vg(R_{\text{drug}}, I_{\text{glaucoma}})$

(c) An expression for the condition resulting in a truth value (scope): $\in(x_1, M_{\text{prescription drug}})$.

Expressions containing quantifiers must be in prenex normal form, i.e. quantifiers must always appear as the leftmost part of an expression.

3 Premises for language analysis in data base systems

The main purpose of data base systems is to provide tools for the management and retrieval of large volumes of data that are maintained on peripheral storage devices. Access by natural language can only be justified if it does not consume an inordinate amount of resources such as storage space or processing time. Consequently a number of restrictions must be imposed on a natural language interface in a data base system as compared to the interface of a general language understanding system.

(1) The natural language interface should be describable in terms of a simple syntax model.
This suggests to limit the syntax model to context-free grammars. Previous research has shown that context-free grammars are inadequate for the purpose of defining natural language, but the examples used in the literature for demonstrating the need of more complex grammars are of a rather exotic nature, at least as far as their applicability in data base systems goes. Indeed, Kratzer [45] defined a comparatively large subset of natural German by means of a context-free grammar without indicating any need for restricting the semantics of his subset. Therefore one would expect a context-free definition to be justified all the more in connection with formal MS and the restrictions of the semantics corresponding to it. The work by Malhotra [18] also indicates that there is no need for an extensive language definition in the data base area. Hence the application of context-free languages does not seem to place unreasonable constraints on the formulations a user may be able to use.

(2) Simple procedures should be chosen for morphemic analysis.
The analysis of natural language, and German in particular, introduces the problem of morphemic analysis [20,46]. Depending on the permissible error rate (incorrectly reduced word forms) costs and efforts for solving this problem may rise arbitrarily high (e.g. [21]). Preferably, simple procedures should be chosen here again, the error rate resulting from even very simple procedures (masking [47]) is surprisingly low (~30 %).

(3) Verbs should be omitted from the interface.
Both requirements (1) and (2) can be justified all the more, since, in defining a language for data base systems, verbs may be omitted to a large extent. Obviously, verbs are indispensible as soon as a MS accounts for temporal relationships and, consequently, permits the

description of dynamic processes (e.g. see REL [40]). Data bases of that kind, however, have so far never gone beyond pilot studies; data base systems in practical use do not include them yet.

(4) The parser should be simple and, on the average, fast.
Like (1) and (2), this requirement influences the complexity of the total system. In the literature a number of parsers for context-free languages are given [48,49,50]. Their efficiency is measured in terms of an upper limit of the time needed for processing sentences containing n words (in general the efficiency is proportional to kn^3). However, for queries to a data base system n is comparatively small, so that for choosing a parser the factor k becomes of major importance.

(5) The semantic validity test should be performed only after a syntactic analysis.
The semantic validity of a query may be controlled in combination with the retrieval. Concurrent access to the data base would have a far more negative effect, since all dead ends during the analysis would add to the total retrieval time although not to the result. Inspite of well-known objections [51] quite a number of authors working at natural-language access to data base systems [17,32] defend the principle of postponing the validity test. The number of syntactically correct but semantically meaningless constructions may be reduced by a special structure of the grammar (see 4.1).

Based on the above demands a subset of the German language was defined for accessing the KAIFAS data base system by means of a context-free grammar (4.1). Following the works by Schott [20] a procedure for simplified morphemic analysis (without verbs) was developed. The parser was derived from the M.Kay-parser [52] since it best met the requirements of (4) (see 4.3, [38]). The translation from the natural language to the set algebraic language (MS in KAIFAS) follows traditional approaches. This process consists of the four steps:

(a) lexical analysis
(b) syntactical analysis
(c) code generation
(d) transformations.

Fig. 3-1 illustrates the interaction between the steps. During each of these the following functions are performed.

(a) The query is divided into terminal symbols. When searching a dictionary on those, their corresponding representations on the set-language level is found.

(b) The parser completes the syntactical analysis by means of the grammar.

(c) If the query is parsed to a sentence, the code generation will form an expression of the set-language using the terminal representations and the code fragments generated by the parser.

(d) Then, transformations will be applied to this expression according to certain rules which will be explained in chapter 4.5.

4 Translation: Natural language into set language

4.1 Type and form of the German grammar

4.1.1 Vocabulary

As pointed out earlier a context-free formalization of the natural language interface in KAIFAS was chosen. While a suitable subset of the German language can be described as a context-free language, it is just as important that this description be practicable, i.e. comprehensible and transparent to the designer and user, and easy to implement by the system. Practicability can only be achieved by using some additional tools.

Each context-free grammar contains a number of non-terminals in order to describe the syntactical phenomena of a language. In many natural languages these tend to be quite extensive, see e.g. the combinations of case gender and number. In order to limit the set of non-terminals in the grammar, so-called complex categories (based on REL [40,53]) are introduced. These may be considered schemas for non-terminals, and consist of a main category and a number of features. Traditionally ([40,54,55]), the main categories are related to syntactical phenomena such as noun, noun phrase, whereas features refer to secondary phenomena such as number or case. The values of a feature correspond to such phenomena, e.g.:

number (1) = singular
case (2) = genitive

Schemas denote sets of non-terminals, e.g.

$$N_{num,cas,gen}$$

denotes a set of 24 non-terminals all of them nouns. Complex categories may be partially ordered by assigning values to the features:

$$N_{num,cas(2,3),gen(1,2)}$$

is a more restricted schema than $N_{num,cas,gen}$, and denotes a set of only 8 non-terminals, since only two values are possible for each, cas(2,3) and gen(1,2). Assigning a single value to each feature of a complex category results in a single non-terminal.

The treatment of complex categories in KAIFAS is different from already existing approaches in several respects:

(a) Because of the restricted semantics in KAIFAS, main categories are chosen in accordance with semantical aspects (e.g. main category for sets: ME, for relations: RE). In this way we make sure that only semantically valid constructions are described by the productions of the grammar.

(b) A grammar whose main categories are based on semantical terms does not "naturally" reject sentences containing major errors such as missing congruence in number, gender and case of adjectives and nouns, since these concepts are based on the traditional syntactical categories. The necessary syntactical aspects will be assigned to the features. As a result KAIFAS closely follows the correspondences

main categories - semantical aspects
features - syntactical aspects.

For practical reasons this classification cannot always be maintained. The set language, for example, contains (semantically) different types of quantifiers which in many productions are handled in the same (syntactical) way. The number of main categories and hence productions can be reduced by expressing the difference in type on the feature level so that only one main category will be defined for quantifiers.

(c) Only binary features are allowed:

case features: *num, gen, dat, acc*
gender features: *mas, fem, neu*
number features: *sin, plu*

The binary values are designated by +/-. Then, operations with features may easily be expressed by logic formulas.

Fig. 4-1 provides a list of the main categories and features of the KAIFAS grammar. It is apparent from the figure that the main categories fall into two classes,

(a) object-categories
(b) operator-categories,

corresponding to the classification of the set-theoretic language into objects and operators.

Applying the same distinction to the terminals of the grammar results in

(a) object symbols
which represent instances of the object types
(b) operator symbols
which represent the operators of the set-theoretic machine (the environment of the language in the sense of [56]).

Both because the set of terminal symbols is variable and large (approximately 50.000 objects in the pharmaceutical area) terminal productions are not made part of the grammar, but are maintained by means of a dictionary (lexical analysis is described in chapter 4.2). The operator symbols form a fixed set, but some concordances can be identified, such as all operator symbols for quantifiers to which only one main category will be assigned (see above). The operator symbols are also included in the dictionary.

4.1.2 Productions

The use of complex categories requires a similar extension of productions into complex productions:

$$NP_{cas,gen,num} \rightarrow Det_{cas,gen,num} \; N_{cas,gen,num}$$

This is a production schema from which one may derive a set of context-free productions when substituting suitable non-terminals for the complex categories. In doing so, the feature values have to meet certain conditions (e.g. congruence in case and number). Consequently, the complex rules are separated into a rewrite rule defined on main categories only, and a feature program specifying which combination of feature values may be assigned to the complex categories in this rule. The feature program consists of a test section specifying the conditions that the feature values of the complex categories in the right-hand part of the production have to meet in order to apply the rule, and an assignment section defining the feature values for the left-hand complex category. Test and specification could be done in list form ([45]) or by means of programs in a special programming language such as in KAIFAS.

In summary, a complex rule may be defined as follows:

(1) $\bar{V}_o \rightarrow \bar{V}_1 \; .... \; \bar{V}_p$	rewrite rule
(2) $A(V_1,...,V_p)$	feature program (test)
(3) $Z(V_1,...,V_p)$	feature program (assignment of the features of V_o)
(4) $S(V_1,...,V_p)$	semantical part of the rule

V_o, V_1,... V_p denote complex categories, $\bar{V}_o$, $\bar{V}_1$,... $\bar{V}_p$ their main categories.

Fig. 4-2 provides a summary of the operators used in feature programs.

The semantical part is a term for defining the meaning of the complex rule. It consists of set-language symbols, and place-markers for the semantics of the complex categories in the rule. Since some semantical aspects are treated on the feature level, the semantical part may depend on conditions concerning features. These dependencies are defined by feature programs as well. Thus the semantical part $S(V_1,\ldots,V_p)$ of a complex rule may alternatively be phrased as

$$A(V_1,\ldots,V_p) \Rightarrow S'(V_1,\ldots,V_p) \quad \text{(dependencies on features)}$$

or

$$S'(V_1,\ldots,V_p) \quad \text{(no dependencies)}$$

Fig. 4-3 gives an example of a complex rule.

A complex rule may be applied in the following steps (further details are provided in chapter 4.3):

(1) Matching the input string with the right-hand side of the rule
(2) Testing the right-hand features for acceptance
(3) If yielding "true", reduction to left-hand side and assignment of features and semantics

4.2 Lexical analysis

4.2.1 Assignment of complex categories

The dictionary contains all the object-symbols and all those operator-symbols which have been classified into types. Since the set of object-symbols is chosen in a user- or application-dependent fashion, these will not be defined until a user actually works with the system.

The lexical analysis fulfills two functions:

(a) assignment of a complex category to a terminal
 (a_1) assign a main category
 (a_2) assign feature-values,
(b) assignment of semantics (i.e. a terminal symbol of the set language).

A large number of syntactical ambiguities may be expressed within one complex category, such as the ambiguity arising by the German word "ein" (*+nom* or *+acc*):

ein $\xrightarrow{\textit{lexical analysis}}$ *QU-mas-fem+neu+nom-gen-dat+acc+sin-plu*

where the list of feature-values may be considered a conjunctive logical expression. If disjunction is needed as well, a conjunctive normal form is used.

Example from German language:

drageeförmigen → { *ME+mas-nom+gen+dat+acc+sin-plu*
ME+fem+neu-nom+gen+dat-acc+sin-plu

Here the accusative case is allowed for the gender of masculinum, but not for neutrum or femininum.

4.2.2 Morphology

The multitude of inflections in German language does not allow for storing in a dictionary all word forms to be derived from a large user-vocabulary. Rather, the dictionary only contains the word stems. Reduction from inflective form to word stem is done by algorithmic means (morphological analysis). The exclusion of verbs simplifies the problem. A word stem is defined as follows:

(a) nouns: nominative-singular form
(b) adjectives: attributive form

Also, the morphological analysis must determine the syntactical structure of a terminal (gender, case, etc.). Different approaches have been published for solving this problem for the German language ([20]), but all of them require that extensive linguistic information be supplied with each word in the dictionary which can hardly be expected from a casual user. Therefore, when defining a word stem in KAIFAS the user will only be required to specify a minimum of information, namely:

(1) object-class of a word
(2) gender
(3) noun/adjective
(4) singular and plural forms of the word

The word may then be assigned to a specific morphemic class (see [20]). This class contains all morphemic endings that may be attached to the word stem. Each morphemic ending will determine one or more syntactical structures (set of feature values) for all these terminals that contain this ending. By explicitly storing the plural forms of terminals the highly problematical reduction of terminals involving mutation of vowels becomes unnecessary. The additional storage space required may be tolerated, since plural forms occur in case of set- and relation-identifiers only. Fig. 4-4 presents an example of a morphemic class. In order to save storage space in the dictionary, the syntactical structure of a word stem will also be defined by morphological analysis.

Thus any morphemic class will contain an entry for the null ending "ε".

In fig. 4-5 the complete lexical analysis of a query is illustrated. The syntactical structure of a terminal can be highly ambiguous due to the lexical analysis. The feature programs, however, allow for easy disambiguation as demonstrated by the example of fig. 4-6.

4.2.3 Lexical analysis: algorithm

Lexical analysis for a word $x=x_1...x_k$ is carried out according to the simple algorithm outlined below:

For $l = 0,1,2,..., \min(k-1,3)$:

$x' = x/x_{k-l}...x_k$ (delete $x_{k-l}...x_k$ from x)

If x'is found in the dictionary and $x_{k-l}...x_k$ belongs to the morphemic class of x',

then assign to x':

(1) the main category of the dictionary entry

(2) the features of the dictionary entry

(3) the features defined by the entry of $x_{k-l}...x_k$ in the morphemic class

(4) the semantics specified in the dictionary.

This algorithm is applied to each terminal of a query. The result will be converted to a form suitable for the ensuing parsing process.

4.3 Parser

The parser completes the syntactical and semantical analysis of a query. According to what has been said so far it has to meet the following conditions:

(1) The parser has to recognize context-free languages.

(2) It must be able to operate on complex categories and rules.

(3) The storage space and execution time required for the analysis should be kept small in comparison to the requirements of the entire retrieval process.

(4) Furthermore a syntax-directed approach is needed for parsing which is independent of a special grammar. This is due to the fact that constructing a grammar for natural languages is an approximative process. The grammar will be continuously modified and enlarged, in order to eliminate wrong constructions or to extend the set of permissible sentences.

Several parsers are known to meet conditions (1) and (4), whereas an adaptation to (2) is always necessary. Amongh these, Earley's parser for cfg's suggests itself [48]. However, adapting an improved version of this parser to complex categories and rules resulted in an unwieldy algorithm violating condition (3) (see [57]).

Therefore a parser based on the ideas of Kay [52] was developed. The original algorithm is capable of operating on general rewrite rules but was restricted to context-free grammars expressed in our complex notation. Only a short introduction to this parser will be presented, for details we refer to [38].

Fig. 4-7 represents a typical parsing graph as generated by the parser. The graph contains n+1 vertices for a query consisting of n words. Every edge of the graph is labelled by a complex category and its semantics.

During lexical analysis an initial parsing graph is constructed (heavy lines in fig. 4-7). It contains edges only between vertices k and k+1 $(1 \leq k \leq n)$. The number of edges between two vertices is l, where l the number of complex categories assigned to the k-th terminal in a query.

The parser operates on the initial parsing graph as follows: Starting at vertix k, for all sequences of edges from k to vertices k' $(k < k' \leq n+1)$ the parser compares the main categories within the labels with the right-hand sides of all complex rules. On total agreement with a rule r, the parser performs the following steps:

(a) The feature program of rule r operates on the complex categories in the sequence of edges.
(b) If the test yields "true", the parser produces a new edge between the starting and ending vertices of the sequence of edges. The new edge is labelled by the left-hand side of the rewrite rule and by the features obtained from the assignment section in the feature program of r.
(c) The edge is additionally labelled by the semantics of the rule with all place markers replaced by pointers to the semantics of the complex categories in the sequence of edges.

This process is repeated for all vertices from right to left down to vertix 1.
The parsing of a query will prove successful, if there is an edge between vertices 1 and n+1, which is labelled by the axiom of the grammar (in this case SA).

In fig. 4-8 a special numbering (①, ②) shows the order by which the edges have been generated. The exact structure of the parse can be derived by means of the pointers which connect the semantics. Obviously, the pointer structure saves storage space over a solution generating complete code fragments for each edge.

4.4 Code generation

On code generation the fragments are assembled into one or more expressions of the set-theoretic language depending on the ambiguity of the query. These expressions form the result of query translation.

4.5 Transformations

Applying the code generation process to the parsing graph in fig. 4-7 results in the following expression:

$\subset$ (DB(x,M$\cap$ (M25,M4),#), Ng(R8,I128))

This expression is not well-formed, since the quantifier is not the leftmost operator (prenex normal form). # serves as a placemarker for the scope.

Problems of this kind and other syntactical properties of the set language pose difficulties when handled by the translation mechanism introduced above [38]. Other examples of this nature are the following:

(a) Nesting of quantifiers in the set language is subject to certain rules which control their relative position within an expression: set quantifiers like DB must appear in front of logical quantifiers like AL, EI.

(b) Difficulties arise from the difference in relative position of operator symbols for quantifiers within natural German and in that of their corresponding quantifiers within the set-theoretic equivalent:

Which remedies for which diseases are prescription drugs?

$DB(x_1,M_{diseases}, DB(x_2,Vg(R_{remedy},x_1), \in (x_2,M_{prescription\ drug})))$

These problems can be solved by means of grammar rules, but then the grammar proves impractical (see [38]). Thus these problems are defered to an analysis phase that takes place after completion of the parsing process and hence after application of the grammar rules.

A solution could be based on the tree-like pointer structure of the semantical fragments, which we shall call a semantical tree. The semantical tree has then to be transformed by suitable rules such that the linear expression derived by code-generation puts the quantifiers in right order. Transformations of parsing-trees are usually formulated by means of transformational grammars, but implementing these requires large efforts in time and personell [58].

Moreover, the problems just discussed form a trivial subset of the general transformation problem. It can be shown that for every transformation rule defined on semantical trees and needed here there exists a corresponding rule defined on the linear form, the expression. In place of the traditional approach where basic trees are given as arguments, these rules contain an expression pattern which must be contained in the expression to be transformed. For example, the pattern

(a) $DB_1(x_1, Vg(R, DB_2(x_2, M, \#)))$

is transformed into:

$$DB_2(x_2, M, DB_1(x_1, Vg(R, x_2), \#))$$

Manipulations of linear expressions are easier to do than transformation of trees. Thus the transformations are postponed until after code generation. The transformations may be formulated by means of a string-manipulation language forming a set of procedures. (Our work in this direction is discussed in [59]). These procedures are integrated in the system and executed after code generation.
Fig. 4-8 shows some examples of transformations.

5 Conclusions

The linguistic techniques discussed in this paper have been implemented at the University of Karlsruhe on a Burroughs 6700 as part of the KAIFAS information system. Some experience in their usefulness has been gained by applying the system to a pharmaceutical data base containing data on a part of the drugs available on the German pharmaceutical market (about 8000 [60]). This data base was applied by experts inexperienced in data processing via the natural German interface.

One of the purposes of this implementation was to test the premises in chapter 3 for their validity. A context-free definition of the natural language interface proved sufficient for this application. Whether this is true in general can only be decided if one included verbs in the interface. The descriptive power of the cf-grammar in the system was even unnecessarily large, because the users when working with the system tended to use successively several short queries instead of a single long one, i.e. they solved their problems in steps. For this reason relative clauses could eventually be excluded from the query language. Instead, the possibility of references to queries stated before is needed involving solutions to the well-known problem of pronouns.

The morphological analysis proved to be sufficient, too. All correct inflectional forms were detected and reduced. The simple approach will not guarantee, however, that a syntactical incorrect inflectional form will be refused under any circumstances.

The M.Kay-parser, which we restricted to cf-languages, turned out to be a very simple algorithm. One can show that the algorithm is superior to Earley's parser with respect to processing time for short sentences in the neighbourhood of ten words or less. Consequently, the M.Kay parser is particularly suited to the stepwise user approach mentioned above.

Fig. 2-1

Object types

I	Individuals, e.g. Thomapyrin, Perphyllon
M	Sets, e.g. drugs, diseases Lists of individuals
R	Relations, e.g. indication, contraindication, manufacturer Lists of pairs of individuals (Work is under way to cover n-ary relations)
Z	Numbers
D	Measures, e.g. 4 tablets/day
F	Measure functions, e.g. dosage Lists of ordered n-tuples whose last component is a measure
B	truth values

Operands

I_1, I_2, I_3,...., I_n, M_1, M_2, M_3, ..., M_k, R_1,....

Fig. 2-2

Operators

on sets:

$Mb(I_1, \ldots, I_n)$	set construction
$M\cup(M_1, M_2)$	union
$M\cap(M_1, M_2)$	intersection
$Km(M_1, M_2)$	set difference
$Kz(M_1)$	cardinality

on relations:

$Ko(R_1)$	converse
$Rb(R_1, M_1)$	restriction $(\{(x,y) \mid (x,y) \in R_1 \wedge x \in M_1\})$
$Rp(R_1, R_2)$	product
$R\cup(R_1, R_2)$	union

reduction of binary relations:

$Vo(R_1)$	domain $\{x \mid \exists y: (x,y) \in R_1\}$
$Na(R_1)$	range $\{x \mid \exists y: (y,x) \in R_1\}$
$Vg(R_1, I_1)$	individual domain $\{x \mid (x, I_1) \in R_1\}$
$Ng(R_1, I_1)$	individual range $\{x \mid (I_1, x) \in R_1\}$

reduction of measure functions:

$Fw(F_1, I_1)$	measure number

logical operators:

$\in(I_1, M_1)$	test on set membership
$\subset(M_1, M_2)$	test on set inclusion

Fig. 3-1

Translation to set language

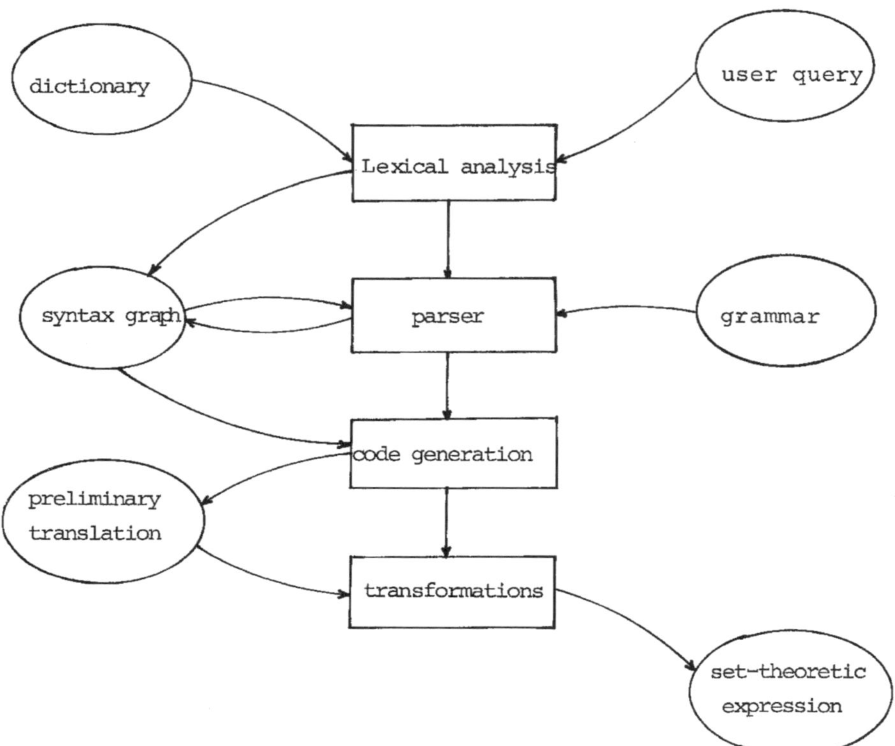

Fig. 4-1

Main categories

AF	AL - quantifier
DZ	measures
ED	term for evaluating measures
EI	measure units
IN	proper name
ME	set
MF	measure function
PR	operators: relations → sets (prepositions)
RE	relations
RP	DB-quantifier
RS	restriction of sets (relative clause)
SA	sentence
SF	EI / KE - quantifier
QU	other quantifiers
VO	relational operator
ZA	number

Features

syntactical aspects:

mas	masculinum
fem	femininum
neu	neutrum
nom	nominative
gen	genitive
dat	dative
acc	accusative
sin plu	number
adj	adjective/noun
att	attributive
ajm	adjective-modified
pdt	predetermined (the drug)
prm	premodified (Peter's friend)
pom	postmodified (friend of Peter)
std	strong declination
svk	stops genitive concatenations

semantical aspects:

qua	quantified
neg	negation-quantifiers (no: KE)
frw	interrogative (who, what)
mul div exp add	for arithmetic operators

Fig. 4-2

Operators in feature programs:

(1) test part:

test (<complex category>,<list of feature-values>)
yields true, if the complex category has associated with it the feature-values specified, else false.

meq (<complex category>,<complex category>,<list of features>)
yields true, whenever at least one of the listed features agrees in both complex categories specified.

equ (<complex category>,<complex category>,<list of features>)
same as *meq*, but all features must agree.

$\wedge$,$\vee$ logical connectives

(2) assignment part:

(all assignments are to the complex category of the left rule part)

zuw (<list of feature-values>)
assigns the feature-values specified.

cop (<complex category>,<list of features>)
copies the values of the features of the denoted complex symbols.

and (<complex category>,<complex category>,<list of features>)
assigns those feature-values which agree in both complex categories.

Fig. 4-3

(1)	ME $\rightarrow$ ME ME	rewrite rule
(2)	*test* (ME^2, *+adj-att*) $\wedge$ *test* (ME^3,*-adj*) $\wedge$ *meq* (ME^2,ME^3, *sin,plu*) *meq* (ME^2,ME^3, *nom,gen,dat,acc*) $\wedge$ *meq* (ME^2, ME^3,*mas,fem,neu*);	feature program (test)
(3)	*zuw* (*-adj*), *and*(ME^2,ME^3,*sin,plu*), *and*(ME^2,ME^3,*mas,fem,neu*) *and* (ME^2,ME^3, *nom, gen, dat, acc*);	feature program (assignment)
(4)	M$\cap$ (ME^2,ME^3)	semantical part

The upper index (ME^2) serves for disambiguation of the complex categories of the production. The feature test excludes those adjectives and nouns which do not agree in number and in at least one of gender or case. The resulting complex category is treated like a noun *(-adj)*,most of the possible ambiguities in gender and noun are solved by the *and*-operator. The semantics of the production is the set-intersection.

Fig. 4-4

Morphemic class for articles singular (e.g. "kein")

ending	syntactical structure
" ε "	+mas-fem-num+nom-gen-dat-acc -mas-fem+neu+nom-gen-dat+acc
"e"	-mas+fem-neu+nom-gen-dat+acc
"es"	+mas-fem+neu-nom+gen-dat-acc
"em"	+mas-fem+neu-nom-gen+dat-acc
"en"	+mas-fem-neu-nom-gen-dat+acc
"er"	-mas+fem-neu-nom+gen+dat-acc

Fig. 4-5

Result of lexical analysis for an entire sentence

Word	Main category	features	set-theoretic representation
Welche	QU	+mas+fem+neu+nom+acc+plu	DB
	QU	+fem+nom+acc+sin	DB
drageeför-migen	ME	+mas+neu+gen+dat+acc+sin	M25
	ME	+fem+neu+gen+dat+sin	M25
	ME	+mas+fem+neu+nom+gen+dat+acc+plu	M25
Psycho-pharmaka	ME	+neu+nom+gen+acc+plu	M4
haben	<terminal>	-	
Depression	IN	+nom+dat+acc	I64
als	<terminal>	-	Ng
Indikation	RE	+fem+nom+gen+dat+acc+sin	R8

Fig. 4-6

Disambiguation

Rule: $ME_1 \rightarrow ME_2 \quad ME_3$

$Meq(mas,fem,neu,ME_2,ME_3) \wedge Meq(nom,gen,dat,acc,ME_2,ME_3) \wedge$
$Meq(sin,plu,ME_2,ME_3);$
$And(mas,fem,neu,ME_2,ME_3), And(nom,gen,dat,acc,ME_2,ME_3),$
$And(sin,plu,ME_2,ME_3);$
$M\cap(2,3);$

applied to

(1) ME +mas-fem-neu-nom+gen +dat+acc+sin-plu (drageeförmigen)

(2) ME -mas+fem+neu-nom+gen +dat-acc+sin-plu "

(3) ME +mas+fem+neu+nom+gen +dat+acc-sin+plu "

(4) ME -mas-fem+neu+nom+gen -dat+acc-sin+plu (Psychopharmaka)

Because of number (sin,plu) the feature test accepts combinations (3) and (4) only. The feature-assignment yields:

(5) ME -mas-fem+neu+nom+gen -dat+acc-sin+plu (drageeförmigen Psychopharmaka)

Rule: $ME_1 \rightarrow QU_2 \quad ME_3$

$Meq(mas,fem,neu,QU_2,ME_3) \wedge Meq(nom,gen,dat,acc,QU_2,ME_3) \wedge$
$Meq(sin,plu,QU_2,ME_3);$
$And(mas,fem,neu,QU_2,ME_3), And(nom,gen,dat,acc,QU_2,ME_3),$
$And(sin,plu,QU_2,ME_3):$
2(x,3,#)

applied to

(6) QU +mas+fem+neu+nom-gen-dat +acc-sin+plu (welche)

(7) QU -mas+fem-neu+nom-gen-dat +acc+sin-plu "

(5) ME -mas-fem+neu+nom+gen -dat+acc-sin+plu (drageeförmigen Psychopharmaka)

Only combination (6) / (5) is accepted.

Result: ME -mas-fem+neu+nom-gen -dat+acc-sin+plu (welche drageeförmigen Psychopharmaka)

Thus all ambiguities with the exception of case (nominativ/accusative) are resolved.

Fig. 4-7

Parsing-graph

Only those features are listed which prevent a rule from being applied.

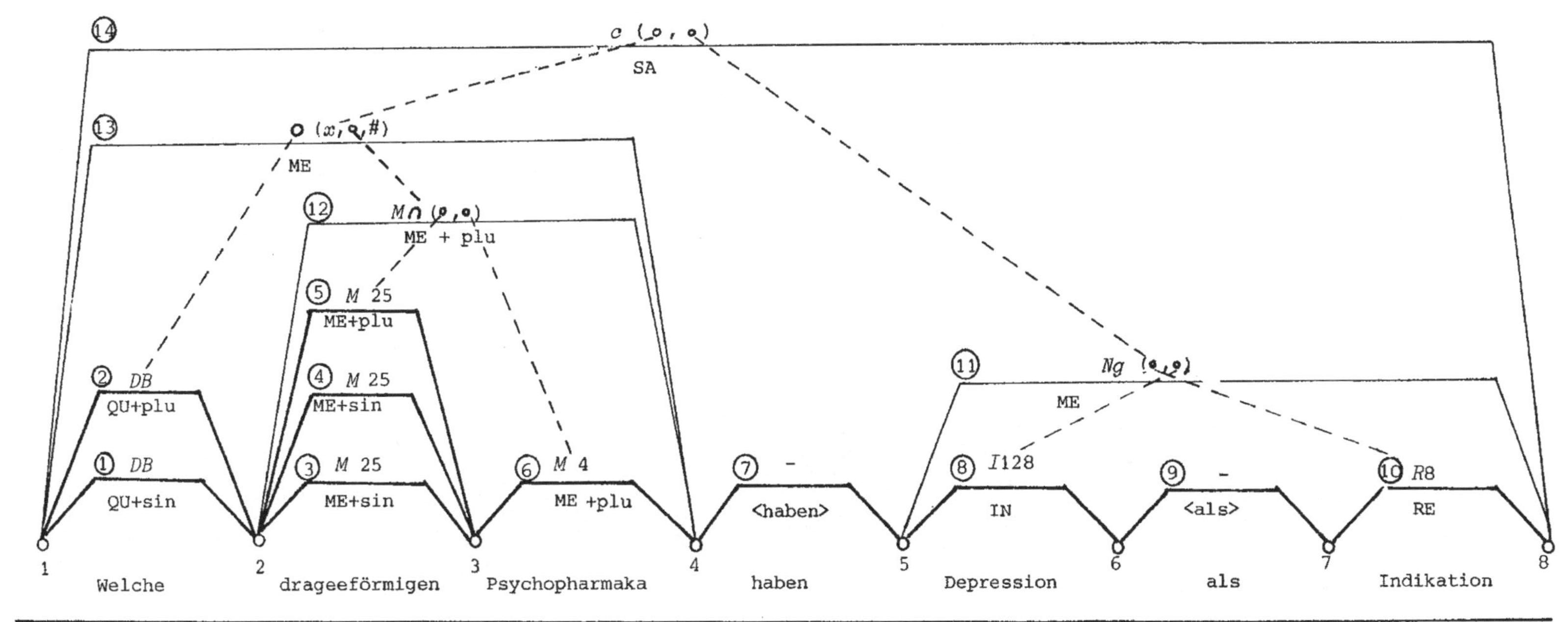

Grammar rules applied (the rewrite rule and semantics only):

$ME \rightarrow IN$ als RE;
$Ng(RE, IN)$

$ME_1 \rightarrow ME_2\ ME_3$;
$M\cap(ME_2, ME_3)$

$ME_1 \rightarrow QU\ ME_2$;
$QU(x, ME_2, \#)$

$SA \rightarrow ME_1$ haben ME_2;
$c(ME_1, ME_2)$

Only those rules are stated whose application do not result in dead-ends.

Fig. 4-8

Transformations

1) Welche drageeförmigen Psychopharmaka haben Depression als Indikation?

   Preliminary translation

   $\subset$ (DB(x,M$\cap$ (M25,M4),#), Ng(R8,I128)

   Transformation: Quantifier DB is placed in front of the expression, $\subset$ transformed to $\in$.

   DB(x,M$\cap$ (M25,M4), $\in$(x,Ng(R8,I128)))

2) Welche Indikationen welcher Medikamente sind Psychosen?

   Preliminary translation:

   $\in$ (DB(x_1,Vg(R8,DB(x_2,M29,#)),#), M30)

   Transformation: Both quantifiers are placed in front but in reverse order.

   DB(x_2,M29,DB(x_1,Vg(R8,x_2), $\in$ (x_1,M30)))

[1] T.Winograd: Five Lectures on Artificial Intelligence. Computer Science Department, Stanford University (Sept. 1974)

[2] L.C.Smith: Artificial Intelligence in Information Retrieval Systems. Information Processing & Management, Vol.12, pp.189-222, Pergamon (1976)

[3] R.Quillian: Semantic Memory. In M.Minsky (ed.): Semantic Information Processing. MIT Press, Cambridge, Mass. (1968)

[4] R.Schank: Identification of Conceptualizations Underlying Natural Language. In Schank and Colby (eds.): Computer Models of Thought and Language, pp. 187-248, Freeman (1973)

[5] E.Charniak: Toward a Model of Children's Story Comprehension. MIT Artificial Intelligence Laboratory, Cambridge, Mass. (1972)

[6] V.Cherniavsky: On Algorithmic Natural Language Analysis and Understanding. Advanced Course on Data Base Languages and Natural Language Processing, Freudenstadt (Sept. 1976)

[7] Procs.IFIP-TC-2 Working Conference on: Modelling in Data Base Management Systems, Freudenstadt, 5.-9.1.1976

[8] R.Durchholz, G.Richter: Concepts for Data Base Management Systems. Procs.IFIP-TC-2 Working Conference on "Data Base Management Systems", Cargese, Corsica, North-Holland Publishing Co. (1974)

[9] E.F.Codd: A Relational Model of Data for Large Shared Data Banks. Comm. ACM 13 (1970), pp. 377-387

[10] R.W.Taylor, R.L.Frank: CODASYL Data Base Management Systems. ACM Computing Surveys, Vol.8, Nr.1 (1976), pp. 67-104

[11] CODASYL-DBTG, Data Base Task Group Report, New York (1971)

[12] J.R.Abrial: Data Semantics. Procs.IFIP-TC-2 Working Conference on "Data Base Management Systems", Cargese, Corsica, North-Holland Publishing Co. (1974)

[13] C.J.Date: An Introduction to Database Systems. Addison-Wesley Publ. Company (1975)

[14] C.A.Montgomery: Is Natural Language an Unnatural Query Language? Proc. ACM Natl. Conf. 1972, pp. 1075-1078

[15] Procs.of the Advanced Course on Data Base Languages and Natural Language Processing, Freudenstadt (Sept. 1976)

[16] K.D.Krägeloh, P.C.Lockemann: Hierarchies of Data Base Languages: An Example. Information Systems, Vol.1, pp.79-90, Pergamon Press (1975)

[17] E.F.Codd: Seven Steps to Rendezvous with the Casual User. Procs. IFIP-TC-2 Working Conference on "Data Base Management Systems", Cargese, Corsica, North-Holland Publishing Co. (1974)

[18] A.Malhotra: Design Criteria for a Knowledge-Based English Language System for Management: An Experimental Analysis. MIT Project MAC, Cambridge, Mass. (1975)

[19] Data Base. Vol.8, Nr.2 (1968)

[20] G.Schott: Automatische Analyse der Flexionsmorpheme deutscher Substantive. Technische Universität München, Abteilung Mathematik, Gruppe Informatik, Bericht Nr.7210 (1972)

[21] Zur maschinellen Syntaxanalyse. Forschungsberichte, Institut für Deutsche Sprache, Mannheim, Bd. 18.1, 18.2, 19., Narr-Verlag, Tübingen (1974)

[22] G.Salton: Automatic Information Organization and Retrieval. McGraw Hill Book Co., New York (1968)

[23] H.L.Josselson: Automatic Translation of Languages Since 1960: A Linguist's View. In: Advances in Computers 11 (1971), pp. 1-58

[24] A.M.Turing: Computing Machinery and Intelligence. Mind (1959), 59, pp. 433-460

[25] J.A.Fodor, J.J.Katz: The Structure of a Semantic Theory. In: Fodor/Katz (eds.): The Structure of Language. Prentice Hall (1964), pp. 170-210

[26] D.G.Bobrow: A Question-Answering System for High School Algebra Word Problems. In Procs. AFIPS 1964 Fall Joint Comp. Conf., Vol. 26, pp. 591-614

[27] B.Raphael: SIR. In Procs. AFIPS 1964 Fall Joint Comp. Conf., Vol. 26, pp. 577-589

[28] B.F.Green et al.: BASEBALL. In F.A.Feigenbaum, J.Feldman (eds.): Computer and Thought. McGraw Hill, New York (1963), pp. 207-216

[29] J.Weizenbaum: ELIZA. Communications of the ACM, Vol.9 (1966), pp. 36-45

[30] L.Coles, L.Stephen: An On-Line Question Answering System with Natural Language and Pictorial Input. In Procs. ACM 23rd Natl. Conf. (1968), pp. 157-167

[31] T.Winograd: Understanding Natural Language. Academic Press Inc., New York (1972)

[32] W.A.Woods: Procedural Semantics for a Question Answering Machine. Procs. AFIPS Fall Joint Comp. Conf., 33 (1968), pp. 457-471

[33] W.A.Woods: Progress in Natural Language Understanding - An Application to Lunar Geology. Procs. National Comp. Conf. (1973), pp. 441-450

[34] J.Mylopoulos, S.Schuster, D.Tsichritzis: A Multi-Level Relational System. Procs. National Comp. Conf. (1975), pp. 403-408

[35] M.M.Astrahan et al.: System R: Relational Approach to Database Management. ACM Transactions in Database Systems, Vol.1, Nr.2 (1976)

[36] IMS 2. In: Kurzbeschreibung von Information Storage and Retrieval Systemen, Gesellschaft für Mathematik und Datenverarbeitung, St.Augustin (1973)

[37] S.Todd: Integrated Architecture for Transaction Specification and Optimization in Relational Data Base Systems. Summer School on Data Base Technology, GMD St.Augustin (1976)

[38] K.D.Krägeloh: A Multi-Level System Architecture with Natural Language Interface (in German). Ph.D.Thesis, University of Karlsruhe (1976)

[39] C.H.Kellog: A Natural Language Compiler for Online Data Management. AFIPS 1968 Fall Joint Comp. Conf., Vol.33, pp.473-493

[40] F.B.Thompson, P.C.Lockemann, B.Dostert, R.S.Deverill: REL: A Rapidly Extensible Language System. Procs. 24th National ACM Conference (1969), pp. 399-417

[41] C.W.Bachman: The Programmer as Navigator. Communications of the ACM, Vol.16, Nr.11 (1973), pp. 653-658

[42] M.Lacroix, A.Pirotte: ILL: An English Structured Query Language for Relational Data Bases. M.B.L.E. Research Laboratory Report, Brussels (1976)

[43] J.A.Feldman, P.P.Rovner: An ALGOL-Based Associative Language. Communications of the ACM, Vol.12, Nr.8 (1969), pp. 439-449

[44] G.Goos: Programmkonstruktion. Interner Bericht, Universität Karlsruhe (1974)

[45] A.Kratzer, E.Pause, A.v.Stechow: Einführung in die Theorie und Anwendung der generativen Syntax. Athenaeum Verlag, Frankfurt (1974)

[46] PASSAT. Systembeschreibung Siemens PBS4004, München (1973)

[47] I.Steinacker: Dokumentationssysteme. De Gruyter, Berlin, New York (1975)

[48] J.C.Earley: An Efficient Context-Free Parsing Algorithm. Ph.D. Thesis, Carnegie-Mellon University, Pittsburgh, Pennsylvania (1968)

[49] T.Kasami: An Efficient Recognition and Syntax Analysis Algorithm for Context-Free Languages. University of Illinois (1966)

[50] D.H.Younger: Recognition and Parsing of Context-Free Languages in Time n^3. Information and Control 10 (1967), pp. 189-208

[51] R.F.Simmons: Natural Language Question Anwering Systems: 1969. Communications of the ACM, Vol.13, Nr.1 (1970), pp. 15-30

[52] M.Kay: Experiments with a Powerful Parser. Deuxième Conference sur le Traitement automatique des langues, Grenoble (1967)

[53] B.H.Dostert, F.B.Thompson: How Features Resolve Syntactic Ambiguity. Procs. of the Symposium on Information Storage and Retrieval, University of Maryland (1971)

[54] K.Brockhaus: Automatische Übersetzung. Vieweg Verlag, Braunschweig (1971)

[55] H.Wulz: ISLIB - Ein Informationssystem auf linguistischer Basis. Interner Bericht, Institut für Deutsche Sprache, Abteilung Linguistische Datenverarbeitung, Mannheim (1975)

[56] F.B.Thompson: English for the Computer. Procs. AFIPS Fall Joint Comp. Conf. (1966), pp. 349-356

[57] W.Wohlleber: Ein Parser für die Analyse natürlicher Sprache. Diplomarbeit, Universität Karlsruhe (1973)

[58] J.Friedman: A Computer Model fo Transformational Grammar. American Elsevier Publishing Company Inc., New York (1971)

[59] C.Mathis: Entwurf und Implementierung einer textverarbeitenden Sprache. Diplomarbeit, Universität Karlsruhe (1975)

[60] ROTE LISTE 1975. Herausgeber: Bundesverband der pharmazeutischen Industrie, Frankfurt, EDITIO CANTOR, Aulendorf/Württ. (1975)

AN OVERVIEW OF P L I D I S

A PROBLEM SOLVING INFORMATION SYSTEM WITH GERMAN AS QUERY LANGUAGE*)

G.L. Berry-Rogghe
H. Wulz

Institut für deutsche Sprache
Postfach 5409, D-6800 Mannheim 1

1. Background and application of the system

PLIDIS (Problemlösendes Informationssystem mit Deutsch als Interaktionssprache) is a natural language information system which is being designed in the context of a project in automated language processing at the Institut für deutsche Sprache sponsored by the Ministry for Research and Technology for the years 1976-77. The present project is in many ways an extension of a previous two-year project which achieved the construction of the experimental question-answering system ISLIB (Informationssystem auf linguistischer Basis) (e.g. KOLB & WULZ 1975) based on the simulated problem domain of the stock-exchange. Within this framework theoretical foundations were investigated and different approaches experimented with. The PLIDIS project differs from its predecessor in its intention to implement an actual system, whereby our emphasis lies on the adaptation of the methods tried out in the pilot-study to a real problem domain and on enhancing the problem solving capacities of the system.

The field of application of PLIDIS will be the control of water pollution. A pilot version of the system is being developed in co-operation with the regional 'department of the environment' at Stuttgart, who supervise industrial wastes lead into the rivers of Northern-Württemberg

*) The research reported here is supported by the German Federal Republic's "Bundesminister für Forschung und Technologie" under grant Nr. 081 5900 69 within the "3. DV-Programm der Bundesregierung".

**) The authors are endebted to W.Brecht, W.Dilger, R.Guntermann, D.Kolb, M.Kolvenbach, A.Lötscher, H.D.Lutz, K.Saukko, G.Zifonun who collaborate within the PLIDIS-project and who did a lot of the research reported here.

In the control of water pollution several bodies co-operate, such as the Waterboard of the Land and the various local authorities; PLIDIS is therefore to be used by a wide variety of people dealing with different aspects of the supervision of industrial waste water.

The following sets of actions are involved in the process of controlling a particular firm:

- the authorities regularly inspect the firms in order to collect and verify data about their production process, the waste products generated, the type and functioning of the sewage treatment plant, etc.,
- at regular intervals sewage samples are taken and sent for analysis to a neutral laboratory,
- the firm is sent a report containing the results of the analysis.

With reference to this field of application, PLIDIS is scheduled to be used in the following capacities:

- as supervision system, e.g. to check the chemical composition of the samples, to compare the current sample with previous samples from the same firm and to issue appropriate warnings if a norm has been transgressed,
- as information system, e.g. to answer queries concerning the composition and toxicity of certain chemicals, the characteristics of the production processes of the firms involved etc.,
- as investigation system, e.g. to detect where pollution may have originated and possibly suggest plans of actions to be taken.

2. General design of PLIDIS

The PLIDIS information system is composed of, on the one hand, a linguistic-logical part which translates the German input into an internal representation modelled on the predicate calculus, and, on the other hand, a problem-solving part which, in addition to performing the usual storage and retrieval functions, involves problem domain-specific regularities in the deduction process.

The design of the system is largely modular and allows extensive user-interaction between the various execution phases. This modularity is an essential prerequisite for efficient teamwork as each member of the group can be allocated a specific part and possible changes in personnel take place smoothly. From the same point of view, interactive facilities are essential to facilitate experimentation and debugging.

Figure 1 is a diagrammatic representation of the system's main components showing the flow of information between them.

The PLIDIS-user has several choices of access to the system, some of which are designed especially for a more naive user and some which are destined for the system designer and administrator.

The natural language processor (NLP) enables the user to formulate problem descriptions as natural language questions or to use natural language for the input of shorter pieces of information such as rules about his problem domain or data for updating.

For the input of stereotyped data of larger quantities, the user may have data-sheets on his terminal, which are processed by the processor of formatted input (FIP). This processor provides also facilities accessible by the system's command language (CL) to define new data-sheets and procedures for plausibility checks of the formatted input.

The natural language processor and the formatted input processor have the same task to perform i.e. to translate the input into the language of internal representation (IR), an extension of first order predicate calculus.

The processor for informations and problem descriptions (PIP) either stores the incoming information or activates problem solving mechanisms in the case of problem descriptions, according to the type of question asked.

In the current state of the system, the processor for answer-formulations (PAF) generates only some sort of 'pretty-print' from the formulas of internal representation, which contain the information found by the PIP-component as answer to the users questions. It would be desirable at a future stage that this component be replaced by procedures which generate natural language sentences out of IRL-formulas.

The interaction of these components is guided by the PLIDIS-supervisor which processes the command language statements and accepts also INTERLISP-code.

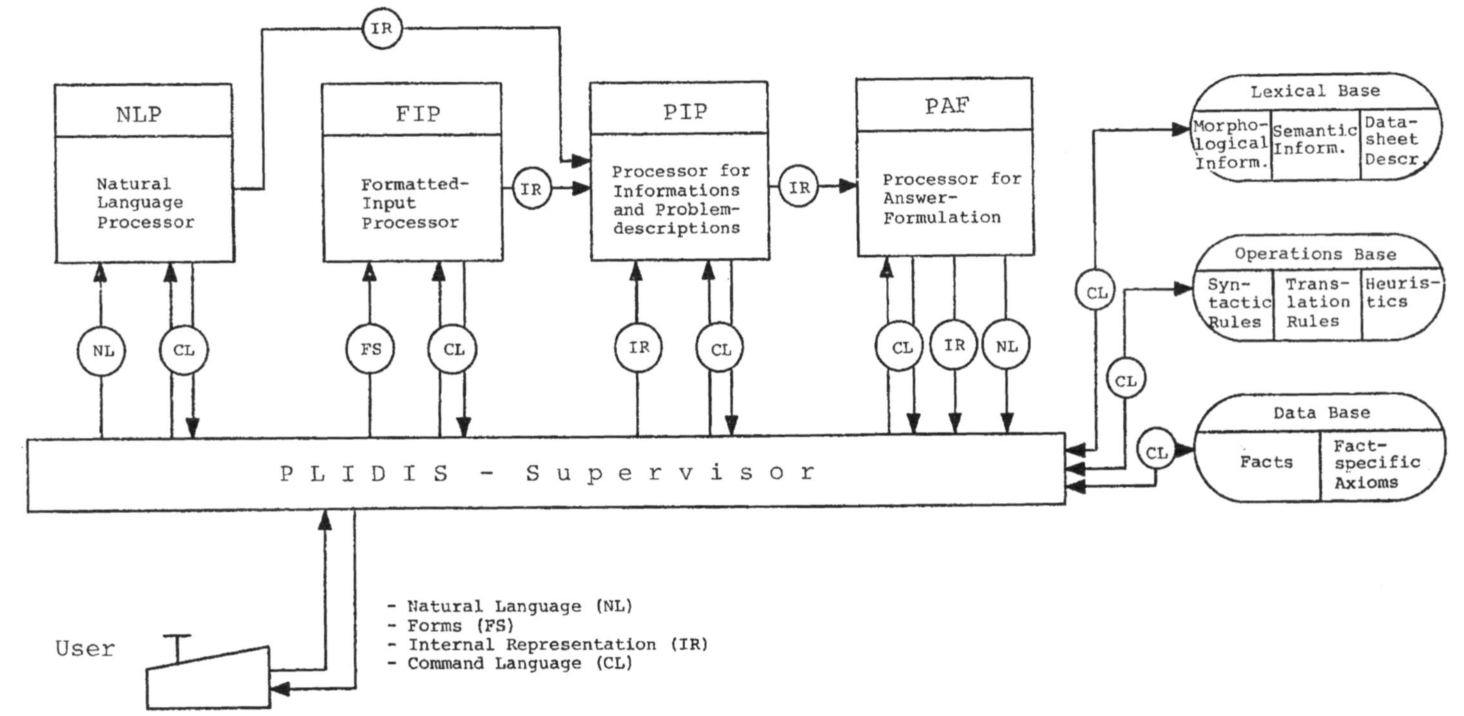

• fig.1 PLIDIS - main components and information flow

The command language gives the non-naive user access to various interactive facilities, which are helpful for testing and debugging. The algorithms draw on lexical and operational information contained in external data bases, which are supplied by the user/designer:

- The morpho-syntactic lexicon contains at the moment some 10,000 entries of non-lemmatised word-forms with their morpho-syntactic features such as tense, number, gender etc.
- The semantic lexicon contains informations about a word's equivalent in the internal representation such as relational symbol, operational symbol, individual term..., its 'sort' (see section 3), the number and sort of the arguments for each predicate, and so on.
- The data-sheet inventory contains the various data-sheets for entering mass-data such as laboratory reports, particulars about the firms, etc....
- The syntactic rules specify a grammar for German as an 'Augmented Transition Network'.
- The translation rules specify 'transformations' of the parsings of the NL-sentences into the internal representation.
- Heuristics specify syntactic and semantic criteria to guide the problem-solver.

The data base proper or the 'knowledge' of the system is a collection of atomic formulas in the internal representation stating the following information about the problem domain: (i) mass-data about samples of river water, the legal norms of the allowed concentrations, the composition of various chemicals, their toxicity, etc..., information about the firms being controlled (type of plant, production processes, treatment of waste...), (ii) axioms stating general logical implications as well as specific regularities in the world-model such as "x is greater than y implies that x is not equal to y" and "if a chemical interferes with the river-flora, it is toxic".

At the present stage in the development of the system, the natural language component and the formatted input processor are more or less completed, as they were largely conceived in a previous project. Some adaptation of the internal representation to specific problems in the domain of application are still in progress. A new concept for a more efficient and theoretically sounder based mechanism for translating the output of the syntactic analysis into the internal representation is being discussed at the moment. The bulk of work that still remains to be done is in the problem solving component.

3. The internal representation in KS

3.1. General considerations

The choice of an appropriate internal representation (IR) for the knowledge within the PLIDIS-system was not motivated solely by theoretical considerations but by the use it is to be made of, namely the effective retrieval of answers to queries stated in natural language. An IR for a QA-system must have the following properties:

- expressive power to match the complexity of natural language,
- world-modelling capacity to describe all situations, events, actions, and changes of states occurring in a given micro-world,
- deductive capacity pertaining to the solution of problems put to the system.

The broad aspects can be made more explicit in the following specific requirements.

(I) Like natural language, the IR must be an 'object language', ie it should not describe regularities of the German language, but should act on the same referential level as natural language. This entails that it should not contain metalinguistic symbols such as set theoretical ones, cases...

(II) The IR should be able to describe arbitrary microworlds; ie for any given concrete micro-world, it should have the means to designate all typical entities existing in that world: individuals, sets of individuals, events, processes, actions, etc. Similarly, it should be able to express time, temporal relations and causality.

(III) The syntax of the IR must be explicitly described in a grammar. This grammar guides automatic mapping processes of natural language structures into IR structures and allows the problem-solver to operate on the syntactic level of the IR.

(IV) With the IR must be associated a formal semantic interpretation which accounts for the way in which IR formulas correspond to particular arrangements in the external world and furthermore allows one to decide about the equivalence of formalisms (HAYES 1974).

(V) It should be suited to the application of general formal deduction mechanisms, so that it is not necessary to program specific deduction algorithms for each deduction (in the sense of "methods") - which does not of course exclude the use of heuristics.

In particular, points (IV) and (V) indicate the use of a predicate calculus for the internal representation, as PC is interpreted by a formal semantics in the form of Tarskian model theory and a general 'theorem prover' mechanism operates on it.

The standard first-order predicate calculus does, however, not fulfill all the above requirements (for example, condition (V)). Therefore a symbolic language (in German 'Konstruktsprache', abbreviated to KS) was designed modelled on the first-order predicate calculus but incorporating a number of extensions described below.

In the discussion below, we distinguish between the formal representation language KS, which according to requirement (I) is independent of the given micro-world, and concrete KS-languages defined by a world-specific vocabulary. The general construction rules of the IR-language KS are described in 3.2; a preliminary outline of the concrete language KS-water-pollution-control is given in 3.4.

3.2. Short description of the syntax of KS

In addition to the usual sets of symbols in a predicate calculus - namely predicate symbols, individual symbols, connectives and quantifiers - the vocabulary of KS contains the set S of sorts:

S = {uni, obj, int, sit, per, ort, zus, akt...}

(These names can be understood as abbreviations for the German: 'Universal, Objekt, Intervall, Situation, Person/Personenkörperschaft, Ort, Zustand, Aktion'.)

The set SV of sort-indexed variables is the Cartesian product of the set $V = \{x_1,...,x_n\}$ of variables and the set S of sorts.

KS-terms can be constructed with the aid of operation and relation symbols. For each such symbol, the sorts of its arguments are specified. The sort of the term thus constructed is determined by the sort of the last argument of the operation or relation symbol.

The following conditions of well-formedness for terms are defined:

(1) Sort-indexed variables from SV are terms.

(2) Individual constants are terms. To each constant is assigned a member of the set S.

(3) Let F be an n-place operation symbol, to which is assigned an n+1-tuple of sorts:

$$\langle a_1,\ldots,a_n,a_{n+1}\rangle \quad (a_i \in S)$$

Let $t_1^{a_1},\ldots,t_n^{a_n}$ be terms of the sorts $a_1,\ldots,a_n$ respectively. Then

$$(F\ t_1^{a_1},\ldots,t_n^{a_n})$$

is a term of the sort a_{n+1}. Operational terms are in general individual terms. If the nth argument term $(t_n^{a_n})$ is of the sort 'int' (interval), then the term designates individuals with reference to a particular time. Such individuals are states of the world, actions processes, and so on. They are terms of the sort 'sit' (situation) and are made up of an operation symbol followed by the following tuple of sorts:

$$\langle a_1,\ldots,a_{n-1},\mathrm{int},\mathrm{sit}\rangle$$

(4) Let R be an m-place relation symbol, to which is assigned an m-tuple of sorts:

$$\langle a_1,\ldots,a_m\rangle \quad (a_i \in S)$$

Let $t_1^{a_1},\ldots,t_{m-1}^{a_{m-1}}$ be terms of the sort $a_1,\ldots,a_{m-1}$.

Then $(R\ t_1^{a_1},\ldots,t_{m-1}^{a_{m-1}})$ is a term of the sort a_m. Relational terms are 'list terms'. Such terms designate sets of individuals (see 3.3)

Atomic formulas in KS are constructed according to the following conditions of well-formedness:

(5) Let F be an n-place operation symbol with the tuple of sorts $\langle a_1,\ldots,a_n,a_{n+1}\rangle$.

Let $t_1^{a_1},\ldots,t_n^{a_n},t_{n+1}^{a_{n+1}}$ be terms of the sorts $a_1,\ldots,a_{n+1}$. Then

$$(F\ t_1^{a_1},\ldots,t_n^{a_n};t_{n+1}^{a_{n+1}})$$

is an operational atomic formula.

(6) Let R be an m-place relation symbol with the tuple of sorts $<a_1,\ldots,a_m>$.

Let $t_1^{a_1},\ldots,t_m^{a_m}$ be terms of the sorts $a_1,\ldots,a_m$. Then

$$(R\ t_1^{a_1},\ldots,t_m^{a_m})$$

is an relational atomic formula.

Non-atomic formulas are constructed according to the usual construction rules of predicate calculus. A more detailed description of the syntax of KS can be found in ZIFONUN 1974 and ZIFONUN 1976.

3.3. Special features of KS

a. many-sortedness

The set S of sorts, described in 3.2, can be extended as demanded by the requirements of specific fields of application. The sorts underlie a hierarchical structure which is made use of in problem-solving.

The sortal structure of KS imposes semantically motivated conditions of syntactic well-formedness - in the sense of Katz-Fodor 'selection restrictions'. But the specification of the number and sorts of the arguments of a predicate is made in function of the world-model, rather than being guided by linguistic principles.

The advantages of a sortal structure in a representation language were indicated in HAYES 1971. A logical sortal calculus with linguistic considerations was proposed by THOMASON 1972.

b. Complex term building

The notion of 'term' in KS is defined recursively, so that it is possible to embed terms within terms, thus reflecting more closely some natural language constructs, such as complex noun groups.

Example: "the mother of the neighbour of the friend of Hans" becomes in KS: (MOTHER (NEIGHBOUR (FRIEND HANS)))

In the framework of the concrete KS-language with reference to social relations, MOTHER would have been defined as a 1-place operation symbol taking the tuple of sorts <per, per>. FRIEND and NEIGHBOUR would have been defined as 2-place relation symbols also with the tuple <per, per>.

c. Quantification

In KS are defined the natural language quantification symbols VIELE, MANCHE, EINIGE (many, several, some). They describe the size of sets of entities. The same applies to the natural numbers which can also be used as quantification symbols. They underlie the following conditions of well-formedness:

Let QU be a quantification symbol, let $(R\ t_1^{a_1},\ldots,t_{m-1}^{m-1})$ be a list term of the sort a_m, then

$$(QU\ (R\ t_1^{a_1},\ldots,t_{m-1}^{a_{m-1}}))$$

is a quantified list term of the sort a_m.

d. Plurality

Singular and plural objects can be designated in KS by 'individual terms' and 'list terms' respectively. As an example the KS-representation of the sentences "*der Nachbar der Mutter von Hans ist Fritz*" and "*die Nachbarn der Freunde von Hans sind Franz und Egon*" is given:

(NACHBAR (MUTTER HANS); FRITZ)
(NACHBAR (FREUND HANS);(LISTE FRANZ EGON))

f. Arithmetic operations

KS incorporates arithmetic operations such as PLUS, DIFFERENCE, TIMES... which can be interpreted as LISP functions.

3.4. The KS-language for the control of water pollution

In PLIDIS is defined a concrete KS-language deriving its vocabulary from the field of application in the control of water pollution.

The set S of sorts given in 3.2. has been accordingly extended. A preliminary partial sort tree for the domain of water pollution is shown in figure 2.

Some examples of the vocabulary of KS-water-pollution-control are given below:

- individual constants: ARSEN (sort : 'stoffkoll')
  ZYANID (sort : 'stoffkoll')
- operation symbols:
  - PROBE (2-place; sortal tuple : <betrieb, int, stoffkoll>)

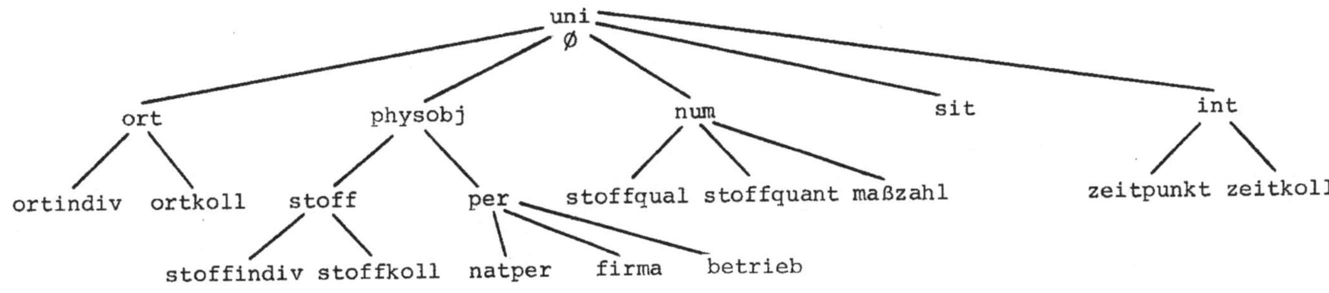

ortkoll:	GEWAESSER, RHEIN, FRANKFURT, ...
stoffindiv:	ARSEN, ...
stoffkoll:	PROBE, ...
stoffqual:	TEMPERATUR, PH-WERT, ...
stoffquant:	ANTEIL, GROESSE, ...
maßzahl:	(Ø.3 MG/L), ...

• fig.2 Preliminary sort tree of KS-water-pollution

- PROBENEHMER (1-place; sortal tuple : <stoffkoll, per>)
- ANTEIL (3-place; sortal tuple : <stoff, stoffkoll, physobj, num>)
- LABORBERICHT (3-place; sortal tuple : <perkörp, stoffkoll, int, physobj>)
- BETRIEB (2-place; sortal tuple : <firma, ort, betrieb>)

- relational symbol:
  - GIFTIG (1-place; sortal tuple : <stoff>)

The above predicates can be 'translated' into English as follows:
PROBE = 'sample', PROBENEHMER ='sampler', ANTEIL = 'amount', LABORBERICHT = 'laboratory report', BETRIEB = 'firm', GIFTIG = 'toxic'.

The following is an example of a KS-term:

(PROBE (BETRIEB MAX-MÜLLER STUTTGART) 76.Ø1.13.14.ØØ)

"The sample taken from the firm Max Müller in Stuttgart on 13.1.197 at 14.00 hours."

The following is an example of a KS-formula:

```
(ANTEIL ZYANID (PROBE (BETRIEB MAX-MÜLLER STUTTGART) 76.Ø1.13.)
        (LABORBERICHT (BETRIEB CHEM-UNTERSUCHUNGSANSTALT PLOCHINGEN)
                      (PROBE (BETRIEB MAX-MÜLLER STUTTGART) 76.Ø1.13
                      76.Ø1.15.)
        ; (O,5 mg/l ))
```

"The amount of cyanide contained in the sample taken from the firm Max Müller in Stuttgart on 13.1.76, according to the laboratory report of the chemical analysis centre in Plochingen produced on 15.1.76 amounted to 0.5 milligram pro liter."

4. Natural-language analysis in PLIDIS

The requirement of modularity in a system such as PLIDIS is dictated not only by organizational reasons, but also, from a more systematic point of view, it was desirable to maintain a strict separation between components, which are theoretically or methodologically well understood or which are of no central interest to the project, and those which are topics of genuine effort and experimentation and where research is still going on.

Thus the natural language processor is separated into three passes (see fig. 4): a PASSØ for the morphological identification, a PASS1 for syntactic analysis and a PASS2 for code generation, i.e. translation into the language of internal representation.

4.1. PASSØ: Morphological identification

In an earlier stage of the system PASSØ was a program for morphological analysis which operated with a lemmatized dictionary. For each german word of the system's vocabulary there existed only one dictionary entry, the basic form of the word. A certain class of verbforms for example were represented by their infinitive form.

It was the task of the program to apply morphological rules to inflected forms of words and to reduce them to their basic form, which then allowed a dictionary look-up for further information. This analysis technique was very time consuming and it was replaced by a very simple program which works with a non-lemmatized dictionary. Each inflected form of a word has an entry in the dictionary with its full morphological information such as basic form of the inflected word, wordclass, gender, tense etc. (see fig. 3).

```
MORPHOLOGISCHE BESCHREIBUNG VON  'PROBEN':

   ((N NF PROBE KNG 7690 K (NOM GEN DAT AKK)
       PN 6 G F)
    (VERB NF PROBEN KNG 7831 PN (2 5)
          MOD BEF TEMP GE DIA AKT)
    (VERB NF PROBEN KNG 8191 TEMP IN)
    (VERB NF PROBEN KNG 7727 PN (4 6)
          MOD (IND KONJ) TEMP GE DIA AKT))


MORPHOLOGISCHE BESCHREIBUNG VON  'PRODUZIERT':

   ((VERB NF PRODUZIEREN KNG 8191 TEMP P2 HS HABEN
          PAS 1 REFL (NER AKK))
    (ADJU NF PRODUZIERT S POS))
```

fig.3 Sample entries of the non-lemmatized morphological dictionary.

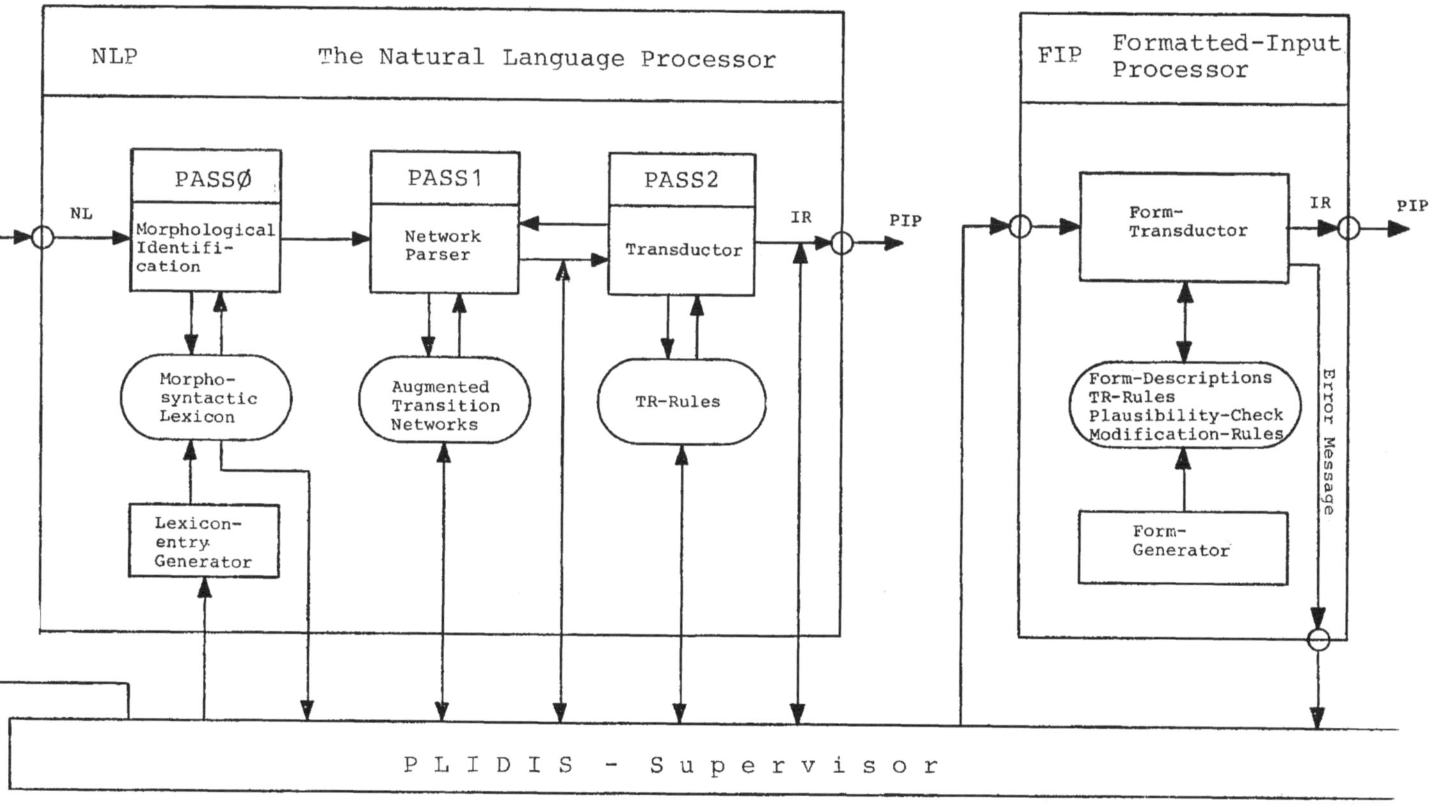

• fig.4 PLIDIS components for processing natural language input and input by data-sheets.

The dictionary is stored on an external device with index sequential access such that time required for morphological identification of a word is rather small.

The amount of work necessary for entering all inflected forms of a word into the dictionary is reduced by a special function of PASSØ, which generates from a dictionary entry of a basic form the entries for the inflected form.

Finally a HELP-routine of PASSØ enables even a user with little linguistic knowledge to write the dictionary entry for a basic wordform.

4.2. PASS1: Morpho-syntactic analysis

In the framework of the PLIDIS project, the following requirements were laid down for a syntax analysis component:

- the grammar should be formulated independent from the parsing algorithm. This requirement ensures ease of modification and enables the formulation of the grammar rules to be carried out by linguists unversed in programming;
- the grammar must allow the formulation of certain context-sensitive features, in particular it must be able to deal effectively with discontinuous constituents, which are very common in the German language;
- as the output of the syntactic analysis should be only one parsing, the parser must be equiped with adequate backtracking facilities to find alternative parsings if requested by subsequent components of the system.

4.2.1. General characterisation of an ATN

Bearing the above requirements in mind, it was decided to adopt the model of an 'augmented transition network' (ATN) (WOODS 1973). An ATN is a context-sensitive extension of a 'basic transition network' (BTN). The latter is equivalent to a 'push-down store' automaton or a context-free PSG. To illustrate a BTN consider the following small context-free grammar with the following rules:

S → NP VP
NP → DET N | NPR
VP → V
DET → der

N → *Hund*
NPR → *Hans*
V → *schläft*

Whereby S is the start symbol; NP, VP, DET, N, NPR, V are non-terminal symbols; *der, Hund, Hans, schläft* are terminal symbols.

The finite-state-transition-diagram for this grammar can be represented as shown in fig. 5.

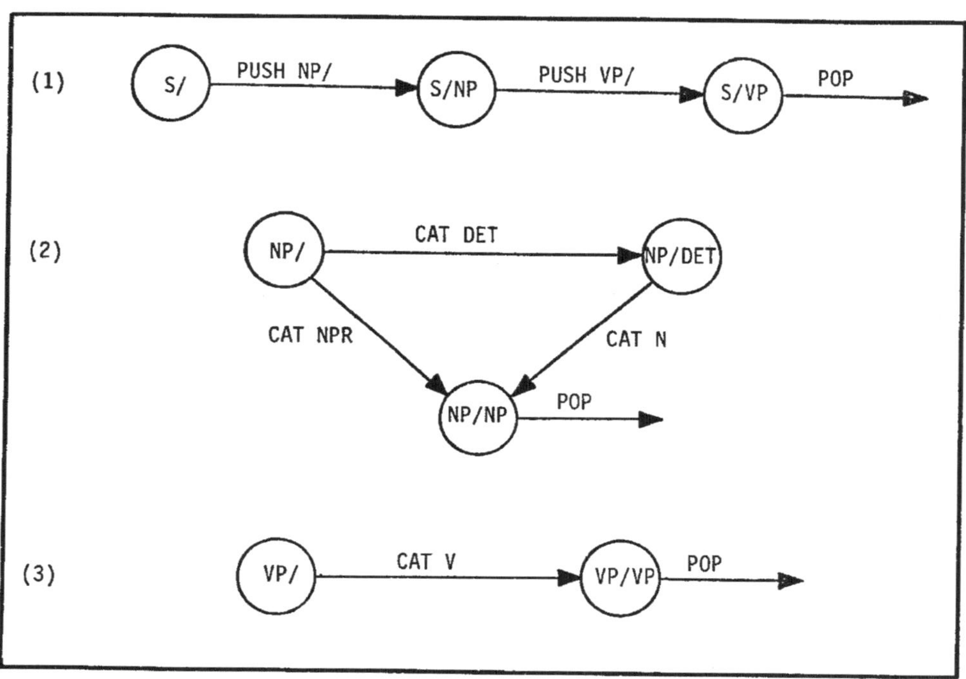

fig.5 A sample basic transition network

The two basic concepts of a BTN are 'state' and 'arc'. An arc represents the transition from $state_i$ to $state_j$. There are the following main types of arcs:

A CAT-arc represents a transition that can be taken if the word in the input sentence which is being pointed at belongs to the syntactic category indicated on the arc.

A PUSH-arc introduces recursion in the network. The transition can be taken if a substring of the input string is accepted by the state indicated on the arc. When leaving this state, the scanner points to the last word in the accepted phrase.

A POP-arc should be interpreted in conjunction with a PUSH-arc. After successfully reaching the state indicated on the PUSH-arc, it leaves the current level of recursion and goes up one level. It is a 'pseudo' arc, in the sense that it does not lead to a next state, but marks the state it leaves as being final. It will also specify the structural representation being given to the substring analysed.

An ATN is a context-sensitive extension of a BTN in the sense that <u>conditions</u> on the arcs can be stated to control the transition from one state to the next. For example, in the above sample BTN it could be stated that the transition from state S/NP to state S/VP is only allowed if the category "number" of subject and verb agree.

Furthermore, structure-building <u>actions</u>, i.e. the construction of parts of a parsing tree can be formulated when the transition to a state has been achieved.

To achieve the desired context-sensitivity, an ATN is augmented with a number of registers which can be used to store intermediate results and thus allow for the treatment of discontinuous results.

To enable the grammar-writer to deal more conveniently with this problem, a further arc, namely a VIR arc was introduced. In addition, there is a TST-arc, which allows the transition to the next state only if the word currently being scanned satisfies a given condition, and a JUMP-arc which is like a TST-arc, except that it does not consume any of the input string.

The purpose of the registers is also to store intermediate results of the structure building actions. Normally, the structure a parser assigns to the input string corresponds directly to the sequence of the transitions (i.e. corresponds to the surface structure). The actions allow one to build up new structures, picking up constituents out of order, and thus to represent 'deep structures' or even semantic representations. Because of this feature, an ATN was also used in an earlier version of PLIDIS for the translation from natural language to internal representation.

Another major advantage of an ATN to represent the grammar of a natural language is its 'open endedness'. New arcs, tests and actions can be formulated to meet the requirements of the specific language being analysed.

4.2.2. Augmented transition networks for German

The following describes briefly how the ATN concept, proposed by WOODS, was adapted to suit the specific structures of the German language (e.g. KOLB & LUTZ 1975).

The inventory of arcs was augmented by an LCAT and an LWRD arc, allowing right-to-left analysis, which is particularly required by the German verbphrase. LCAT stipulates that the last word in the sentence be a past participle of a verb-form, and LWRD looks for the form worden to complete a passive verbphrase.

The table below describes the formats for all arcs used in the currently implemented ATN for German:

(CAT <category> <test> <action>*)
(LCAT <category> <test> <action>*)
(MCAT (<category>*) <test> <action>*)
(VIR <category> <stack> <test> <action>*)
(VIRL <category> <stack> <test> <action>*)
(TST <label> <test> <action>*)
(WRD <word> <test> <action>*)
(LWRD <word> <test> <action>*)
(MEM (<word>*) <test> <action>*)
(PUSH <state> <test> <preaction>* <action>*)
(POP <form> <test>)
(JUMP <state> <test> <action>*)
(TO <state> <test> <action>*)

Disadvantages of using an ATN for German became apparent, mainly due to its complex morpho-syntactic structure. Since morpho-syntactic ambiguity is extreme, particularly in the case of very common articles, the parsing is slowed down considerably due to the extensive amount of backtracking required. For example, the article der has the following morpho-syntactic interpretations:

nom sing masc
gen sing fem
dat sing fem
gen plur masc
gen plur fem
gen plur neut

Another, more general disadvantage of an ATN is that the tests are formulated as constants so that it is not possible to vary a test according to the path in the analysis followed so far except by an excessively complex aparatus of register setting.

Nevertheless there seems to be no alternative parsing technique within the domain of natural language parsing, which is as well studied as ATN-parsing and which at the same time may be handled easily by linguists without a special programming training.

Diagrams of a part of the ATN grammar of the German noun phrase and verb phrase can be seen in figs. 6-1ff. This grammar is very weakly structured for noun phrases. Whereas a linguist would like to have a structure resembling to something like fig. 7 PASS1 produces an analysis like fig. 8 for the sentence

"Der Anteil an Cyanid in der Probe der Firma Müller betrug 2 mg/l." (The amount of cyanide contained in the sample of the firm Müller was 2 mg/l.)

In the present version, the parser is able to recognise the majority of German sentence structures, including complex sentences containing all types of subordinate clauses: relative clauses, adverbial clauses, object and subject clauses. There is, however, a restriction imposed on the position of adverbial clauses, which have to occur either at the beginning or at the end of the sentence.

The following main sentence-constituents are recognized:

- noun phrases (NG)
- prepositional noun phrases (PNG)
- adjectival attributes (ADJG)
- adverbs (ADV)
- verb phrases (VK)

Complex noun phrases having inflected participal constructions as attributes, such as 'Das von der Firma Müller in den Rhein eingeleitete Abwasser' can be handled as well.

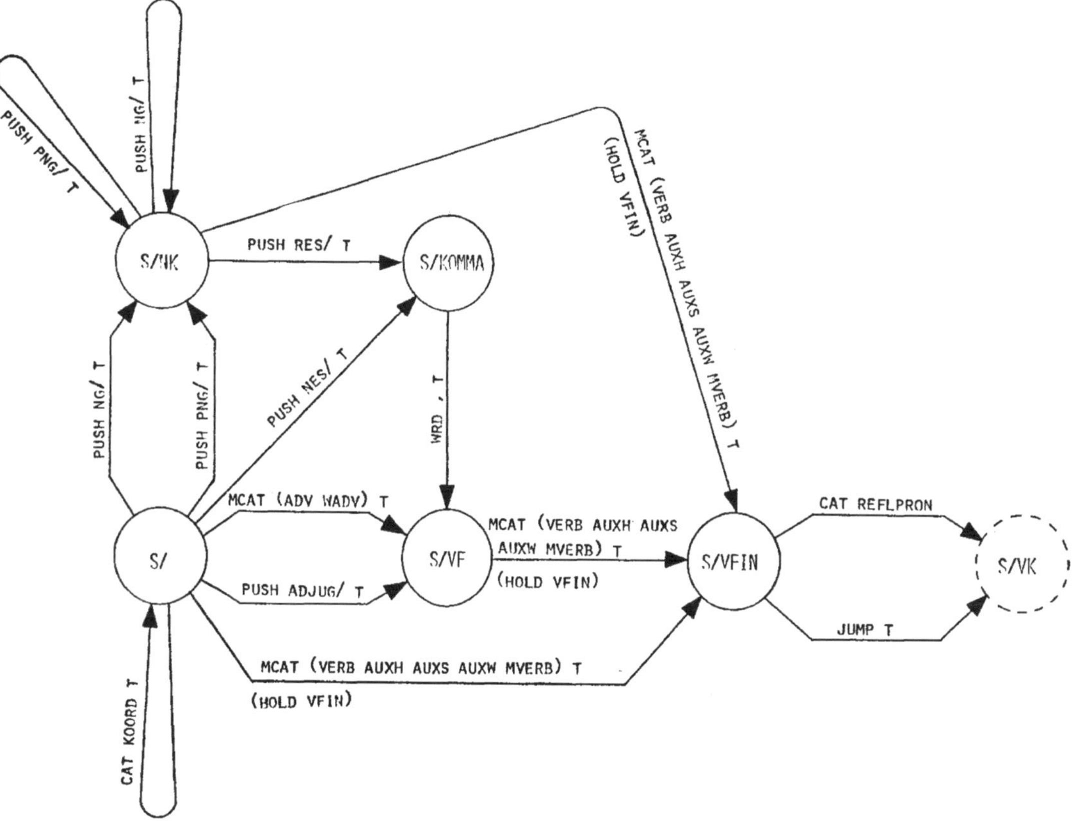

fig.6-1 ATN for German (Hauptsatz)

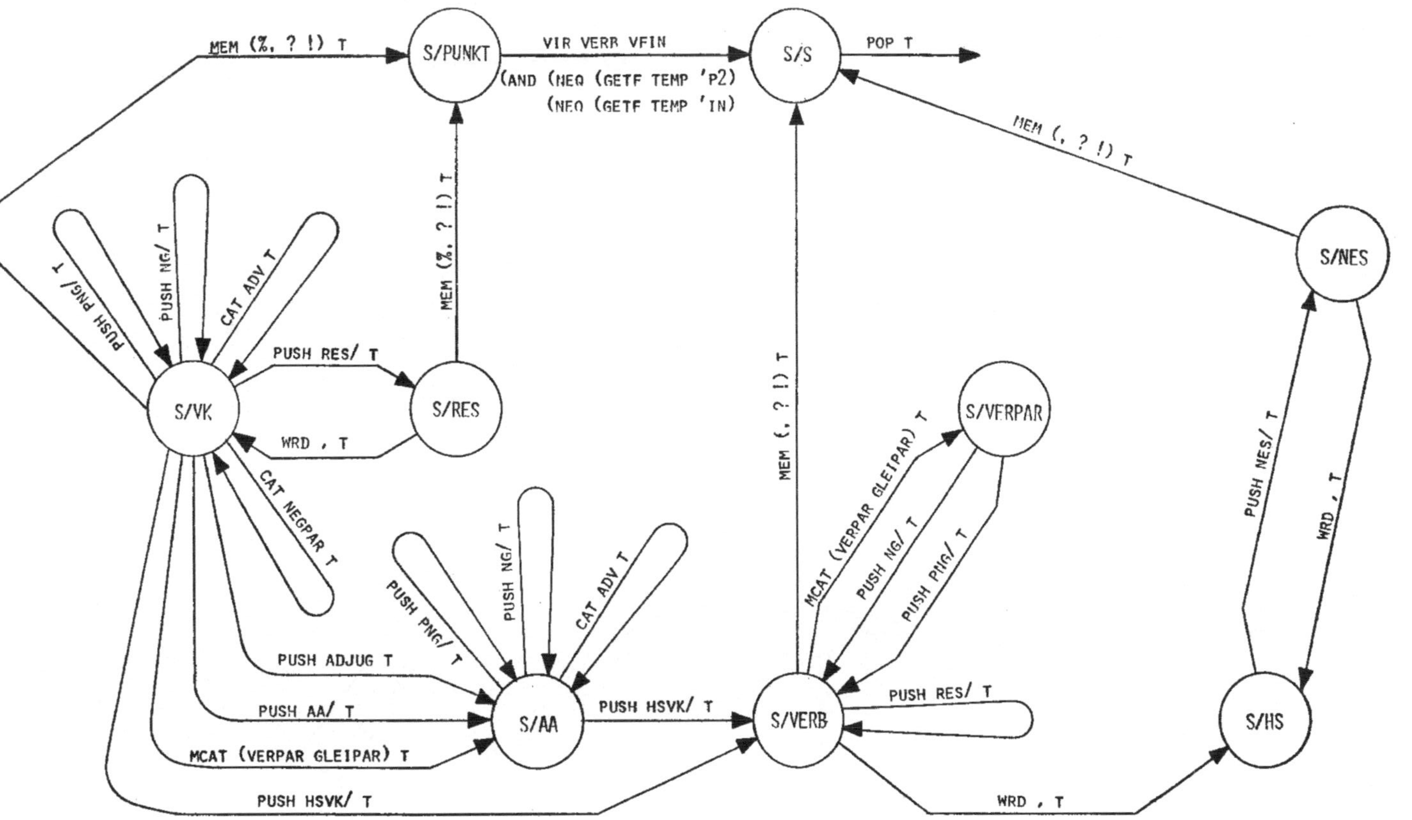

fig.6-2 ATN for German (Hauptsatz)

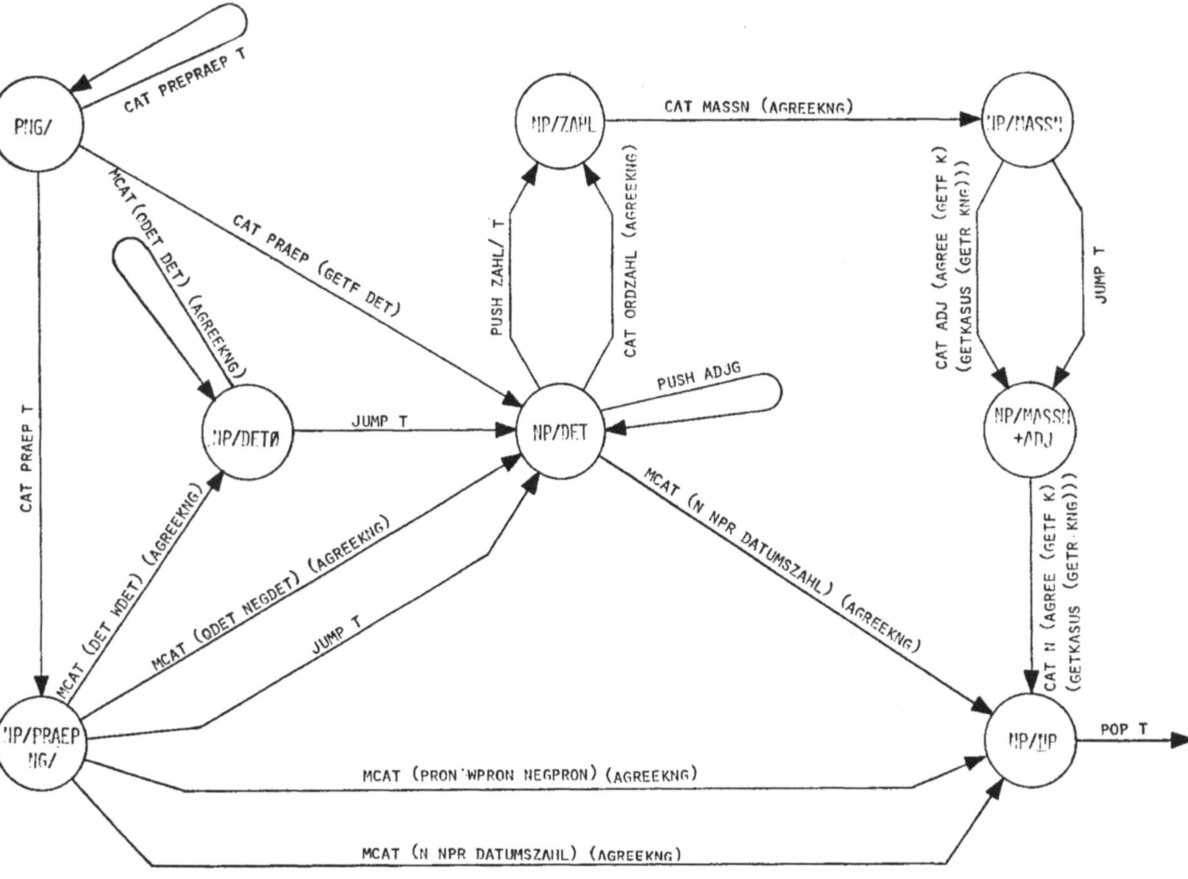

fig.6-3 ATN for German (praepositionale Nominalgruppe)

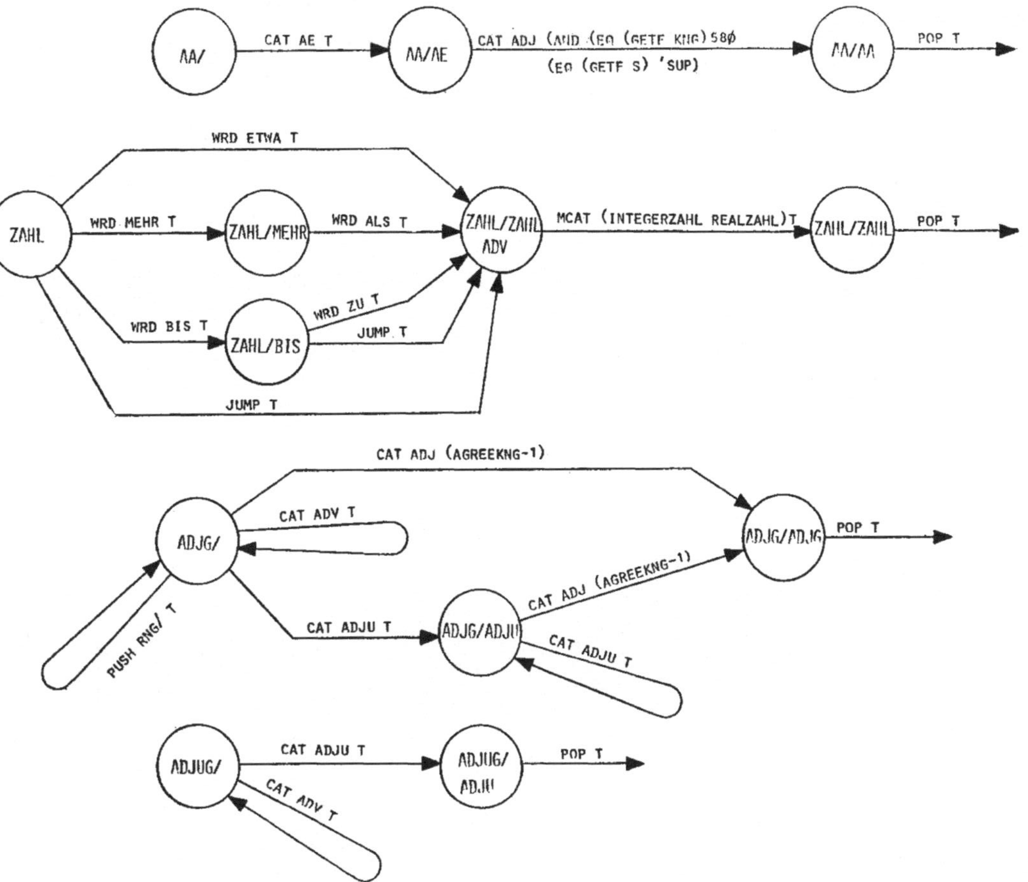

fig.6-4 ATN for German (Artangabe; Zahlgruppe; Adjektivgruppe flektiert; Adjektivgruppe unflektiert)

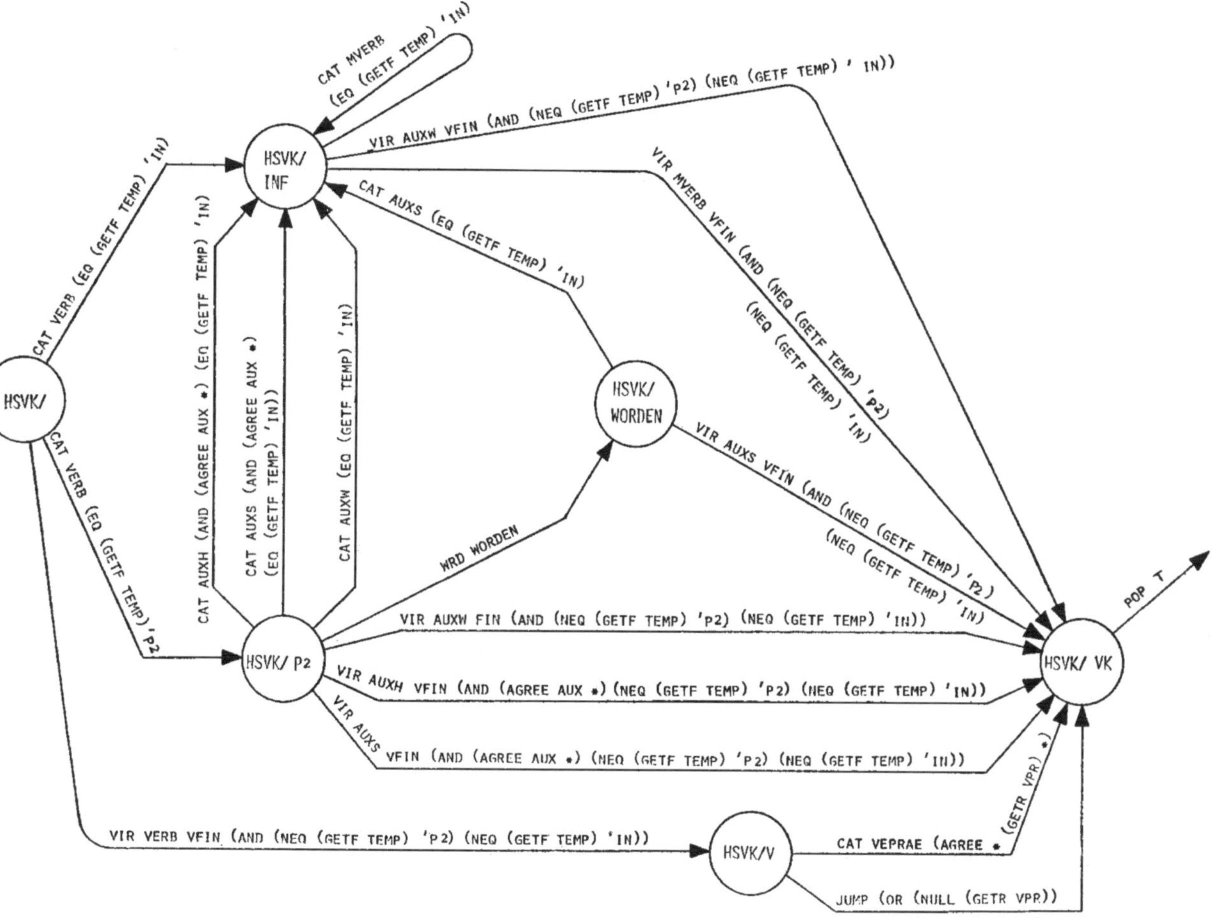

fig.6-5 ATN for German (Hauptsatzverbkomplex)

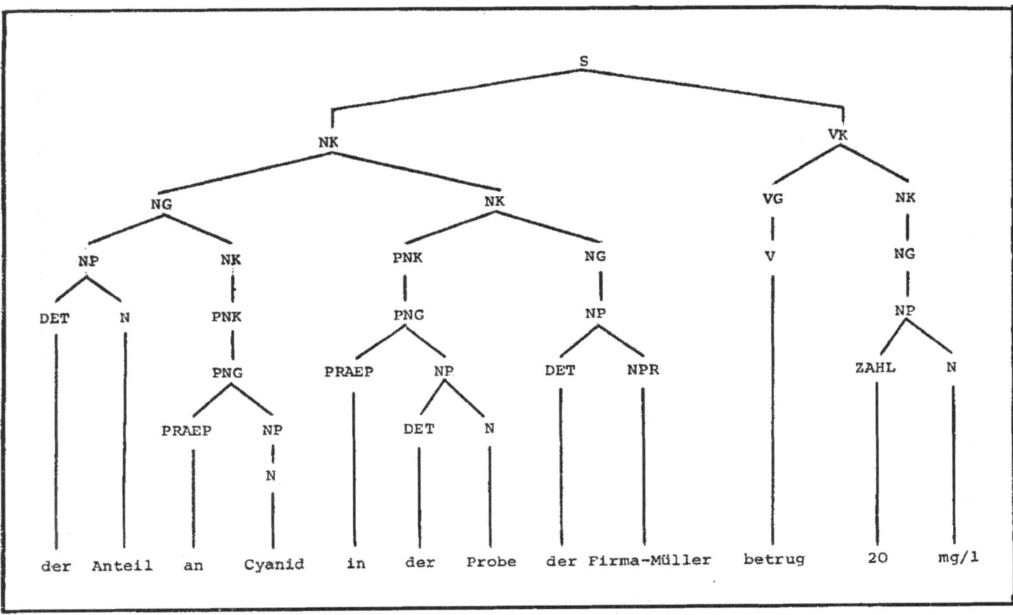

fig.7 Example for desirable syntactic structuring within the domain of noun groups.

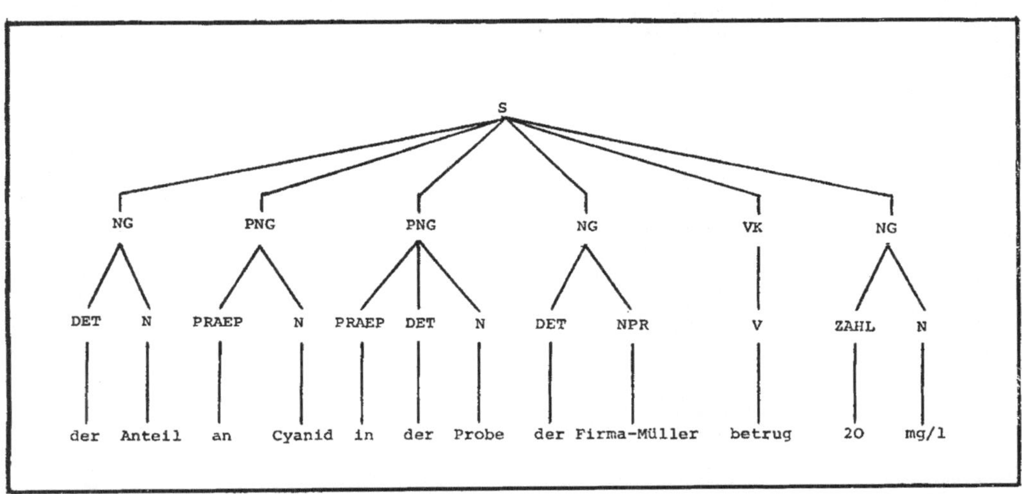

fig.8 Example for structuring capacity of the PLIDIS natural language parser.

```
ERGEBNIS DER MORPHO-SYNTAKTISCHEN ANALYSE (PASS1):

    (S ((TYPE . AUSSAGE)
        (DIATHESE . AKTIV)
        (NS . (DER ANTEIL AN ZYANID IN DER PROBE DER FIRMA-MUELLER
                   BETRUG 2 MG/L .)))
       (VK ((PN . (1 3)))
           (V ((TEMP . VE))
              BETRAGEN))
       (NG ((KNG . 4164)
            (K . NOM)
            (PN . 3)
            (G . M)
            (NS . (DER ANTEIL)))
           (DET NIL
                DER)
           (N NIL
              ANTEIL))
       (PNG ((KNG . 1601)
             (K . (DAT AKK))
             (PN . 3)
             (G . N)
             (NS . (AN ZYANID)))
            (PRAEP NIL
                   AN)
            (N NIL
               ZYANID))
       (PNG ((KNG . 1090)
             (K . DAT)
             (PN . 3)
             (G . F)
             (NS . (IN DER PROBE)))
            (PRAEP NIL
                   IN)
            (DET NIL
                 DIE)
            (N NIL
               PROBE))
       (NG ((KNG . 3138)
            (K . (GEN DAT))
            (PN . 3)
            (G . F)
            (NS . (DER FIRMA-MUELLER)))
           (DET NIL
                DIE)
           (NPR NIL
                FIRMA-MUELLER))
       (VERB ((NS . BETRUG))
             BETRAGEN)
       (NG ((KNG . 7745)
            (K . (NOM GEN DAT AKK))
            (PN . 3)
            (G . N)
            (NS . (2 MG/L)))
           (ZAHL NIL
                 (INTEGERZAHL NIL
                              2))
           (N NIL
              MG/L)))
```

fig.9 Sample output of PASS1

The verbphrase may contain a main verb in any tense or mode, with the exclusion of the conjunctive mood.

Because of their inherent ambiguity, which cannot be resolved by purely syntactic criteria, some constructions had to be excluded:

- coordination between noun phrases (eg 'Die alten Männer und Frauen')
- 'elliptical' noun phrases, i.e. noun phrases without a nominal head (eg 'Er nannte das billigste gut')

Certainly it would be possible to push the noun phrase analysis further by extending the syntactic categories and by using informations such as dependency frames of verbs. But since deeper noun phrase analysis needs sooner or later semantic information it was decided to restrict the syntactic analysis to the generation of a list of the main constituents of the input sentence with a minimal dependency structure and to pass the burden of semantic interpretation to the translation component in PASS2.

4.3. PASS2: Semantic analysis component

Within the PLIDIS-system semantic analysis is viewed as the problem of translating natural language sentences into formulas of the internal representation language KS, more precisely: to generate KS-code from the parsing trees, which are produced by the network-parser of PASS1.

In the earlier ISLIB-approach augmented transition networks were used to state the rules for KS-code generation. As stated earlier, this approach turned out to be not very efficient and remained at an ad-hoc level, since it was not possible to find a theoretical foundation which would have allowed to reduce the amount of rules needed within this approach.

The new concept for the natural-language-to-KS translation starts from the concept of a translation grammar for a pair of languages L_1, L_2, where L_1 is the source language and L_2 the goal language of the translation (WULZ 1976). PASS2 then can be viewed as a program which interprets the translation grammar rules.

The translation grammar may be compared with a transformational grammar (GINSBURG/PARTEE 1969), the rules of which operate on already existing derivation trees of a phrase structure grammar of the source language, i.e. German in the PLIDIS system. The nodes of these trees are labelled with non-terminal (syntactic categories of the grammar) and terminal symbols (source language words) of the phrase-structure grammar. In a similar way the translation grammar rules are applied to the derivation trees of the source language which correspond within the context of PLIDIS to the lists of bracketed and labelled constituents from the parsing of natural language sentences.

For the sake of simplicity and clarity, the translation grammar is explained here by simplified examples and in an abbreviated terminology of derivation trees.

The translation grammar disposes of three types of rules:

(1) rules for the replacement of source language symbols - i.e. in general natural language words - by the context-pattern of their goal-language equivalent

(2) insertion rules for the goal language context-pattern

(3) pattern raising rules.

The rules are based on the concept that it will be possible to define for each goal language symbol something what we will call a <u>context pattern</u>. The context pattern of a symbol is a prediction about the syntactical context in which this symbol will occur. Thus the writer of a translation grammar for German to KS may state in a rule of type (1), that the KS-symbol PROBE may correspond to the german word "Probe" (sample). The grammar of KS defines, that PROBE may be used within a two-place <TERM> of the sort <stoffkoll>, where the first argument has to be a <TERM> of the sort <firma> and the second argument a <TERM> of the sort <int>. Thus in any context where the german "Probe" is translated by the KS-symbol PROBE, it will be followed by two terms specified as above and the context pattern for PROBE can be defined as a structure like fig. 10.

The rule of type 1 for the german word "Probe" would state then, that "Probe" is to be replaced by the context pattern of fig. 10.

In the context pattern of PROBE, <TERM ; stoffkoll> is viewed as the head of the context pattern, whereas the non-terminal KS-symbols <TERM ; firma> and <TERM ; int> are considered as "slots" and it is the task of the type (2) rules of the translation grammar, to define, how to fill in these slots. A distributional analysis of the context

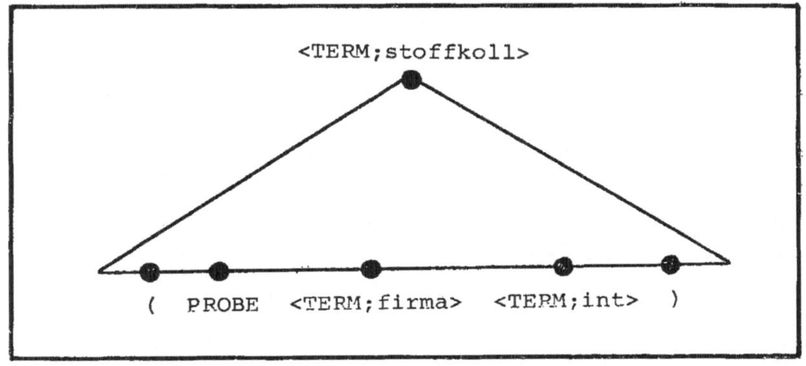

fig.10 Context pattern of PROBE

of german "Probe" will show that the nominal attributes of "Probe", i.e. a noun-group in the genitive case or a prepositional noun-group following "Probe", are the constituents, the translations of which has to be inserted into the slots of the PROBE context pattern. Thus the insertion rules for the KS-context pattern assigned within the translation of a natural language sentence to german "Probe" would state that e.g. the slot with the name <TERM ; int> has to be filled with a context pattern of the same name, resulting from the translation of a prepositional noun-group following "Probe", specifying also possible prepositions like "am" or "vom".

<u>Example</u>:

Let RR_1, ..., RR_6 denote some rules of type (1) for the replacement of german words by the context pattern of their KS-equivalent,

IR_1, IR_2 rules of type (2) for the insertion into context patterns;

let E denote the empty context pattern, consisting of no symbols;

the application of these rules onto german "Probe" within the context "die Probe bei Müller & Co vom 15.12.76" (the sample from Müller & Co of 12/15/76) can be represented schematically as shown in fig. 11, where the arcs stand for the application of the rules which label the arc.

The use of the sorts of KS for disambiguation within the translation can be shown if one considers "die Probe <u>von</u> Müller & Co <u>am</u> 15.12.76"

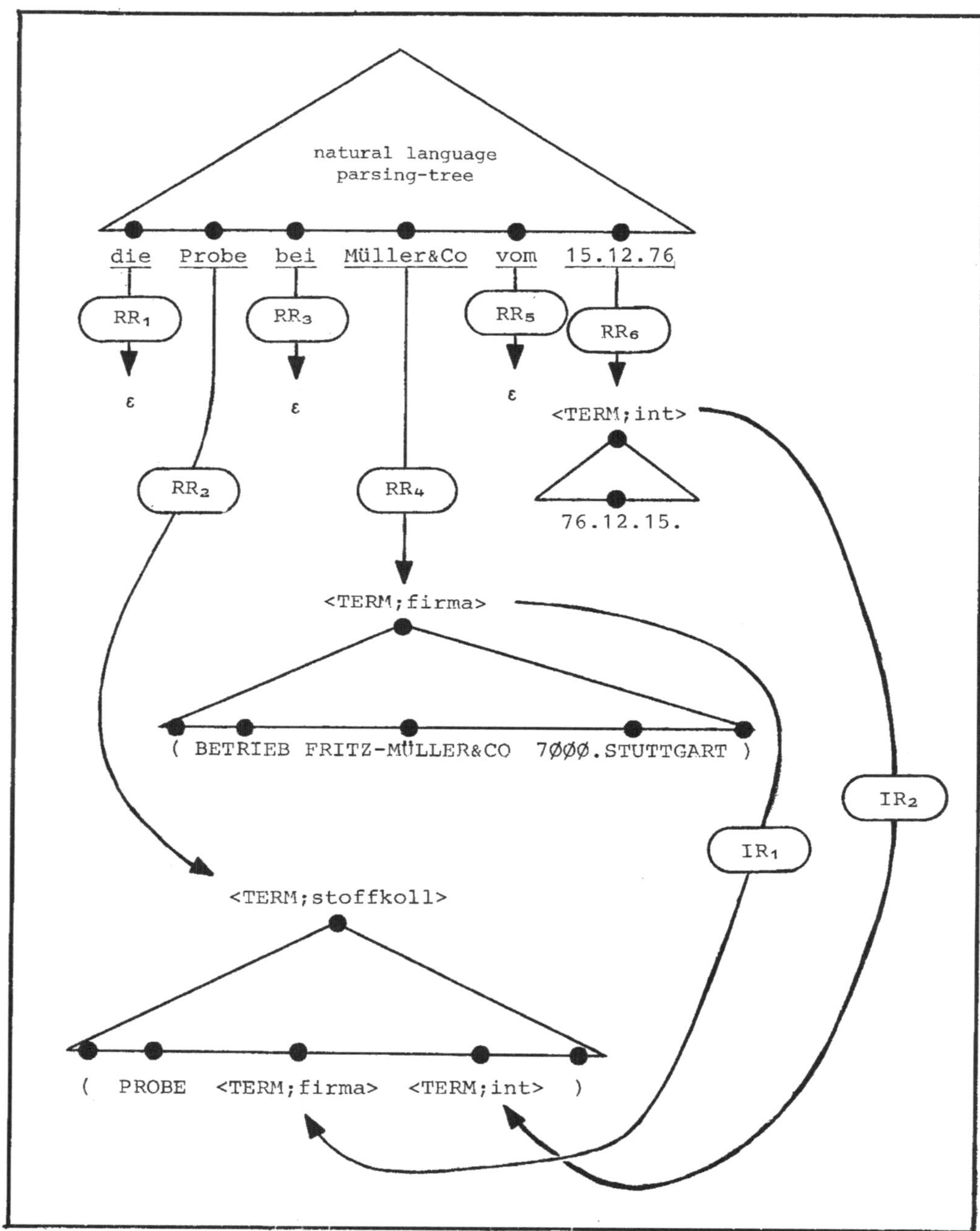

fig.11 Simplified illustration of the application of replacement rules (RR) and insertion rules (IR).

as alternative formulation for "die Probe bei Müller & Co vom 15.12.76". As insertion rule IR2 requires the translation of a prepositional noun-group with the preposition "von" or "am" to be inserted as tense argument into the context pattern assigned to "Probe", the translation of "Müller & Co" would take the place of the second TERM within the PROBE-pattern. But since the KS-equivalent to "Müller & Co" is a TERM of the sort <firma>, a check of the sort consistency will block the insertion at the place of a TERM with the sort <intervall>.

For each insertion rule there is a side effect defined. If a filled-in context-pattern is inserted into the slot of another pattern, it is deleted at its original place i.e. replaced by the empty pattern E (see fig. 12 for illustration).

If all terminal symbols i.e. all natural language words of a derivation tree are replaced by the context-pattern of their KS-equivalent and if all slots of these patterns are filled in, the pattern raising rules may be applied to the remaining structure in the following ways:

(1) A non-terminal symbol x of the source language grammar can be replaced by a filled in context pattern if this pattern is dominated by x and if all other context patterns, which are dominated by x, are equal to the empty context pattern.

(2) If a non-terminal symbol x of the source language grammar dominates only empty patterns, then it is replaced by the empty pattern.

(3) If the top node of the remaining tree structure is labelled by a symbol of the grammar of the goal language, a head y of a context pattern can be replaced by the string which results from the concatenation of the symbols dominated by the head y under the condition that y does not dominate another head of a context pattern.

For simplicity we will illustrate the application of the pattern raising rules with an abstract example.

Example:

Let A, B, C, D be some non-terminal symbols of a source language grammar and a, b, c, d, e, f symbols of the goal language grammar; let PR_1, PR_2, PR_3 denote the pattern-raising rules as described above in (1), (2), (3) respectively. Fig. 13 then illustrates the application of these rules to the tree, whose top is labelled by A and where a and d are the heads of context patterns. The numbers preceding the rule names

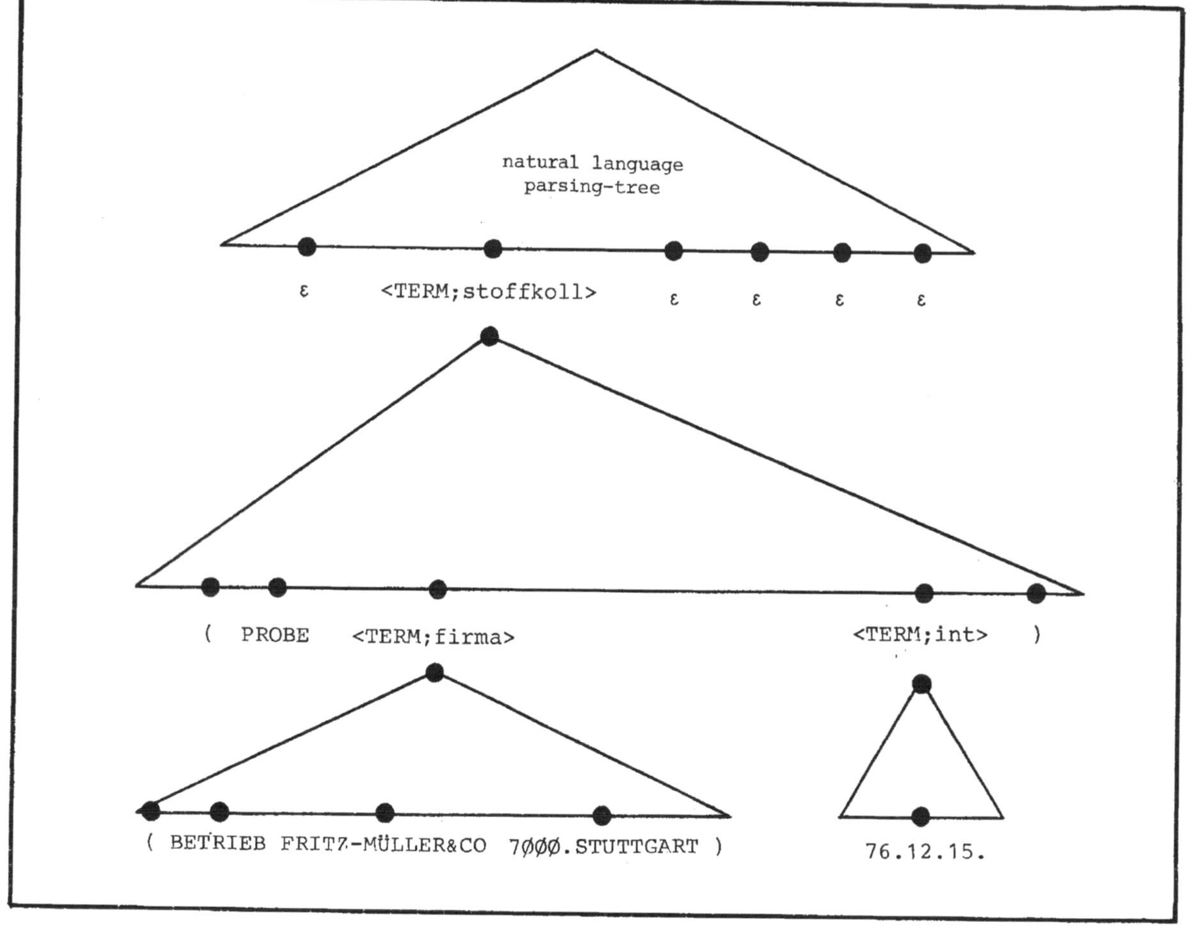

fig.12 Result of the application of the rules of type 1 and 2 on "die Probe bei Müller & Co vom 15.12.76".

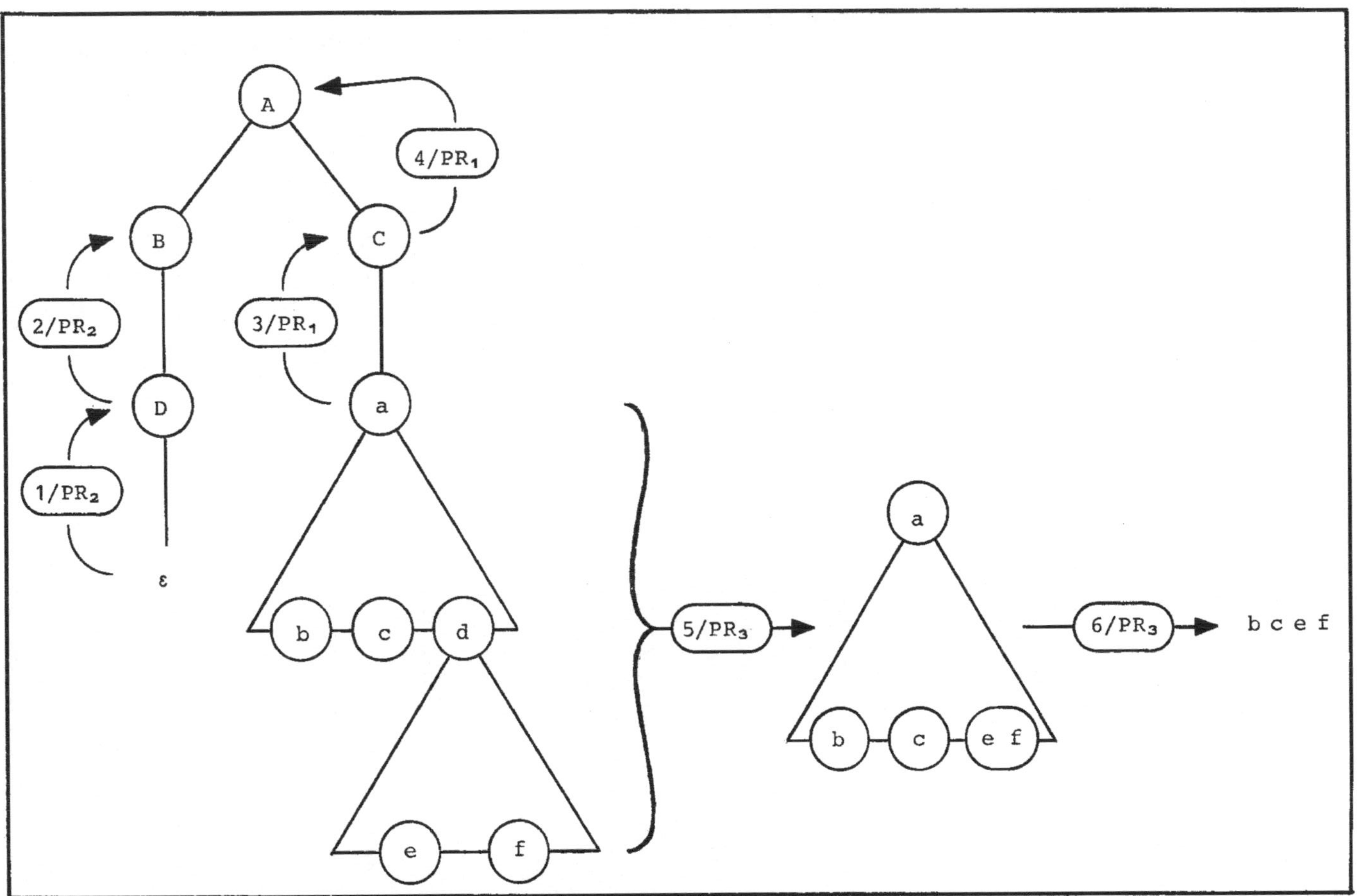

• fig.13 Application of pattern raising rules (PR).

indicate the order, in which these rules were applied.

If the string resulting from the application of the pattern raising rules consists of terminal symbols of the goal language grammar, then a translation has been found.

Since various details of a translation grammar for a subset of German into KS are still subject of experimentation the PASS2 program which interprets the translation rules has not yet reached its definitive form.

5. Information handling and problem-solving

The processor for informations and problem descriptions (see fig. 14) consists of, on the one hand, data base management procedures for storing the symbolic data into the data base; and, on the other hand, 'problem-solving procedures' for the answering of questions. This section deals primarily with the latter, as data base management problems are not within the main topics of the PLIDIS development and will arise only in the "real-life" application of the system, when mass-data have to be processed. For the case that the PLIDIS data base management will be too weak to handle these problems, the component may be replaced by adaptions of already existing data base management systems.

5.1. An outline of Data base management

It is the task of the data base management component of PLIDIS to 'normalise' the KS-formulas representing the system's knowledge in such a way as to ensure easy retrieval. Its other task is to ensure the security of the data so that access is only given to authorized persons.

The normalising process includes skolemising of the existential quantifiers and subsequently reducing the KS-formulas into sets of literals. Certain argument-terms, such as those of the type 'stoffkoll' are replaced by skolem constants, for example (PROBE MÜLLER 13.10.76) might be replaced by the constant $Ø1Ø9.STOFFKOLL, denoting the number of this specific sample. This presupposes that the formula (PROBE MÜLLER 13.10.76 ; $Ø1Ø9.STOFFKOLL) is also stored.

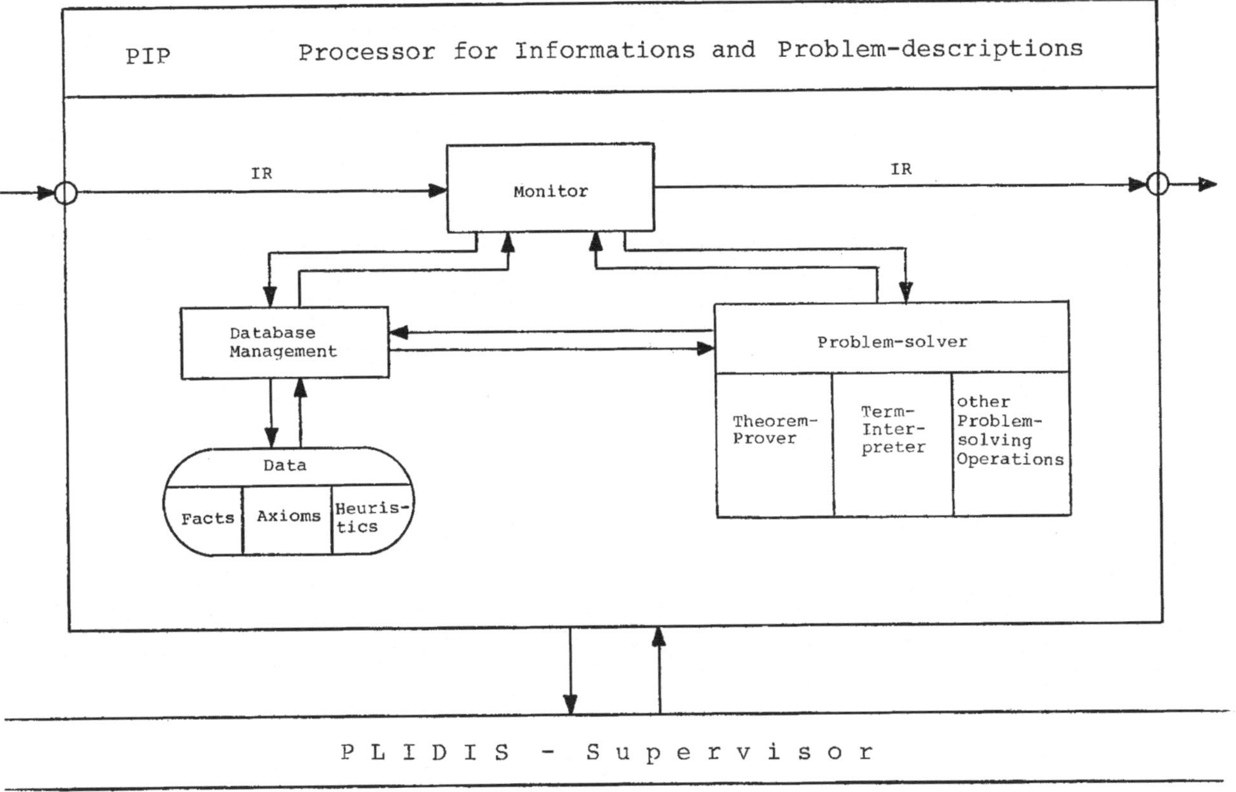

fig.14 Structure of the PLIDIS component for information processing and problem solving.

The data base is divided into two sections:

- the primary base, containing the items
- the secondary base, containing the 'modes of access' to the items.

Both data bases are in the form of ISAM-files. Each item to be stored gets prefixed with the security-key of the user entering the item. The security-keys of all users are organised in a dependency tree. A user is allowed access only to those items prefixed with his own key or with the key of a user on a dependent node. This ensures that only authorized persons have access to specific data.

5.2. Characteristics of the problem-domain for PLIDIS

First it should be made clear what is meant by 'problem-solving' in the context of the QA system PLIDIS. Defined in a negative sense the problem-domain excludes the area of mathematical theorem proving, game playing, and robot reasoning. The emphasis is rather on retrieving the appropriate answer for a question from a large data base with a minimal number of deductions.

The sorts of problems the system will have to deal with are:

1. The retrieval of facts explicitly or implicitly contained in the data base. An example of a question asking for an explicit fact would be: 'how high is the level of arsenic in a specific sample'. An example asking for an implicit fact: 'which toxic materials were contained in sample y'; whereby it has to be deduced what is meant by 'toxic' from such statements of facts as 'a stuff which impedes the growth of plants in the river is toxic'; 'the growth of plants is impeded by chemicals which reduce the level of oxygen in water'.

2. The performance of arithmetic operations on the data retrieved, such as 'the average level of cyanide over a specified period'.

3. The reconstruction of some processes. For example, an excessive level of cyanide was detected in a river at place x, which firm could have caused this? To arrive at an answer, it has to be deduced which firms, located upstream from place x might have produced cyanide as a waste product; this information itself might not be explicitly given, but it might have to be deduced from the chemical processes involved in the production process.

4. The controlling of pollution. Incoming data about the composition of water samples is immediately checked against the legal norms, and if a norm is found to be transgressed, appropriate action is taken. This action involves checking of previous samples to find out if it is a 'first offence', and so on.

From the above catalogue, it follows that the problem solving component of PLIDIS must be able to perform the following operations:
- matching operations
- set-theoretic operations
- deduction operations
- arithmetic operations

The choice of the appropriate matching operations depends in the first place on the techniques used in the 'data base management' component for storage of mass-data (hash-coding, pattern-matching...).

As natural language questions put to the system usually involve the use of plural noun phrases, it should be possible to ask for the extension of sets (of individuals or of mass-terms). This task is performed by a component called '<u>Terminterpreter</u>' (TI), which reformulates the KS-question into set-theoretic terms and subsequently evaluates this term with set-theoretic operators. The deduction process proper is done by means of a theorem-prover based on the resolution principle.

Arithmetic operations present no particular problem, as they are represented as KS-operators which are evaluated as LISP functions. The components which perform the above operations interact with each other in the process of solving a particular problem. This interaction is guided by a 'monitor'. An illustrative example of the operation of the problem-solver is shown in section 5.4.

5.3. Problem-solving with an automatic 'theorem-prover'*)

Since PLIDIS disposes of a 'declarative' internal representation of its knowledge consisting of a set of KS-formulas, it seemed indicated to adopt as deduction mechanism an automatic theorem-prover (TP) based on the resolution principle offering the advantages of a universal, uniform system with provable properties (cf. CHANG & LEE 1970).

---

*) for further information see DILGER 1976a

Without giving a detailed analysis of the respective merits of different problem-solving approaches, it may be argued that the justification for the choice of a theorem-prover against its alternative, namely a programming language with deductive capacity, lies primarily in its adaptability to different problem-domains. Nevertheless the latter method may achieve greater efficiency where the problem-domain is clearly defined and the sorts of answers expected are known in advance.

Theorem-provers have in the past been heavily critised for their inefficiency. Recent research on improved searching strategies have significantly increased their efficiency. A more deep reaching criticism is probably that all knowledge cannot be adequately presented in first-order predicate calculus. In our opinion, the extensions incorporated in KS, which were described earlier, have considerably improved the power of first-order predicate calculus. Another objection by advocates of a 'procedural' approach is that a theorem-prover operates on a static world-model whereas in a real-world model, it is often required to be able to remove data from the data base to reflect changed states of the world. In PLIDIS there is no need to remove data since all facts and actions are characterised by situational and temporal variables.

Most important in the evaluation of the efficiency of a TP is the extent to which it can be guided by appropriate heuristics which not only evaluate syntactic features but also semantic ones.

The theorem-prover based on the resolution principle proceeds in two main stages: normalization and resolution.

The process of normalising consists in reducing the KS-formulas into sets of literals obtained out of clauses in conjunctive normal form, the existential quantifiers having been replaced by skolem-constants or -functions.

For greater efficiency, normalising takes place when the formulas are entered into the data base, so that it only needs to be carried out once. Questions must of course still be normalised by the TP.

The process of resolution proper generally involves two important aspects: i) search strategies and ii) heuristics.

Under the heading of search strategies fall such alternative techniques as 'state space' versus 'problem reduction', 'depth-first' versus 'breadth-first' analysis, and the use of connection graphs as described by KOWALSKI (1975), supported by methods such as the Waltz-algorithm.

Each of these techniques presents advantages for particular types of problems. It was deemded important in the PLIDIS implementation of the TP to allow the deduction strategies to be kept variable, according to the type of problem at hand.

In a QA system, for example, 'the problem reduction' method (such as 'input resolution') has the advantage that the question being asked (i.e. the conclusion) can be taken as the starting clause, thus ensuring that only clauses containing a predicate relevant to the question is resolved upon. Because of the incompleteness of input resolution conclusions from false premises ('ex falso quodlibet') is avoided.

On the other hand, where the TP is to be used for controlling pollution, the goal-state is in general not known and a 'state-space' deduction method is hence indicated.

The 'default' implementation of the PLIDIS theorem-prover functions in state-space mode with breadth-first analysis. It is possible to change the operation mode to either 'unit resolution' or 'input resolution', by specifying the appropriate parameters.

The axioms being resolved upon are linked by a connection graph.*) It is envisaged to construct connection graphs when the data is entered in the data base. The set of clauses can thus be divided into subsets linked by a connection graph, representing different mini-world models of related axioms. As a further extension, heuristics could be similarly connected into subsets, which would aid the selection function.

Whether the entire system's knowledge can thus be neatly divided into subsets has not yet been empirically verified. On a preliminary investigation, it seems that at least certain coherent bodies of knowledge can be distinguished, such as legal norms, geographical data, composition of chemicals etc.

At each step in the deduction process, the selection of the next pair of clauses to be resolved upon is guided by a 'selection function'. This function calls upon semantic as well as syntactic heuristics.

---

*) cf. DILGER 1976b

In the context of resolution by means of connection graphs, heuristics can be defined as functions which evaluate links by some syntactic or semantic criteria so that the 'optimal' pair of clauses is chosen to be resolved upon.

Such heuristic functions could be viewed as functions operating on the subsets of the set of links, having as values fuzzy sets of links defined as follows:

Let $K = \{k_1, \ldots k_n\}$ be the set of links in the connection graph and FS the fuzzy set consisting of the union of all fuzzy sets FS(K'), whereby K' denotes a subset of K: $FS = \bigcup_{K' \subset K} FS(K')$. (A fuzzy set FS of K' is a function: $f : K' \to [0,1]$).

A heuristic function is a partial function from the powerset of K into the set FS:

$$h : 2^K \to FS$$

whereby $h(K') \in FS(K') \qquad (K' \subseteq K)$

This means that a heuristic function does not need to yield a value for all subsets of K. In the case of a 'depth-first' method of analysis, for example, only those links are evaluated which end in the same clause.

In general, for a particular subset K' of K, several heuristic functions will be defined. It is necessary to allow the user the possibility of adding new heuristic functions to the system, required by his problem.

An example of a syntactic heuristic would be a function computing the size of the unifier, i.e. the number of substitutions (e.g. if the unifier of the link k contains p elements then $f(k)=\frac{1}{p}$); another example would be the use of resolution with unit clauses (the value of this function would be either '0' or '1').

Semantic heuristics take into account the semantic characterisation of the predicate and the arguments of the literal. Such heuristics must be formulated in terms of the world-model and the problem at hand.

Finally, the PLIDIS problem-solver makes use of the sortal structure of KS in selecting a unifier for a set of clauses. Before a substitution is carried out, it is checked if the sort of the constant is compatible with the sort of the argument, as is illustrated by the following two clauses:

¬(AT x y)v¬(MOVE x y z) v (AT x z)
(AT table (PLACE table))

The following unifier can be established together with a specification of the sortal characterisation of the substitutions

(table PHYSOBJ)/x,((PLACE table)LOC)/y

yielding the following resolvent:

¬(MOVE table (PLACE table)z) v (AT table z)

The above clause is ill-formed as the first argument of MOVE has to be of the sort 'animate'; the substitution must hence be rejected.

5.4. Illustrating the problem-solving component of PLIDIS

The theorem-prover is only part of the problem-solving component of the question-answering system PLIDIS. There is constant interaction between the four components described in section 5.2., namely retrieving and matching functions, set theoretic operations, arithmetic operations and the theorem-prover.

The following is a brief semantic characterisation of the kind of questions put to PLIDIS.

(1) Questions asking whether or not something is the case (Yes/no question)

(2) Questions asking for specific information (what/which/who... questions)

(3) Questions asking about 'processes' or sequences of actions needed to reach a goal (how/why questions)

In all these cases a theorem-prover can be called upon, as all of them can be reduced to the form: 'can q be deduced from the formulas representing the system's knowledge?'.

In the case of type 2 questions, the variable whose extension is being questioned is 'traced' by adding an 'answer-predicate' which is implied by the conclusion. The deduction is completed if instead of the empty clause the 'answering clause' is derived. This consists of only one formula with the answer predicate, the argument of which constitutes the answer. In the case of type 3 questions, the procedure is similar, but the argument of the formula of the answering clause is not an individual variable but a term, which denotes the sequence of actions collected in the deduction process.

The following two examples show the similarity of the KS-representation of a type 1 and a type 2 question. ('?' is a pragmatic operator indicating a yes/no question)

- "Has the firm Müller already been checked three times this year?"

$$
\begin{array}{l}
(?(\text{ANZAHL}\ (\text{LAMBDA}\ x_1^{int} \\
\quad (\text{EXIST}\ x_1^{stoffkoll} \\
\quad (\text{UND}\ (\text{PROBE}\ (\text{BETRIEB MÜLLER \& CO 7000.STUTTGART}) \\
\qquad\qquad x_1^{int}\ ;\ x_1^{stoffkoll}) \\
\qquad (\text{IN 1976.}\ x_1^{int})))) \\
\quad 3))
\end{array}
$$

- "How often has Müller been checked this year?"

$$
\begin{array}{l}
(\text{LAMBDA}\ x_1^{zahl} \\
\quad (\text{ANZAHL}\ (\text{LAMBDA}\ x_1^{int} \\
\qquad (\text{EXIST}\ x_1^{stoffkoll} \\
\qquad (\text{UND}\ (\text{PROBE}\ (\text{BETRIEB MÜLLER \& CO 7000.STUTTGART}) \\
\qquad\qquad x_1^{int}\ ;\ x_1^{stoffkoll}) \\
\qquad\quad (\text{IN 1976.}\ x_1^{int})))) \\
\quad ;\ x_1^{zahl}))
\end{array}
$$

The interaction between the various components of the problem-solving part of PLIDIS will be illustrated by means of a ficticious example, wherein the KS-formulas appear in a somewhat simplified format. The predicates have been 'translated' into English, to ensure greater ease of readability to the non-German reader. Input to the system is the following question:

'Which toxic materials were contained in the samples of the firm Müller taken on 24.5.75 and on 7.9.75?'

The internal representation of this question in KS would take the following form (making allowance for the translation of the predicates and individual terms):

$$
\begin{array}{l}
(\text{LAMBDA}\ x^{stoff}\ (\text{UND}(\text{COMPONENT}(\text{SAMPLE MÜLLER}(\text{LISTE 24.5.75 7.9.75})) \\
\qquad\qquad x^{stoff}) \\
\qquad (\text{TOXIC}\ x^{stoff})))
\end{array}
$$

The data base contains following axioms defining 'toxic' material in the context of water pollution, which might be called upon for the deduction:

- toxic are such materials which interfere directly or indirectly with the fauna or flora in the river.
- poisons interfere directly with the flora and fauna of the river.
- materials which reduce the oxygen level of the water interfere indirectly with the flora and fauna.
- chemicals which stimulate growth excessively or slightly oxidising materials reduce the oxygen content of the water.

The above axioms are formalised as follows:

(1) (FUERALL x^{stoff} (IMPLIK(ODER(DIRINTERFER x^{stoff})
(INDIRINTERFER x^{stoff}))
(TOXIC x^{stoff})))

(2) (FUERALL x^{stoff} (IMPLIK(POISON x^{stoff})
(DIRINTERFER x^{stoff})))

(3) (FUERALL x^{stoff} (IMPLIK(REDUCEOXYGEN x^{stoff})
(INDIRINTERFER x^{stoff})))

(4) (FUERALL x^{stoff} (IMPLIK(ODER(STIMULGROWTH x^{stoff})
(OXIDISING x^{stoff}))
(REDUCEOXYGEN x^{stoff})))

Apart from these axioms, the database contains entries about the composition of the samples taken from the firm Müller on 24.5.75 and on 7.9.75, as well as information about the properties of certain chemicals, for example that nitrate excessively stimulates plant growth and that arsenic and cyanide are poisons:

(5) (COMPONENT(SAMPLE MUELLER 24.5.75)
(LISTE OXYGEN SULPHATE CYANIDE))

(6) (COMPONENT(SAMPLE MUELLER 7.9.75)
(LISTE NITRATE CYANIDE LEAD))

(7) (STIMULGROWTH NITRATE)

(8) (POISON(LISTE ARSENIC CYANIDE))

In order to deduce the answer the following steps are required:

(i) The 'TI' component reformulates the KS-question into a set-theoretic formula, whereby the operators ET and VEL denote set-theoretic intersection and union, respectively.

```
(9)  (ET(VEL(COMPONENT(SAMPLE MUELLER 24.5.75))
             (COMPONENT(SAMPLE MUELLER  7.9.75)))
        (TOXIC))
```

(ii) The extension of the individual set terms contained in the formula has to be defined:

```
A : (COMPONENT(SAMPLE MUELLER 24.5.75))
B : (COMPONENT(SAMPLE MUELLER  7.9.75))
C : (TOXIC)
```

The matching operations called by TI obtain from (5) and (6) give the following answers to A and B:

```
A = (LISTE OXYGEN SULPHATE CYANIDE)
B = (LISTE NITRATE CYANIDE LEAD)
```

Since no entry for the predicate TOXIC is found, the theorem-prover is called at this point.

(iii) The conclusion to be deduced by the TP is:

```
(LAMBDA x (TOXIC x))
```

which is normalised as:

```
(10)  ((NEG(TOXIC x))(ANS x))
```

The normalisation process changes sentences (1-4) into the following clauses:

```
(a)  ((NEG(DIRINTERFER X))(TOXIC X))
(b)  ((NEG(INDIRINTERFER X))(TOXIC X))
(c)  ((NEG(POISON X))(DIRINTERFER X))
(d)  ((NEG(REDUCEOXYGEN X))(INDIRINTERFER X))
(e)  ((NEG(STIMULGROWTH X))(REDUCEOXYGEN X))
(f)  ((NEG(OXIDISING X))(REDUCEOXYGEN X))
```

From (10) and (a-f) can be deduced:

```
(g)  ((NEG(DIRINTERFER X))(ANS X))  (a), (10)
(h)  ((NEG(POISON X))(ANS X))       (c), (g)
```

At this stage, the TP does not find a positive literal with the predicate POISON. Instead of continuing the deduction, control is passed to TI in order to retrieve from the data base the extensions of all entries about toxic materials, yielding:

(LISTE ARSENIC CYANIDE)

Control is passed back again to the TP which makes the following further deductions:

(i) ((NEG(INDIRINTERFER X))(ANS X)) (10), (b)
(j) ((NEG(REDUCEOXYGEN X))(ANS X)) (d) , (i)
(k) ((NEG(STIMULGROWTH X))(ANS X)) (e) , (j)

At this point, TI retrieves from the data base the answer:
NITRATE

A further deduction step is:

(l) ((NEG(OXIDISING X))(ANS X)) (f) , (j)

In this case no entry is found in the data base so that the final answer to C is:

C = (LISTE ARSENIC CYANIDE NITRATE)

Evaluation by TI of the expression:

(ET(VEL A B)C) yields the final answer to question (10):
(LISTE CYANIDE NITRATE)

6. Implementation of PLIDIS

PLIDIS is written in SIEMENS-INTERLISP, which is an implementation of Uppsala-INTERLISP (URMI 1975) on a SIEMENS-4004/151 running under the BS 2000 operating system. Uppsala-INTERLISP is itself an implementation of INTERLISP (TEITELMAN 1974) for an IBM 360/370 configuration. No specific SIEMENS-INTERLISP features were used so that the system will almost certainly run in other INTERLISP implementations.

REFERENCES

IdS Institut für deutsche Sprache, Mannheim

Chang, C.L. & Lee, R. (1970): Symbolic Logic and Mechanical Theorem Proving. - Academic Press, New York.

Dilger, W. (1976a): Ein Frage-Antwort-System auf der Basis einer prädikatenlogischen Sprache. - Proceedings of the workshop in 'Dialoge in natürlicher Sprache und Darstellung von Wissen', Freudenstadt, 1976, p. 31ff.

--- (1976b): Verbindungsgraph und Auswahlfunktion. - unpubl. working paper, IdS, Mannheim.

Ginsburg, S. & Partee, B. (1969): A Mathematical Model of Transformational Grammars. - In: Information and Control 15 (1969), pp. 297-334.

Hayes, P.J. (1971): A Logic of Actions. - In: B. Meltzer & D. Michie (eds.): Machine Intelligence 6. Edinburgh.

--- (1974): Some Problems and Non-problems in Representation Theory. - Proceedings of the 1974 AISB Summer Conference, pp. 63ff.

Kolb, D. & Lutz, H.D. (1975): Verarbeitung von Netzwerken. - ISLIB-Info I-4, IdS, Mannheim.

--- & Wulz, H. (1975): Allgemeine Beschreibung und Kurzanleitung für die Benutzung von $\text{ISLIB}_{\text{Börse}}$. - ISLIB-Info I-1, IdS, Mannheim.

Kowalski, R. (1975): A Proof Procedure Using Connection Graphs. - In: Journal of the ACM, 22(4).

Teitelman, W. (1974): INTERLISP Reference Manual. - XEROX Palo Alto Research Center, Palo Alto.

Thomason, R. (1972): A Semantic Theory of Sortal Incorrectness. - In: Journal of Philosophical Logic 1, pp. 209-258.

Urmi, J. (1975): INTERLISP /360 and /370 User Reference Manual. - Uppsala University Data Center, Uppsala.

Woods, W.A. (1973): An Experimental Parsing System for Transition Network Grammars. - In: Rustin, R. (ed.): Natural Language Processing. New York.

Wulz, H. (1976): Konzept einer Theorie einer Übersetzungsgrammatik. - unpubl. ms., IdS, Mannheim.

Zifonun, G. (1974): KS: eine formale Sprache zur kanonischen Darstellung natürlicher Inhalte in einem automatischen Frage-Antwort-System. - Arbeitspapier LDV-MA-73-3, IdS, Mannheim.

--- (1976): Die Konstruktsprache KS. Entwurf eines Darstellungsmittels für natürlichsprachlich formulierte Information. - working paper, IdS, Mannheim.

METAMORPHOSIS GRAMMARS

A. COLMERAUER

GROUPE D'INTELLIGENCE ARTIFICIELLE
U.E.R. Scientifique de Luminy
Université d'Aix-Marseille II
70, Route Léon Lachamp
13288 MARSEILLE (FRANCE)

This work was completed with the help of a grant from SESORI (Research Convention 73047).
Let us also indicate that the Artificial Intelligence Group is an Associated Research Group of the CNRS.

Abstract : We present some very general grammars in which each re-writing rule is of the type : "replace such and such sequence of trees by such and such another sequence of trees". Within the framework of programming in first-order logic, we propose axioms for these grammars which produce efficient parsing and syntheses algorithms. We illustrate this work by the programming-language PROLOG and by two important examples : writing of a compiler and writing of an intelligent system conversing in French.

Key-words : Grammars, syntactic analysis, 1st order logic, predicate calculus, automatic demonstration, compilation, natural language.

INTRODUCTION

In 1970 I was trying to perfect a particular kind of non-determinist programming-language : q-systems (4). This work concerned a formal system allowing us to write complex grammars, to which was associated an interpreter in order to analyse or synthesise structures conforming to these grammars. The basis of the formal system was composed of re-writing rules.

These rules were very general : on the one hand they were not necessarily of the "context-free" type, i.e. one could re-write any sub-sequence of any length in any sequence ; on the other hand, instead of working on sequences of simple symbols, one could work on sequences of complex symbols (more precisely, trees). A system of formal parameters allowed us to transmit into each symbol any information required.

The formal aspect of this work was very satisfactory : here was an example of a powerful language, based on few but very systematic principles. It allowed us to complete all the stages of our process of English/French translation : morphology and analysis of English sentences, stages of transference from the English deep structure to the French deep structure, synthesis and morphology of the French sentences.

Having become more interested subsequently in the semantics of language and in mechanisms of deduction, I abandoned q-systems and turned to techniques of automatic demonstration, basing my work on J.A. Robinson's principle of resolution (cf. 10 and 8).

I then collaborated in the elaboration of a programming-language PROLOG (cf. 11 and 1). Originally conceived to resolve deductive problems in a system conversing in French (6), this language found immediately a number of applications : let us quote among others, formal integration (3), robotic (12) and speech-recognition (2). However, although this language was superior in many fields to the q-systems, the latter were simpler and clearer as far as the treatment of syntax was concerned. It was to remedy this situation that we conceived metamorphosis grammars : these involve an axiomatisation into 1st-order logic of the associativity of the concatenation in order to obtain in PROLOG the facilities of the q-systems, thus obtaining a very powerful instrument for all syntactic and semantic treatment of languages.

This article is divided into two parts : a theoretical part in chapters 1 and 2, and a practical part in the last 3 chapters.

The first chapter introduces our terminology and proposes some ideas which may be considered a better basis for PROLOG than "SL-resolution" (8). We take up here ideas suggested in (9).

The 2nd chapter is devoted to metamorphosis grammars.

The third chapter gives a brief outline of PROLOG and of the way in which metamorphosis grammars are treated in that language. For more details we refer the reader to the PROLOG-Manual (11).

Chapter 4 illustrates by an example the way in which we can write a compiler by means of metamorphosis grammars.

In chapter 5 metamorphosis grammars are used to treat the problem which interests us most of all : conversing in French with a machine capable of reasoning. The example proposed is described very briefly, but is based on an extensive study of the role of articles in French. This study follows the general line of R. Pasero's work on the representation of French in logic.

CHAPTER 1

A SUBSET OF 1ST-ORDER LOGIC AS A PROGRAMMING-LANGUAGE

1.1 BASIC TERMINOLOGY

In all that follows we suppose that to each symbol s is associated a integer $i \geqslant 0$ called its order. We write

$$\text{order}[s] = i$$

Let F be a set of symbols called functional symbols and let there be a finite set of variables. Each formula constructed as follows is called a term on F :

(1) if v_i is a variable then v_i is a term

(2) if $f \in F$ and $\text{order}[f] = 0$ then f is a term

(3) if $f \in F$ and $\text{order}[f] = n$ and $t_1, t_1, \ldots, t_n$ are terms then $f(t_1, t_2, \ldots, t_n)$ is a term.

We write $\hat{H}[F]$ or simply $\hat{H}$, the set of terms, and $H[F]$ or simply H the set of terms containing no variables. H is often called a Herbrand universe.

The elements of the Herbrand universe are none other than the "good" trees of the computer scientist constructed on F but respecting the order of each symbol.

A formula or set of formulae p has as its value any p' obtained by substituting for each variable of p a tree, i.e. an element of the Herbrand universe.

Let R be another set of symbols called relational symbols ; we call atomic each formula constructed as follows :

(1) if $r \in R$ and $\text{order}[r] = 0$ then r is atomic

(2) if $r \in R$ and $\text{order}[r] = n$ and $t_1, t_2, \ldots, t_n$ are terms then $r(t_1, t_2, \ldots, t_n)$ is atomic.

If p is atomic, then $+p$ and $-p$ are literals.

A clause is a set of literals.

A (Herbrand) interpretation I is a set of atomic formulae without variables. To each relational symbol r of order n , it associates the n-ary relation ρ between the elements of the Herbrand universe :

$\rho[t_1,t_2,\ldots,t_n]$ iff $r(t_1,\ldots,t_n) \in I \quad \forall t_1,t_2,\ldots,t_N \in H$

in the case where $n = 0$, ρ is reduced to the boolean value :

ρ iff $r \in I$

An interpretation I is smaller than an interpretation J iff $I \subset J$

We consider that

(1) a set of clauses is a conjunction $(\wedge)$ of clauses

(2) the variables of a clause are universally quantified at its head

(3) a clause is a disjunction $(\wedge)$ of literals

(4) the sign + marks affirmation and the sign - negation.

We therefore define the notion of satisfaction as follows :

An interpretation I satisfies

(1) a set of clauses iff it satisfies each clause of the set. The empty set of clauses is considered as always satisfied.

(2) a clause iff it satisfies each value of the clause.

(3) a clause without variables iff it satisfies at least one literal of the clause. The empty clause is never satisfied.

(4) a literal without variables $+p$ iff $p \in I$

a literal without variables $-p$ iff $p \notin I$

Between two sets of clauses A and B we define the relation $\models$ by

$A \models B$ iff each interpretation which satisfies A satisfies B .

1.2. REGULAR SETS OF CLAUSES AND THE SMALLEST INTERPRETATION SATISFYING THEM

We are accustomed to considering a "programme" as the definition of a certain function f . The "machine" which executes it permits us to "compute" this function by giving the result $f[x]$ for every x which is given as input.

Let E be a set of clauses in which appears a certain n-ary relational symbol r. Let us suppose that there exists a smallest interpretation I which satisfies E . This interpretation I therefore associates to the symbol r an n-ary relation ρ between the trees. We can therefore consider E as a "programme" defining the relation ρ , provided we have at our disposal deductive rules which play the part of a "machine" allowing us to "compute" this n-ary relation by enumerating all the n-uplets of trees which satisfy it and which may interest us.

From this point of view, our programmes will be sets of clauses of a peculiar type, called "regular".

Definition : A clause is said to be regular iff it contains one and only one positive literal. A set of clauses is said to be regular iff it contains only regular clauses.

A regular set of clauses always admits an interpretation I which satisfies it. We need only take as I the set of all atomic formulae without variables.

One can also show that if E is regular and if I and J satisfy E , then I ∩ J also satisfies E . (This is not always true for an non-regular set : {{+a,+b}} is a counter-example).

If we now consider the intersection of all the interpretations which satisfy a regular set, we can deduce from it the following property :

Property 1. If E is a regular set of clauses, then there exists a smallest interpretation, written Imin[E], which satisfies it.

Example

F = {a,b,nil,.} order[a] = order[b] = order[nil] = 0 order[.] = 2

R = {conc} order[conc] = 3

variables : e,x,y,z,...

E =

+conc(nil,y,y)

+conc(.(e,x),y,.(e,z)) -conc(x,y,z)

(each line represents a clause, each clause is written by writing its literals one after the other).

The alert reader will verify that the smallest interpretation satisfying E in this example associates to conc the ternary relation

conc'[u,v,w] iff u is of the form

v is of any form

w is obtained by substituting v for the nil at the bottom of u.

The notion of smallest interpretation satisfying a set of clauses takes on all its interest only when one notes the second property, which follows.

Property 2. Let E be a set of clauses having a smallest interpretation Imin[E] satisfying it. For each atomic formula without variables, we have

$$E \models \{\{+p\}\} \text{ iff } p \in \text{Imin}[E]$$

The rules of deduction needed to calculate relations will therefore be those used in automatic demonstration.

1.3 RULES OF DEDUCTION

The rules of deduction presented here are a simplification of Robinson's principle of resolution (10), reasoning on regular sets of clauses. They are formulated taking into account the fact that the notion of a sequence of elements lends itself more easily to programming than that of a set of elements.

Let L be the set of all the literals. We will call ordered clause any sequence of literals $a_1a_2\ldots a_n$ with $n \geq 0$. When $n=0$, we write this sequence Λ. The set of ordered clauses (including Λ) is written L^*.

For each $x,y \in L^*$, we agree that

$$x\,y = a_1a_2\ldots a_nb_1b_2\ldots b_n \text{ if } x = a_1a_2\ldots a_n \text{ and if } y = b_1b_2\ldots b_n$$
$$x\,\Lambda = \Lambda x = x$$

Let E be a regular set of clauses and Eord a set of ordered clauses obtained by substituting for each clause

$$\{+p_0,-p_1,-p_2,\ldots -p_n\}$$

of E an ordered clause

$$+p_0\ -p_1\ -p_2\ \cdots\ -p_n$$

where the positive literal is placed at the head.

Definition : for each $x,y \in L^*$ we note

$x \vdash_{Eord} y$ iff (a) $\exists +p \in L$ $\exists u,v \in L^*$ such that $x = u\ {-p}\ v$

(b) $\exists s \in$ Eord and $+q\ t$ is a variant of s obtained by renaming the variables of s in such a way as to have no common variable with x

(c) $y = [u\ t\ v]\ \sigma$ where σ is a most general unifier (in Robinson's sense) of the set $\{p,q\}$

$x \vdash^n_{Eord} y$ iff $\exists u_0,u_1,\ldots,u_n \in L^*$ such that

$$x = u_0 \vdash_{Eord} u_1 \vdash_{Eord} u_2 \cdots \vdash_{Eord} u_n = y$$

Since this is not the main purpose of this paper, we ask the reader to admit that :

<u>Theorem</u> : for any atomic formula p

$E \models \{\{+r\}\}$ and r is a value of p

iff

there exists $n > 0$ and there exists an atomic formula q such that

$-p\ +p \ \vdash^{n}_{Eord}\ +q$ and r is a value of q.

By using proposition 2 of the preceding paragraph, we obtain :

<u>Corollary</u> : for any atomic formula p

$r \in Imin[E]$ and r is a value of p

iff

there exist $n > 0$ and there exist an atomic formula q such that

$-p\ +p \ \vdash^{n}_{Eord}\ +q$ and r is a value of q

Let us consider again the preceding example and try to calculate x such that

conc'[.(a,nil),.(b,nil),x]

Since

-conc(.(a,nil),.(b,nil),u) +conc(.(a,nil),.(b,nil),u) $\vdash_{Eord}$

-conc(nil,.(b,nil),z) +conc(.(a,nil),.(b,nil),.(a,z)) $\vdash_{Eord}$

+conc(.(a.nil),.(b,nil),.(a,.(b,nil)))

we deduce according to the corollary

x = .(a,.(b,nil))

If we now try to calculate all the couples x,y such that

conc'[x,y,.(a,nil)]

since

-conc(u,v,.(a,nil)) +conc(u,v,.(a,nil)) $\vdash_{Eord}$

+conc(nil,.(a,nil),.(a,nil))

and since

-conc(u,v,.(a,nil)) +conc(u,v,.(a,nil)) $\vdash_{Eord}$

-conc(x,y,nil) +conc(.(a,x),y,.(a,nil)) $\vdash_{Eord}$

+conc(.(a,nil),nil,.(a,nil))

and since no other deductions are possible, the two solutions are

x = nil y = .(a,nil) and x = .(a,nil) y = nil

Of course, in general, the set of ordered clauses that may be deduced is not necessarily finite and we therefore have only an algorithm of semi-decision. However, in order to restrict the field of research, one can make the preceding theorem more sophisticated by introducing the notion of selection function.

<u>Definition</u> : f is a selection function if to each ordered clause x containing at least one negative literal, it associates a triplet

$$f[x] = [u,-p,v] \quad \text{with} \quad -p \in L \quad u,v \in L^* \quad x = u\ -p\ v$$

<u>Stronger theorem</u> : Let f be any selection function. The preceding theorem is always true if in the definition of $\vdash_{Eord}$ we add to the point (a) the constraint

$$f[x] = [u,-p,v]$$

CHAPTER 2

METAMORPHOSIS GRAMMARS

2.1 STRINGS, STRING-SCHEMAS AND CONCATENATION

We now suppose that the set F of functional symbols contains the binary symbol : "." and the symbol of order 0 "nil" .

We use an infix notation with bracketing from right to left to write any term constructed with the functional symbol ".", i.e. we write

$$a_1.a_2.---.a_{n-1}.a_n$$

instead of

$$.(a_1,.(a_2,---.(a_{n-1},a_n)---))$$

Let V be a subset of H called vocabulary

A string-schema of length n on the vocabulary V is a term of the form :

$$a_1.a_2.---.a_n.\text{nil} \text{ with } n\geq 0 \text{ and } a_i \in V$$

The string-schema of length 0 reduces to "nil". We write V* the set of all string-schemas. For strings of length 1 we introduce the abridged notation

$\underline{a}$ for a.nil

If the vocabulary contains no variables, we speak of strings instead of string-schemas.

In the set of string-schemas V*, concatenation is a law of internal composition written as a product and defined by

if x = nil then xy = y

if $x = a1.a_2.---.a_n.\text{nil}$ then $xy = a_1.a_2.---.a_n.y$

Of course, this is an associative law of which the neutral element is "nil".

Moreover, xy is also defined for a $y\in\hat{H}$ which is not a string-schema .If we use the abridged notation of string-schemas of length 1, we can now write

$$\underline{a_1}\ \underline{a_2}\ ---\ \underline{a_n} \text{ instead of } a_1.a_2.---.a_n.\text{nil}$$

2.2 RE-WRITING RELATION $\rightarrow$ AND RELATIONS $\rightarrow^{i}$ AND $\rightarrow^{*}$

Let $\rightarrow$ be a binary relation between the elements of H and let V be a vocabulary without variables, i.e. $V \subset H$.

The relation $\rightarrow$ is said to be a re-writing relation on V^* iff for each $x,y \in H$

$$x \rightarrow y \quad \text{implies} \quad x,y \in V^*$$

Starting with the re-writing relation $\rightarrow$, we define the following relations between the elements of H.

$x \rightarrow^{0} y$ iff $x = y$ and $x,y \in V^*$

$x \rightarrow^{i+1} y$ iff there exist $u,v,r,s \in V^*$ such that

$x = urv$ and $r \rightarrow s$ and $usv \rightarrow^{i} y$

$x \rightarrow^{*} y$ iff there exist $i \geq 0$ such that $x \rightarrow^{i} y$

Note that these new relations are also re-writing relations.

2.3 METAMORPHOSIS GRAMMAR

Definition : A metamorphosis grammar G is defined by a quintuplet $(F, V_T, V_N, V_S, \rightarrow)$ where

(1) F is a set of functional symbols containing "." and "nil"

(2) V_T is a vocabulary said to be terminal with $V_T \subset H[F]$

(3) V_N is a vocabulary said to be non-terminal with $V_N \subset H[F]$. We suppose that $V_N \cap V_T = \emptyset$ and write $V = V_T \cup V_N$

(4) $V_S \subset V_N$. The elements of V_S are termed starting non-terminals.

(5) $\rightarrow$ is a re-writing relation on V^* with the restriction that $x \rightarrow y$ implies $x \neq \text{nil}$

The language generated by the grammar G is the set of strings on V_T

$$L(G) = \{t \in V_T^* \mid \text{there exist } s \in V_s \text{ with } \underline{s} \rightarrow^{*} t\}$$

If $s \in V_s$, $t \in V_T^*$ and $\underline{s} \rightarrow^{*} t$ then s is called deep structure of t

Example 1 : Here is an example of a metamorphosis grammar

(1) $F = \{$nil,zéro,a,b,suite,bs,suc,.$\}$ with

order [nil] = order [zéro] = order [a] = order [b] = 0

order [suite] = order [bs] = order [suc] = 1

order [.] = 2

(2) $V_T = \{a,b\}$

(3) $V_N = V_S \cup \{ bs(x) \mid x \in H[F]\}$

(4) $V_S = \{suite(x) \mid x \in H[F]\}$

(5) The couples of strings satisfying the re-writing relation → are enumerated by :

$$\underline{suite(x)} \rightarrow \underline{a}\ \underline{suite(suc(x))} \qquad \forall x \in H[F]$$
$$\underline{suite(x)} \rightarrow \underline{bs(x)} \qquad \forall x \in H[F]$$
$$\underline{bs(suc(x))} \rightarrow \underline{b}\ \underline{bs(x)} \qquad \forall x \in H[F]$$
$$\underline{bs(zéro)} \rightarrow nil$$

We obtain

$$\underline{suite(suc(suc(zéro)))} \rightarrow^* \underline{a}\ \underline{b}\ \underline{b}\ \underline{b}$$

Since

$$\underline{suite(suc(suc(zéro)))} \rightarrow^1 \underline{a}\ \underline{suite(suc(suc(suc(zéro))))} \rightarrow^1$$
$$\underline{a}\ \underline{bs(suc(suc(suc(zéro))))} \rightarrow^1 \underline{a}\ \underline{b}\ \underline{bs(suc(suc(zéro)))} \rightarrow^1$$
$$\underline{a}\ \underline{b}\ \underline{b}\ \underline{bs(suc(zéro))} \rightarrow^1 \underline{a}\ \underline{b}\ \underline{b}\ \underline{b}\ \underline{bs(zéro)} \rightarrow^1$$
$$\underline{a}\ \underline{b}\ \underline{b}\ \underline{b}$$

In a general way, we notice that the language generated by this grammar is the set of strings of the form

$$\underline{a}^i\ \underline{b}^j \text{ with } j - i \geqslant 0$$

and that the deep structure associated to each string

$$\underline{a}^i\ \underline{b}^j$$

is the tree

suc(suc(---suc(zéro)---))

where the number of "suc" is equal to $j - i$.

<u>Example 2</u> : Here is another example of a metamorphosis grammar

(1) F = {nil,a,b ,<,>,+,end,formula,value,.} with

order [nil] = order [a] = order [b] = order [<]=
order [>] = order [+] = order [end] = 0
order [formula] = order [value] = 1
order [.] = 2

(2) $V_T = \{a,b,<,>,+\}$

(3) $V_N = V_S \cup \{\underline{\mathrm{end}}\} \cup \{\mathrm{value}(x) \mid x \in H[F]\}$

(4) $V_S = \{\mathrm{formula}(x) \mid x \in H[F]\}$

(5) The couples of strings satisfying the re-writing relation $\rightarrow$ are enumerated by :

$$\begin{array}{l}
\underline{\mathrm{formula(a)}} \rightarrow \underline{a} \\
\underline{\mathrm{formula(b)}} \rightarrow \underline{b} \\
\underline{\mathrm{formula(x)}} \rightarrow \underline{\mathrm{value(x)}} \\
\underline{\mathrm{value(y.z)}} \rightarrow \underline{<}\underline{\mathrm{formula(y)}}\ \underline{\mathrm{end}}\ \underline{\mathrm{value(z)}} \\
\underline{\mathrm{value(nil)}} \rightarrow \underline{\mathrm{nil}} \\
\underline{\mathrm{end}}\ \underline{<} \rightarrow \underline{+} \\
\underline{\mathrm{end}} \rightarrow \underline{>}
\end{array}$$

where y and z designate arbitrary elements of $H[F]$ and x designates an element of $H[F]$ of the form u.v

We therefore obtain among other results

$$\begin{array}{l}
\underline{\mathrm{formula(a)}} \rightarrow^* \underline{a} \\
\underline{\mathrm{formula(a.b.a.nil)}} \rightarrow^* \underline{<}\ \underline{a}\ \underline{+}\ \underline{b}\ \underline{+}\ \underline{a}\ \underline{>} \\
\underline{\mathrm{formula(a.((a.b.nil).nil).nil)}} \rightarrow^* \underline{<}\ \underline{a}\ \underline{+}\ \underline{<}\ \underline{<}\ \underline{a}\ \underline{+}\ \underline{b}\ \underline{>}\ \underline{>}\ \underline{>}
\end{array}$$

which gives a good idea of what this grammar "does".

2.4. METAMORPHOSIS GRAMMAR IN NORMAL FORM

Definition : A metamorphosis grammar is said to be in normal form if it satisfies the restriction :

$$\underline{a}x \rightarrow y \quad \text{implies} \quad a \in V_N \quad \text{and} \quad x \in V_T^*$$

This is the case in the two grammars given in the preceding examples. The restrictio proposed is not very strong, since one can show that :

Property 1 . For each metamorphosis grammar $G = (F, V_T, V_N, V_S, \rightarrow)$ there exists a grammar in normal form $G' = (F', V'_T, V'_N, V'_S, \rightarrow')$ such that for each $a \in V_N$, each $t \in V_T^*$

$$\underline{a} \rightarrow^* t \quad \text{iff} \quad \underline{a} \rightarrow'^* t$$

Here is a way of constructing G' from G

(1) $F' = F \cup \{te, nt\}$ with order [te] = order [nt] = 1

(2) $V'_T = V_T \cup \{te(a) \mid a \in V_N\}$

(3) $V'_N = V_N \cup \{nt(a) \mid a \in V_T\}$

(4) $V'_S = V_S$

(5) The couples of strings satisfying the relation $\rightarrow'$ are all enumerated by

(a) $a \rightarrow' te(a)$ for each $a \in V_N$

(b) $nt(a) \rightarrow' a$ for each $a \in V_T$

(c) $\underline{a}x \rightarrow y$ implies $\underline{a}'x' \rightarrow y'$ with

$a' = a$ if $a \in V_N$

$a' = nt(a)$ if $a \in V_T$

$x' = nil$ if $x = nil$

$x' = \underline{a}'_1\ a'_2 --- \underline{a}'_n$ if $x = \underline{a}_1\underline{a}_2 --- \underline{a}_n$ with

$a'_i = a_i$ if $a_i \in V_T$

$a'_i = te(a_i)$ if $a_i \in V_N$

$y' = nil$ if $y = nil$

$y' = \underline{b}'_1\ \underline{b}'_2 --- \underline{b}'_n$ if $y = \underline{b}_1\underline{b}_2 --- \underline{b}_n$ with

$b'_i = nt(b_i)$ if $b_i \in V_T$ and $\exists x,y \in V^*$ with $\underline{b}_i x \rightarrow y$

$b'_i = b_i$ otherwise

Here is a characteristic property of metamorphosis grammars in normal form.

Property 2. For each $t \in V_T^*$ each $x,y \in V^*$ each $i \geq 0$

$tx \rightarrow^i y$ implies $\exists z \in V^*$ with $x \rightarrow^i z$ and $tz = y$

This property can be demonstrated by induction on i .

2.5 RELATION $\Rightarrow$

Let $G = (F, V_T, V_N, V_S, \rightarrow)$ be a metamorphosis grammar in normal form.

Definition : $\Rightarrow$ is a binary relation between the elements of the Herbrand universe. The set of couples of trees which verify this relation is constructed in this way :

$\forall u \in V^*$, $\forall t_0, t_1, ---, t_n \in V_T^*$, $\forall b_1, b_2, ---, b_n \in V_N$, $\forall v_0, v_1, ---, v_n \in H[F]$

(1) if $u \rightarrow t_0$ then $uv_0 \Rightarrow t_0 v_0$

(2) if $u \rightarrow t_0\underline{b}_1 t_1 \underline{b}_2 t_2 --- b_n t_n$ and if we already have

$\underline{b}_1 t_1 v_1 \Rightarrow v_0$, $\underline{b}_2 t_2 v_2 \Rightarrow v_1$, ... , $\underline{b}_n t_n v_n \Rightarrow v_{n-1}$

then $uv_n \Rightarrow t_0 v_0$

Let us agree that a binary relation $\Rightarrow_1$ is <u>smaller</u> than a binary relation $\Rightarrow_2$ iff $\forall x,y \quad x \Rightarrow_1 y$ implies $x \Rightarrow_2 y$

From the way in which $\Rightarrow$ is constructed we deduce another definition of this relation.

<u>Equivalent definition</u> : $\Rightarrow$ is the smallest binary relation (between the elements of $H[F]$) which satisfies the conditions (1) and (2).
Let us notice that the following property is constantly verified as we construct the couples (x,y) satisfying $\Rightarrow$

<u>Property</u> : For each $x,y \in V^*$ each $u \in H$

$$x \Rightarrow y \quad \text{implies} \quad xu \Rightarrow yu$$

The theorem and the property which follow show that there exists a very simple link between the relation $\Rightarrow$ and the relation $\rightarrow^*$

<u>Theorem</u> : For each $x,y \in H$

$x \Rightarrow y$ iff $\exists a \in V_N$, $\exists s,\ t \in V_T^*$, $\exists v \in H$ such that
$x = \underline{a}sv$, $\underline{a}s \rightarrow^* t$, $tv = y$ and v minimal

By v is minimal, we understand that there does not exist $c \in V_T$ and $w \in H$ such that $v = \underline{c}w$.

The demonstration can be found in paragraph 2.7

If, in the preceding theorem we take $x = \underline{a}$ with $a \in V_N$ we obtain

<u>Corollary</u> for each $a \in V_N$, each $t \in H$

$$a \Rightarrow t \quad \text{iff} \quad \underline{a} \rightarrow^* t \quad \text{and} \quad t \in V_T^*$$

2.6. <u>CALCULATING RELATION $\Rightarrow$</u>

Let $G = (F, V_T, V_N, V_S, \rightarrow)$ be a metamorphosis grammar in normal form.

We make the following hypotheses :

Hypotheses

(1) there exist sets of terms $\hat{V}_T$ and $\hat{V}_N$ such that

x is a value of an element of $\hat{V}_T$ iff $x \in V_T$

x is a value of an element of $\hat{V}_N$ iff $x \in V_N$

we write $\hat{V} = \hat{V}_T \cup \hat{V}_N$

(2) there exists a regular set of clauses E such that $\forall x,y \in H[F]$

$x \rightarrow y$ iff $r(x,y) \in \mathrm{Imin}[E]$

F is the set of functional symbols of E ,

R is the set of relational symbols of E and

r is a relational symbol of order 2 contained in R

(3) no clause in E contains a negative literal of the form $-r(x,y)$ where $x,y \in \hat{H}[F]$

(4) if a clause of E contains a positive literal of the form $+r(x,y)$ then $x,y \in \hat{V}^*$

we also introduce the definitions :

Definition 1. Let d be a new relational symbol of order 2, not contained in R. We define the transformation t by

(1) for each $u \in \hat{V}^*$, each $t_0 \in \hat{V}^*_T$

$t[+r(u,t_0)] = \{+d(uv_0,t_0v_0)\}$ where v_0 is a new variable

(2) for each $u \in \hat{V}^*$, each $t_i \in \hat{V}^*_T$, each $b_i \in \hat{V}_N$

$t[+r(u,t_0\underline{b}_1t_1\underline{b}_2t_2---\underline{b}_nt_n)] =$

$\{+d(uv_n,t_0v_0),-d(\underline{b}_1t_1v_1,v_0),-d(\underline{b}_2t_2v_2,v_1),---,-d(\underline{b}_nt_nv_n,v_{n-1})\}$

where the v_i are new variables.

Definition 2. We designate by $Tr[E]$ the set of clauses obtained by substituting for each clause in E of the form

$\{+r(x,y)\} \cup g$ (r does not appear in g)

the clause

$t[+r(x,y)] \cup g$

F is the set of functional symbols of Tr[E], and (R ∪ {d}) - {r} that of the relational symbols of Tr[E].
We then obtain the following result :

<u>Theorem</u> : For each $x,y \in H[F]$

$x \Rightarrow y$ iff $d(x,y) \in Imin[Tr[E]]$

The demonstration can be found in paragraph 2.8. By using the corollary of paragraph 2.5, we obtain the new corollary :

<u>Corollary</u> : For each $a \in V_N$ and each $t \in H[F]$

$a.nil \rightarrow^* t$ and $t \in V_T^*$ iff $d(a.nil,t) \in Imin[Tr[E]]$

Let us consider again the 2nd example of a metamorphosis grammar given in paragraph 2.3. The re-writing relation → can be defined by the minimal interpretation satisfying the set of clauses E :

```
+r(formula(a).nil,a.nil)
+r(formula(b).nil,b.nil)
+r(formula(x).nil,valeur(x).nil)-egal(x,r.s)
+r(value(x.y).nil,<.formula(x).end.value(y).nil)
+r(value(nil).nil,nil)
+r(end.<.nil,+.nil)
+r(end.nil,>.nil)
+egal(x,x)
```

where r,s,x,y are variables. The other hypotheses of the beginning of this paragraph are satisfied if we take

$\hat{V}_T = \{a,b\}$ $\hat{V}_N = \{formula(x), value(x)\}$

and therefore, according to the preceding theorem, the relation ⇒ is defined by the minimal interpretation satisfying the set of clauses Tr[E] :

$+d(formula(a).v_0,a.v_0)$

$+d(formula(b).v_0,b.v_0)$

$+d(formula(x).v_1,v_0)$ $-egal(x,r.s)$ $-d(value(x).v_1,v_0)$

$+d(value(x.y).v_3,<.v_0)$ $-d(formula(x).v_1,v_0)$ $-d(end.v_2,v_1)$ $-d(value(y).v_3,v_2)$

$+d(value(nil).v_0,v_0)$

$+d(end.<.v_0,+.v_0)$

$+d(end.v_0,>.v_0)$

$+egal(x,x)$

The last corollary and the deductive rules of paragraph 1.3 allow us for example to analyse the string

< a + b >

to obtain the deep structure

formula(a.b.nil)

by the sequence of deductions

-d(formula(x).nil,<.a.+.b.>.nil) +d(formula(x).nil,<.a.+.b.>.nil)

⊢...............⊢

+d(formula(a.b.nil).nil,<.a.+.b.>.nil)

and inversely to produce the terminal string

< a + b >

from the deep structure

formula(a.b.nil)

by the sequence of deductions

-d(formula(a.b.nil).nil,x) +d(formula(a.b.nil).nil,x)

⊢...............⊢

+d(formula(a.b.nil).nil,<.a.+.b.>.nil)

<u>Remark</u> : All atomic formulae constructed with the relational symbol d are always of the form :

d(f(1). 2 , 3)

where f is a precise functional symbol of order n . This is true in a general way and results from the restrictive hypotheses stated at the beginning of the paragraph. We can therefore substitute for each of these formulae the formula :

f'(1 , 2 , 3)

where f' is a new relational symbol of the order n+2 associated to the symbol f.

If we take up our example again, the set of clauses Tr[E] can be written :

+formula'(a,v_o,a.v_o)

+formula'(b,v_o,b.v_o)

+formula'(x.v_1,v_o) -egal(x,r.s) -value'(x,v_1,v_o)

+value'(x.y,v_3,<.v_o) -formula'(x,v_1,v_o) -end'(v_2,v_1) -value'(y,v_3,v_2)

+value'(nil,v_o,v_o)

+end'(<.v_o,+.v_o)

+end'(v_o,>.v_o)

+egal(x,x)

and to obtain, for example, the deep structure

formula(a.b.nil)

of the string

< a + b >

we need only make the sequence of deductions :

-formula'(x,nil,<.a.+.b.>.nil) +formula'(x,nil,<.a.+.b.>.nil)

⊢ ....⊢

+formula'(a.b.nil,nil,<.a.+.b.>.nil)

2.7 DEMONSTRATION OF THE THEOREM CONCERNING THE LINK BETWEEN ⇒ AND →*

Here is the demonstration of the theorem of paragraph 2.5, of wich we repeat the terms.

Theorem for all $x,y \in H$

(1) $x \Rightarrow y$ iff (2) $\exists \underline{a} \in V_N$, $\exists s,t \in V_T^*$, $\exists v \in H$ such that $\underline{a}s \rightarrow^* t$, $x=\underline{a}sv$, $y=tv$ and v minimal

Demonstration, 1st part. Let us demonstrate that (1) implies (2). We need only verify that the implication is true constantly as we construct the couples of trees satisfying the relation ⇒. If

$$x \Rightarrow y$$

two cases present themselves :

(a) the couple (x,y) is constructed by using rule (1) of the definition of ⇒. Because of this, and because we are reasoning on a grammar in normal form, there exists

$$\underline{a} \in V_N,\ u,t_0 \in V_T^*,\ v_0 \in H \quad \text{such that}$$

$$x = \underline{a}uv_0,\ y = t_0v_0,\ \underline{a}u \rightarrow t_0$$

posing

$$v_0 = w_0v \text{ with } w_0 \in V_T^* \text{ and } v \text{ minimal}$$

$$s = uw_0,\quad t = t_0w_0$$

we obtain

$$\underline{a}s = \underline{a}uw_0 \rightarrow^* t_0w_0 = t, \quad x = \underline{a}uw_0v = \underline{a}sv, \quad y = t_0w_0w = tv$$

(b) the couple (x,y) is constructed by using rule (2) of the definition of $\Rightarrow$. Because of this, and because we are reasoning on a grammar in normal form, there exists

$$u, t_0, t_1, \text{---}, t_n \in V_T^*, \; a, b_1, b_2, \text{---} b_n \in V_N, \; v_0, v_1, \text{---}, v_n \in H \text{ such that}$$

$$x = \underline{a}uv_n, \quad y = t_0v_0, \quad \underline{a}u \rightarrow t_0\underline{b}_1t_1\underline{b}_2t_2\text{---}\underline{b}_nt_n$$

$$\underline{b}_1t_1v_1 \Rightarrow v_0, \quad \underline{b}_2t_2v_2 \Rightarrow v_1, \text{ --- }, \underline{b}_nt_nv_n \Rightarrow v_{n-1}$$

the couples $(\underline{b}_it_iv_i, v_{i-1})$ having already been constructed, the implication that we wish to demonstrate applies to them. Posing

$$v_i = w_im_i \text{ with } w_i \in V_T^* \text{ and } m_i \text{ minimal}$$

$$\underline{b}_it_iv_i \Rightarrow v_{i-1} \text{ implies } \underline{b}_it_iw_i \rightarrow^* w_{i-1} \text{ and } m_i = m_{i-1} = v$$

Since

$$\underline{b}_1t_1w_1 \rightarrow^* w_0, \; \underline{b}_2t_2w_2 \rightarrow^* w_1, \text{ --- }, \underline{b}_nt_nw_n \rightarrow^* w_{n-1}$$

we have

$$\underline{b}_1t_1\underline{b}_2t_2\text{---}\underline{b}_nt_nw_n \rightarrow^* w_0$$

and therefore

$$\underline{a}uw_n \rightarrow^* t_0w_0$$

posing

$$s = uw_n, \quad t = t_0w_0$$

we finally obtain

$$\underline{a}s \rightarrow t, \quad x = \underline{a}uv_n = \underline{a}uw_nv = \underline{a}sv, \quad y = t_0v_0 = t_0w_0v = tv$$

<u>Demonstration, 2nd part</u>. Let us demonstrate that (2) implies (1). We therefore have to demonstrate that

$$\forall a \in V_N, \quad \forall s,t \in V_T^*, \quad \forall v \in H$$

$$\underline{a}s \rightarrow^* t \text{ and } v \text{ minimal implies } \underline{a}sv \Rightarrow tv$$

Recalling the property of $\Rightarrow$ cited in paragraph 2.5, we deduce from it that we need only to demonstrate that

$$\forall a \in V_N, \quad \forall s,t \in V_T^*$$

$$\underline{a}s \rightarrow^* t \text{ implies } \underline{a}s \Rightarrow t$$

This last implication is the particular case of the proposition which ensues when $u = nil$

$$\forall a \in V_N,\ \forall s,t \in V_T^*,\ \forall u \in V^*,\ \forall i \geq 0,\ \exists v \in V_T^*,\ \exists j \geq 0 \text{ such that}$$
$$\underline{a}su \rightarrow t \text{ implies } u \rightarrow^j v \text{ and } \underline{a}sv \Rightarrow t \text{ and } j \leq i$$

Let us demonstrate this last proposition by induction on i .
The proposition is true for $i = 0$, since in this case the left side of the implication is false since

$$a \in V_N \text{ and } t \in V_T^* \text{ and } V_N \cap V_T = \emptyset \text{ implies } \underline{a}su \neq t$$

Let us suppose the proposition true for $0 \leq k \leq i$ and let us demonstrate that it is true for $i+1$. If

$$\underline{a}su \rightarrow^{i+1} t$$

there exist $r \in V^*$ such that

$$\underline{a}su \rightarrow^1 r \rightarrow^i t$$

The passage from $\underline{a}su$ to r can be made in three ways :

(a) $\underline{a}su \rightarrow^1 \underline{a}su' = r$ with $u \rightarrow^1 u'$, $u' \in V^*$

since

$$\underline{a}su' \rightarrow^i t$$

there exist $v \in V_T^*$ and $j \geq 0$ such that

$$u' \rightarrow^j v,\ \underline{a}sv \Rightarrow t,\ j \leq i$$

and therefore

$$u \rightarrow^{j+1} v,\ \underline{a}sv \Rightarrow t,\ j+1 \leq i+1$$

(b) $\underline{a}su = \underline{a}s'u \rightarrow^1 t_0u' = r$ with $\underline{a}s' \rightarrow t_0$, $s',t_0 \in V_T^*$, $u' \in V^*$

therefore

$$t_0u' \rightarrow^i t$$

according to the property 2 of paragraphe 2.4, there exists $v_0 \in V_T^*$

such that

$$u' \rightarrow^i v_0,\ t_0v_0 = t$$

therefore

$$su = s'u' \rightarrow^i s'v_0$$

according to the same property of paragraph 2.4, there exists $v \in V_T^*$ such that

$$u \rightarrow^i v,\ sv = s'v_0$$

according to point 1 of the definition of $\Rightarrow$

$$as' \rightarrow t_0 \quad \text{implies} \quad as'v_0 \Rightarrow t_0v_0$$

we therefore finally obtain

$$u \rightarrow^i v, \quad \underline{a}sv = as'v_0 \Rightarrow t_0v_0 = t, \quad i \leq i+1$$

(c) $\underline{a}su = as'u' \rightarrow^1 t_0\underline{b}_1t_1\underline{b}_2t_2---\underline{b}_nt_nu' = r$ with

$as' \rightarrow t_0b_1t_1b_2t_2---b_nt_n, \quad s',t_i \in V_T^*, \quad b_i \in V_N, \quad u' \in V^*$

therefore

$$t_0\underline{b}_1t_1\underline{b}_2t_2---\underline{b}_nt_nu' \rightarrow^i t$$

according to the property of paragraphe 2.4, there exists $v_0 \in V_T^*$ such that

$$\underline{b}_1t_1\underline{b}_2t_2---\underline{b}_nt_nu' \rightarrow^i v_0, \quad t_0v_0 = t$$

the proposition that we wish to demonstrate being supposed true for $k \leq i$, there exists $v_1 \in V_T^*$ and $j_1 \geq 0$ such that

$$\underline{b}_2t_2---\underline{b}_nt_nu' \rightarrow^{j_1} v_1, \quad \underline{b}_1t_1v_1 \Rightarrow v_0 , \quad j_1 \leq i$$

the proposition that we wish to demonstrate being supposed true for $k \leq i$, there exists $v_2 \in V_T^*$ and $j_2 \geq 0$ such that

$$\underline{b}_3t_3---\underline{b}_nt_nu' \rightarrow^{j_2} v_2 , \quad \underline{b}_2t_2v_2 \Rightarrow v_1, \quad j_2 \leq i$$

....

$$u' \rightarrow^{j_n} v_n , \quad \underline{b}_nt_nv_n \Rightarrow v_{n-1} , \quad j_n \leq i$$

since

$$as' \rightarrow t_0\underline{b}_1t_1\underline{b}_2t_2---\underline{b}_nt_n$$

$$\underline{b}_1t_1v_1 \Rightarrow v_0 , \quad \underline{b}_2t_2v_2 = v_1 , \quad --- , \quad \underline{b}_nt_nv_n \Rightarrow v_{n-1}$$

according to point (2) of the definition of $\Rightarrow$

$$as'v_n \Rightarrow t_0v_0$$

we obtain

$$su = s'u \rightarrow^{jn} s'v_n \quad \text{since} \quad u' \rightarrow^{jn} v_n$$

according to property 2 of paragraph 2.4 and since $v_n \in V_T^*$ there exists $v \in V_T^*$ such that

$$u \rightarrow^{jn} v, \quad sv = s'v_n$$

therefore

$$u \rightarrow^{jn} v, \quad \underline{a}sv = \underline{a}s'v_n \Rightarrow t_0v_0 = t , \quad j_n \leq i \leq i+1$$

2.8 DEMONSTRATION OF THE THEOREM ON THE CALCULATION OF $\Rightarrow^*$

Here is the demonstration of the theorem of paragraph 2.6, of which we repeat the terms.

Theorem for all $x,y \in H[F]$

$$x \Rightarrow y \quad \text{iff} \quad d(x,y) \in Imin[Tr]E]]$$

Demonstration. 1st part. Let us demonstrate first that

$$d(x,y) \in Imin[Tr[E]] \quad \text{iff} \quad d(x,y) \in Imin[E \cup Trbis[E]]$$

where Trbis[E] is the set of clauses of the form

$$t\,[+r(u,v)] \cup \{-r(u,v)\} \quad \text{with} \quad +r(u,v) \text{ element of a clause of } E$$

We therefore need only to demonstrate that

$$Tr[E] \models \{\{+d(x,y)\}\} \quad \text{iff} \quad E \cup Trbis[E] \models \{\{+d(x,y)\}\}$$

or that

$$\exists I \text{ satisfying } Tr[E] \cup \{\{-d(x,y)\}\}$$

$$\text{iff}$$

$$\exists J \text{ satisfying } E \cup Trbis[E] \cup \{\{-d(x,y)\}\}$$

If I satisfies $Tr[E] \cup \{\{-d(x,y)\}\}$ we can arrange I in such a way that it contains no formula of the form r(u,v). In that case let G be the set of all the values of the clauses of E not satisfied by I . The interpretation

$$J = I \cup \{r(u,v) \mid \exists g \in G \text{ with } +r(u,v) \in g\}$$

satisfies $E \cup Trbis[E] \cup \{\{-d(x,y)\}\}$

If that were not the case, according to hypothesis (3) of paragraph 2.6, there could only exist a clause-value of the form

$$\text{(a)} \quad t[+r(u,v)] \cup \{-r(u,v)\}$$

which would not be satisfied by J, and therefore

$$r(u,v) \in J$$

According to the definition of J , there therefore exists a clause-value of E of the form

$$\{+r(u,v)\} \cup g \quad (r \text{ does not occur in } g)$$

not satisfied by I . Therefore I does not satisfy g

According to the definition of Tr[E] , there exists a clause-value of the form

$$t[+r(u,v)] \cup g$$

and, by hypothesis, I satisfies it. Since I does not satisfy g , I satisfies

$$t[+r(u,v)]$$

and therefore so does J , which contradicts (a).

If J satisfies E U Trbis[E] U {-d(x,y)} then the interpretation I , obtained by removing from J all the atomic formulae of the form **r**(u,v) , satisfies

Tr[E] U {-d(x,y)}

If that were not the case, there would exist a clause value of the form

t[+r(u,v)] U g

not satisfied by I and therefore not satisfied by J . By hypothesis J satisfies

{+r(u,v)} U g and t[+r(u,v)] U {-r(u,v)}

therefore J satisfies

t[+r(u,v)] U g

which is contradictory.

Demonstration. 2nd part. It remains to demonstrate that for all x,y ∈ H

x ⇒ y iff d(x,y) ∈ Imin[E U Trbis[E]]

Let us first demonstrate that

Imin[E U Trbis[E]] = Imin[E] U Kmin

Kmin = the smallest K ⊂ Id such that Imin[E] U K satisfies Trbis[E]

Id = {d(u,v) | u,v ∈ H}

Indeed, let I be an interpretation satisfying

E U Trbis[E]

Let us pose

I' = Imin[E] U K with K = I ∩ Id

We obtain on the one hand

I' ⊂ I

on the other hand, I' satisfies also

E U Trbis[E]

since I' satisfies E by definition and satisfies Trbis[E] which contains no literals of the form +r(u,v). Therefore

Im[E U Trbis[E]] =

the smallest Imin[E] U K which satisfies E U Trbis[E]

hence the required result.

It remains only to demonstrate that

x ⇒ y iff d(x,y) ∈ Kmin

Let us specify the value of Kmin . The property

"Imin[E] U K satisfies Trbis[E]"

may be written

+r(u,v) element of a value of a clause of E

implies that Imin[E] U K satisfies t[+r(u,v)] U {-r(u,v)}

or

+r(u,v) element of a value of a clause of E and

r(u,v) $\in$ Imin[E]

implies K satisfies t[+r(u,v)]

noticing that

r(u,v) $\in$ Imin[E] implies +r(u,v) element of a value of a clause of E

since, contrary to Imin[E], Imin[E] - {r(u,v)} **does** not satisfy E ; the preceding property can be simplified to

r(u,v) $\in$ Imin[E] implies K satisfies t[+r(u,v)]

and therefore finally

Kmin = the smallest K $\subset$ Id such that for all u,v $\in$ H

u $\rightarrow$ v implies K satisfies t[+r(u,v)]

Let us now notice that to each K $\subset$ Id we may associate **bi**-univocally the relation $\Rightarrow_K$ defined by

$u \Rightarrow_K v$ iff d(u,v) $\in$ K

The relation $\Rightarrow_{Kmin}$ is therefore the smallest relation satisfying the points (1) and (2) of the definition of $\Rightarrow$ in paragraphe 2.5. According to the equivalent definition of the relation $\Rightarrow$ we can therefore deduce

$x \Rightarrow_{Kmin} y$ iff $x \Rightarrow y$

i.e.

d(x,y) $\in$ Kmin iff $x \Rightarrow y$

CHAPTER 3

INTRODUCTION TO PROLOG

3.1 GENERAL MECHANISMS OF PROLOG

PROLOG is a programming language which materialises ideas developed in chapter 1. (In fact, these ideas only became clear after the birth of PROLOG). In this language each instruction is therefore a logical statement and the execution of a programme consists in making deductions.

More precisely, a PROLOG programme will consist in a sequence of clauses. Each clause is a sequence of literals and ends with either a full-stop or an exclamation mark. The clauses ending with a full-stop correspond to instructions to be recorded, while those ending with an exclamation-mark correspond to instructions to be executed immediately. If we take up the example common to paras 1.2 and 1.3, it may be written in PROLOG :

```
+CONC(NIL,*X,*X).
+CONC(.(*E,*X),*Y,.(*E,*Z)) -CONC(*X,*Y,*Z).
-CONC(.(A,NIL),.(B,NIL),*X)) -SORT(*X)!
-CONC(*X,*Y,.(A,NIL)) -SORT(*X) -SORT(*Y)!
```

Let us note in passing that the variables are preceded by an asterisk. The general system, of which a large part is written in PROLOG, reads the first two clauses, records them and launches an execution as soon as it has read a third clause. This execution consists in taking the third clause x as a starting-point and in calculating successively the clauses $y_1, y_2, y_3, \dots$ such that

$$x \vdash_{Eord} y_1 \vdash_{Eord} y_2 \vdash_{Eord} y_3 \vdash_{Eord} \dots$$

where Eord represents the set of the first two clauses (see para 1.3). The selecting function is that which chooses always the left-most literal. If for a y_i there exist several clauses $c_1, c_2, c_3, \dots$ (recorded in that order in Eord) which may be used to construct a y_{i+1} such that

$$y_i \vdash_{Eord} y_{i+1}$$

the system chooses first c_1, and it is only after completing its search in this direction that it will choose c_2 and explore that direction, and so on .... The order in which the clauses are recorded can therefore assume a certain importance.

The literal -SORT(*X) does not behave like the other literals : it is a special literal which, when evaluated, provokes the printing of the term which has been substituted for *X . (This kind of mechanism will be described in the following paragraph.) Therefore, after reading the third clause, the system will print

.(A,.(B.NIL))

then, after reading the fourth clause

NIL.(A,NIL)
.(A,NIL) NIL

3.2 PREDEFINED RELATIONS

In PROLOG there exist a certain number of relational symbols predefined by a standard set of clauses or by sub-programmes (called on in the evaluation of any literal based on one of them). The following are the principal predefined relations :

Input and output

LU(x) reads the next character and unifies it with x.

LUB(x) reads the next character other than a blank and unifies it with x .

ECRIT(x) writes the character x.

LIGNE jumps a line on the output device.

SORT(x) writes the term x .

SORM(x) writes one after the other the characters constituting the string x.

AJOP(",",n,"f") considers that from now on the sequence of characters x is an infixed functional symbol of priority n and that it must be noted according to certain conventions specified by f.

Example : the evaluation of
-AJOP(".",1,"X=(X=X)")
will allow us to note the functional symbol "."
in the usual manner.

Note : It is always permitted to write

"C_1C_2---C_n" instead of $C_1.C_2.$---.C_n.NIL

if the C_i are characters.

Creation of clauses and symbols

AJOUT(x) transforms the term x into a clause and adds it to the list of all the clauses which already exist within the system.

Example : the evaluation of

-AJOUT(+(P(*X)).-(Q(A,*X)).NIL)

creates and adds the clause

+P(*X) -Q(A,*X).

UNIV(x,y) Example : the evaluation of

-UNIV(*X,(T.O.T.O.NIL).F(A).G(B).NIL)

unifies *X with

TOTO(F(A),G(B))

whereas the evaluation of

-UNIV(TOTO(F(A),G(B)),*Y)

unifies *Y with

(T.O.T.O.NIL).F(A).G(B).NIL

Control of the strategy

VAR(x) verifies that x is a variable

/ limits the non-determinism

Example : Let us consider the two clauses

(1) +P(*X) -Q(*X) -R(*X) -/ -S(*X) .

(2) +P(*X) -U(*X) .

To evaluate a literal of the form -P(y) we will first use the clause (1). Two cases then present themselves :

a) If one can evaluate the literals -Q(y) and -R(y) one will evaluate -S(y) but on returning one will not use the clause (2).

(b) If one cannot evaluate all the literals of clause (1) which precede -/ , one will use clause (2).

Treatment of characters and integers

LETTRE(x)	verifies that x is a letter.
CHIFFRE(x)	verifies that x is a digit.
PLUS(x,y,z)	adds the integer x to the integer y and unifies the result with z .
INF(x,y)	verifies that the integer x is strictly smaller than the integer y .

3.3 TREATMENT OF METAMORPHOSIS GRAMMARS IN PROLOG

The programming language PROLOG was conceived to facilitate the definition and use of metamorphosis grammars in normal form. These grammars, of course, must satisfy the hypotheses of para 2.6. The grammar of the example 2 in para 2.4 is written in PROLOG :

```
:FORMULA(A) == #A.
:FORMULA(B) == #B.
:FORMULA(*X) == -EGAL(*X,*R.*S) :VALUE(*X).
:VALUE(*X.*Y) == #< :FORMULA(*X) :END :VALUE(*Y).
:VALUE(NIL) ==.
:END #< == #+.
:END == #>.
+EGAL(*X,*X).
```

The terms which correspond to non-terminals (pseudo-non-terminals) are preceded by ":" while those which correspond to terminals (pseudo-terminals) are preceded by "#" or "£". Literals can be inserted in the right-hand side of each rule. Of course, this set of rules represents nothing other than the set of clauses E which defines the relation →. As these rules are read, they are transformed (by a programme written in PROLOG) in order to obtain finally the set of clauses Tr[E] , but taking into account the remark at the end of para 2.6. Each pseudo-non-terminal is therefore transformed into a literal with two supplementary arguments. The pseudo-terminals are inserted into these supplementary arguments. The literals figuring in the right-hand sides remain unchanged.

To analyse or synthesise a string one must use the predefined relational symbol SYN (abbreviation of synthesis) which plays the same role as d . For instance, the execution of

```
-SYN(FORMULA(*X).NIL,< .A.+.B.> .NIL) -SORT(FORMULA(*X))!
```

will provoke the printing of the deep structure of

```
<.A.+.B.>.NIL
```

whereas the execution of

```
-SYN(FORMULA(A.B.NIL).NIL,*X) -SORT(*X)!
```

will provoke the printing of the terminal sequence of which the deep structure is

```
FORMULA(A.B.NIL)
```

CHAPTER 4

A COMPILER WRITTEN IN PROLOG

4.1 NATURE OF THE PROBLEM

We propose to write a compiler. It will be constituted principally by two metamorphosis grammars, one to analyse the source-program and to furnish a normalised form, the other to synthesise the machine-code by means of this normalised form. The language we will compile is of the ALGOL type. It contains no declarations and each variable within it is of integer type. We simply give its definition in Backus normal form ; the reader may deduce the semantic part from the notations :

```
<program>  ::=  <instruction>.
<instruction>  ::=  begin  <instruction> <instructions> end | <empty> |
                    <identifier>  :=  <arithmetical exp 1> |
                    while  <boolean exp 1>  do  <instruction> |
                    repeat <instruction> until  <boolean exp 1> |
                    read  <identifier> |  write  <arithmetical exp 1> |
                    goto  <identifier> |
                    if  <boolean exp 1>  then  <instruction>
                    else  <instruction> |
                    if  <boolean exp 1>  do  <instruction> |
                    <identifier>  :  <instruction>
<instructions>  ::=  ;  <instruction> <instructions> | <empty>
<arithmetical exp 1>  ::=  <plus or minus> <arithmetical exp 2> |
                   <arithmetical exp 2> |
                   <arithmetical exp 1> <plus or minus> <arithmetical exp 2>
<arithmetical exp 2>  ::=  <arithmetical exp 3> | <arithmetical exp 2> *
                   <arithmetical exp 3>
<arithmetical exp 3>  ::=  <integer> | <identifier> |
                    ( <arithmetical exp 1> )
<plus or minus>  ::=  + | -
<boolean exp 1>  ::=  <boolean exp 2> | <boolean exp 1>
                  or  <boolean exp 2>
```

```
<boolean exp 2>  ::=  <boolean exp 3> | <boolean exp 2>
                      and  <boolean exp 3>
<boolean exp 3>  ::=  not  <boolean exp 3> | ( <boolean exp 1> ) |
                      <arithmetical exp 1> <relation> <arithmetical exp 1>
<relation>  ::= = | less
<integer>  ::=  <digit> | <digit> <integer>
<identifier>  ::=  <letter> | <identifier> <letter> |
                 <identifier> <digit>

<digit>  ::= 0 | 1 |... | g
<letter> ::= a | b |... | z
<empty>  :: =
```

The machine which executes the compiled programme is constituted by a series of memories (numbered from 0) and by an accumulator (which we shall call accu).
Each memory may contain indifferently an instruction or an integer . The execution of the programme starts with the instruction contained in the memory n° 0. Here is the list of the instructions and pseudo-instructions of the machine :

LOAD n load into the accu the contents of memory n° n
STOR n store into memory n° n the contents of the accu
PLUS n add to the contents of the accu the contents of memory n° n
MINU n subtract from the contents of the accu the contents of memory n° n
MULT n multiply the contents of the accu by the contents of memory n° n
GOTO n goto the instruction contained in memory n° n
GOZE n goto n if the contents of the accu = 0 (goto if zero)
GONE n goto n it the contents of the accu $<$ 0 (goto if negative)
GONZ n goto n if the contents of the accu $\neq$ 0 (goto if not zero)
GONN n **goto** n if the contents of the accu $\geq$ 0 (goto if not negative)
WRIT write the integer contained in the accu
READ read an integer and load it into the accu
STOP stop
ALLO EMPTY allocate a memory (pseudo-instruction executed when loading the program)
ALLO n allocate a memory and initialises it with n (pseudo-instruction executed when loading the program).

4.2 PROGRAMME AND EXAMPLES OF COMPILATION

Here is the whole of the programme PROLOG which constitutes this compiler, followed by two examples of program-compilation. In the case of the first example we print intermediate results.

```
-AJOP(".",1,"X£(X£X)")!


** (0) CALL FOR THE DIFFERENT PHASIS.


+COMPILE -LIGNE
   -READING(*U) -PRETREATING(*U,*V) -ANALYSIS(*V,*W)
   -SYNTHESIS(*W,*X) -ASSEMBLING(*X,*Y) -PRINTING(*Y).


** (1) READING OF THE SOURCE-PROGRAM.


+READING(*L.*U) -/ -LUB(*K) -TR(*K.NIL,*L) -READBIS(*L,*U).

+READBIS(DOT,NIL) -/.
+READBIS(BLANK,*U) -/ -READING(*U).
+READBIS(*K,*M.*U) -LU(*L) -TR(*L.NIL,*M) -READBIS(*M,*U).

+TR(".",DOT) -/.                   +TR(" ",BLANK) -/.
+TR("*",STAR) -/.                  +TR("(",LBRACK) -/.
+TR(")",RBRACK) -/.                +TR(*K.NIL,*K).


** (2) PREATREATING OF THE SOURCE-PROGRAM.


+PRETREATING(*U,*V) -SYN(UNITS(*V).NIL,*U) -OUT(*V).

:UNITS(*U.*X) == :UNIT(*U) -/ :SPACE :UNITS(*X).
:UNITS(NIL) ==.

:SPACE == £BLANK -/.               :SPACE ==.

:UNIT(IN(*X)) == £*K -CHIFFRE(*K) -/ :DIGITS(*U)
   -UNIV(*X,(*K.*U).NIL).
:UNIT(*Y) == £*K -LETTRE(*K) -/ :ALPHANUMS(*U)
   -UNIV(*X,(*K.*U).NIL) -CHGT(*X,*Y).
:UNIT(*K) == £*K.

:DIGITS(*K.*U) == £*K -CHIFFRE(*K) -/ :DIGITS(*U).
:DIGITS(NIL) ==.

:ALPHANUMS(*K.*U) == £*K -ALPHANUM(*K) -/ :ALPHANUMS(*U).
:ALPHANUMS(NIL) ==.

+ALPHANUM(*K) -LETTRE(*K) -/.     +ALPHANUM(*K) -CHIFFRE(*K).

+CHGT(*X,*X) -*X -/.              +CHGT(*X,ID(*X)).

+THEN.      +BEGIN.     +WRITE.     +AND.       +DO.        +END.
+LESS.      +UNTIL.     +READ.      +NOT.       +OR.        +REPEAT.
+IF.        +ELSE.      +WHILE.     +GOTO.
```

** (3) ANALYSIS OF THE SOURCE-PROGRAM.

```
+ANALYSIS(*S,*I) -SYN(PROG(*I).NIL,*S) -/ -OUT(*I).
+ANALYSIS(*S,*I) -LIGNE -SORM("SYNTAX-ERROR") -LIGNE -CULDESAC.

:PROG(*I) == :INST(*I) £DOT.

:INST(SEQ.*I.*S) == £BEGIN -/ :INST(*I) :INSTRS(*S) £END.
:INST(ASSIGN.*X.*Y) == £ID(*X) £: £= -/ :EXP(ARIT,1,*Y).
:INST(WHILE.*B.*I) == £WHILE -/ :EXP(BOOL,1,*B) £DO :INST(*I).
:INST(REPEA.*B.*I) == £REPEAT -/ :INST(*I) £UNTIL :EXP(BOOL,1,*B).
:INST(GOTO.*X) == £GOTO £ID(*X) -/.
:INST(READ.*X) == £READ £ID(*X) -/.
:INST(WRITE.*X) == £WRITE -/ :EXP(ARIT,1,*X).
:INST(*IF.*B.*S) == £IF -/ :EXP(BOOL,1,*B) :ENDIF(*IF,*S).
:INST(LABEL.*X.*I) == £ID(*X) £: -/ :INST(*I).
:INST(SEQ.NIL) ==.

:ENDIF(IF1,*I) == £DO -/ :INST(*I).
:ENDIF(IF2,*I.*J) == £THEN :INST(*I) £ELSE :INST(*J).

:INSTRS(*I.*S) == £; -/ :INST(*I) :INSTRS(*S).
:INSTRS(NIL) ==.

:EXP(*T,3,*X) == £LBRACK -/ :EXP(*T,1,*X) £RBRACK.
:EXP(ARIT,3,*X) == £ID(*X) -/.
:EXP(ARIT,3,IN(*X)) == £IN(*X) -/.
:EXP(BOOL,3,NOT.*B) == £NOT -/ :EXP(BOOL,3,*B).
:EXP(BOOL,3,*R.*X.*Y) == -/ :EXP(ARIT,1,*X) £*R -RELATION(*R)
   :EXP(ARIT,1,*Y).
:EXP(*T,*N,*X) == -INF(*N,3) -PLUS(*N,1,*M) :EXP(*T,*M,*Y) -/
   :ENDEXP(*T,*N,*Y,*X).
:EXP(ARIT,1,*X) == :ENDEXP(ARIT,1,IN(0),*X).

+RELATION(=) -/.                    +RELATION(LESS).

:ENDEXP(*T,*N,*X,*Z) == £*R -OPERATOR(*R,*T,*N) -/ -PLUS(*N,1,*M)
   :EXP(*T,*M,*Y) :ENDEXP(*T,*N,*R.*X.*Y,*Z).
:ENDEXP(*T,*N,*X,*X) ==.

+OPERATOR(OR,BOOL,1) -/.            +OPERATOR(AND,BOOL,2) -/.
+OPERATOR(+,ARIT,1) -/.             +OPERATOR(-,ARIT,1) -/.
+OPERATOR(STAR,ARIT,2).
```

** (4) SYNTHESIS OF THE MACHINE-CODE.

```
+SYNTHESIS(*I,*S) -SYN(PRO(*I).NIL,*S) -OUT(*S).

:PRO(*I) == :INS(*I,*U.*V.*W) £CODE(STOP) :ALLOCATION(*V)
   :ALLOCATION(*W).

:INS(SEQ.NIL,*D) == -/.
:INS(SEQ.*I.*S,*D) == -/ :INS(*I,*D) :INS(SEQ.*S,*D).
:INS(LABEL.*X.*I,*U.*V.*W) == £LAB(*E) -/ -ADR(*X,*E,*U)
   :INS(*I,*U.*V.*W).
:INS(ASSIGN.*X.*Y,*U.*V.*W) == -/ -ADR(*X,*E,*V) :EXPARIT(*Y,*V.*W)
   £CODE(STOR.*E).
:INS(WHILE.*B.*I,*D) == £LAB(*E) -/ :IFGO(NOT.*B,*F,*D)
   :INS(*I,*D) £CODE(GOTO.*E) £LAB(*F).
:INS(REPEA.*B.*I,*D) == £LAB(*E) -/ :INS(*I,*D) :IFGO(NOT.*B,*E,*D).
:INS(GOTO.*X,*U.*V.*W) == £CODE(GOTO.*E) -/ -ADR(*X,*E,*U).
:INS(READ.*X,*U.*V.*W) == £CODE(READ) £CODE(STOR.*E) -/
   -ADR(*X,*E,*V).
:INS(WRITE.*X,*U.*V.*W) == -/ :EXPARIT(*X,*V.*W) £CODE(WRIT).
:INS(IF2.*B.*I.*J,*D) == -/ :IFGO(*B,*E,*D) :INS(*J,*D)
   £CODE(GOTO.*F) £LAB(*E) :INS(*I,*D) £LAB(*F).
:INS(IF1.*B.GOTO.*X,*U.*V.*W) == -/ :IFGO(*B,*E,*U.*V.*W)
   -ADR(*X,*E,*U).
:INS(IF1.*B.*I,*D) == :IFGO(NOT.*B,*E,*D) :INS(*I,*D)
   £LAB(*E).

:ALLOCATION(NIL) == -/.
:ALLOCATION((*X.*E).*U) == £LAB(*E) £CODE(ALLO.*Y) -CONTENT(*X,*Y)
   :ALLOCATION(*U).

+CONTENT(IN(*X),*X) -/.           +CONTENT(*X,EMPTY).

:IFGO(OR.*B.*C,*E,*D) == -/ :IFGO(*B,*E,*D) :IFGO(*C,*E,*D).
:IFGO(AND.*B.*C,*E,*D) == -/ :IFGO(NOT.*B,*F,*D) :IFGO(*C,*E,*D)
   £LAB(*F).
:IFGO(NOT.NOT.*B,*E,*D) == -/ :IFGO(*B,*E,*D).
:IFGO(NOT.OR.*B.*C,*E,*D) == -/ :IFGO(AND.(NOT.*B).NOT.*C.*E,*D).
:IFGO(NOT.AND.*B.*C,*E,*D) == -/ :IFGO(OR.(NOT.*B).NOT.*C,*E,*D).
:IFGO(NOT.*R.*S,*E,*D) == -/ :IFGO((NOT.*R).*S,*E,*D).
:IFGO(*R.*X.*Y,*E,*U.*V.*W) == :EXPARIT(-.*X.*Y,*V.*W) £CODE(*Q.*E)
   -HOMOLOGOUS(*R,*Q).

:EXPARIT(*R.*X.*Y,*V.(EMPTY.*E).*W) == -COMPLEX(*Y) -/
   :EXPARIT(*Y,*V.(EMPTY.*E).*W) £CODE(STOR.*E) :EXPARIT(*X,*V.*W)
   £CODE(*Q.*E) -HOMOLOGOUS(*R,*Q).
:EXPARIT(*R.*X.*Y,*V.*W) == -/ -HOMOLOGOUS(*R,*Q) -ADR(*Y,*E,*V)
   :EXPARIT(*X,*V.*W) £CODE(*Q.*E).
:EXPARIT(*X,*V.*W) == £CODE(LOAD.*E) -ADR(*X,*E,*V).

+COMPLEX(*R.*X.*Y).

+HOMOLOGOUS(=,GOZE) -/.           +HOMOLOGOUS(NOT.=,GONZ) -/.
+HOMOLOGOUS(LESS,GONE) -/.        +HOMOLOGOUS(NOT.LESS,GONN) -/.
+HOMOLOGOUS(+,PLUS) -/.           +HOMOLOGOUS(-,MINU) -/.
+HOMOLOGOUS(STAR,MULT).

+ADR(*X,*E,(*X.*E).*U) -/.
+ADR(*X,*E,(*Y.*F).*U) -ADR(*X,*E,*U).
```

** (5) ASSEMBLING OF THE MACHINE-CODE.

```
+ASSEMBLING(*X,*U) -ASS(*X,*U,0).

+ASS(LAB(*N).*X,*U,*N) -/ -ASS(*X,*U,*N).
+ASS(CODE(*C).*X,*C.*U,*N) -/ -PLUS(*N,1,*M) -ASS(*X,*U,*M).
+ASS(NIL,NIL,*N) -/.
+ASS(*X,*U,*N) -SORM("ERROR: TWICE THE SAME LABEL")
   -LIGNE -CULDESAC.
```

** (6) FINAL PRINTING.

```
+PRINTING(*X) -LIGNE -PRI(0,*X) -LIGNE -LIGNE.

+PRI(*N,*X.*Y) -/ -SORT(*N) -SORM("   ") -SORT(*X) -LIGNE
   -PLUS(*N,1,*M) -PRI(*M,*Y).
+PRI(*N,NIL).
```

** (7) PRINTING OF INTERMEDIATE RESULTS.

```
+TRACE -SUPP(+(OK).NIL) -/.
+TRACE -AJOUT(+(OK).NIL).

+OUT(*X) -OK -/ -LIGNE -SORT(*X) -LIGNE.
+OUT(*X).
```

```
-TRACE -COMPILE!

BEGIN
   READ N; READ M;
   IF NOT N=5 AND (M LESS 10 OR M=50) THEN WRITE 0
   ELSE WRITE (2+N)*(10+M)
END.

BEGIN.READ.ID(N).;.READ.ID(M).;.IF.NOT.ID(N).=.IN(5).AND.LBRACK.ID(M)
.LESS.IN(10).OR.ID(M).=.IN(50).RBRACK.THEN.WRITE.IN(0).ELSE.WRITE.LBR
ACK.IN(2).+.ID(N).RBRACK.STAR.LBRACK.IN(10).+.ID(M).RBRACK.END.DOT.NI
L

SEQ.(READ.N).(READ.M).(IF2.(AND.(NOT.=.N.IN(5)).OR.(LESS.M.IN(10)).=.
M.IN(50)).(WRITE.IN(0)).WRITE.STAR.(+.IN(2).N).+.IN(10).M).NIL

CODE(READ).CODE(STOR.*X0).CODE(READ).CODE(STOR.*X1).CODE(LOAD.*X0).CO
DE(MINU.*X2).CODE(GOZE.*X3).CODE(LOAD.*X1).CODE(MINU.*X4).CODE(GONE.*
X5).CODE(LOAD.*X1).CODE(MINU.*X6).CODE(GOZE.*X5).LAB(*X3).CODE(LOAD.*
X4).CODE(PLUS.*X1).CODE(STOR.*X7).CODE(LOAD.*X8).CODE(PLUS.*X0).CODE(
MULT.*X7).CODE(WRIT).CODE(GOTO.*X9).LAB(*X5).CODE(LOAD.*X10).CODE(WRI
T).LAB(*X9).CODE(STOP).LAB(*X0).CODE(ALLO.EMPTY).LAB(*X1).CODE(ALLO.E
MPTY).LAB(*X2).CODE(ALLO.5).LAB(*X4).CODE(ALLO.10).LAB(*X6).CODE(ALLO
.50).LAB(*X8).CODE(ALLO.2).LAB(*X10).CODE(ALLO.0).LAB(*X7).CODE(ALLO.
EMPTY).NIL

0   READ
1   STOR.24
2   READ
3   STOR.25
4   LOAD.24
5   MINU.26
6   GOZE.13
7   LOAD.25
8   MINU.27
9   GONE.21
10  LOAD.25
11  MINU.28
12  GOZE.21
13  LOAD.27
14  PLUS.25
15  STOR.31
16  LOAD.29
17  PLUS.24
18  MULT.31
19  WRIT
20  GOTO.23
21  LOAD.30
22  WRIT
23  STOP
24  ALLO.EMPTY
25  ALLO.EMPTY
26  ALLO.5
27  ALLO.10
28  ALLO.50
29  ALLO.2
30  ALLO.0
31  ALLO.EMPTY
```

```
-TRACE -COMPILE!

BEGIN
   READ N;
   IF 10 LESS N DO GOTO TOOBIG;
   I:=0; F:=1;
   WHILE I LESS N DO
   BEGIN
      I:=I+1; F:=I*F
   END;
   WRITE F;
   TOOBIG:
END.

0   READ
1   STOR.22
2   LOAD.23
3   MINU.22
4   GONE.21
5   LOAD.25
6   STOR.24
7   LOAD.27
8   STOR.26
9   LOAD.24
10   MINU.22
11   GONN.19
12   LOAD.24
13   PLUS.27
14   STOR.24
15   LOAD.24
16   MULT.26
17   STOR.26
18   GOTO.9
19   LOAD.26
20   WRIT
21   STOP
22   ALLO.EMPTY
23   ALLO.10
24   ALLO.EMPTY
25   ALLO.0
26   ALLO.EMPTY
27   ALLO.1
```

4.3 EXPLANATION OF THE PROGRAM

The first clause indicates that the fonctionnal symbol "." will be written in infixed notation with right-to-left parenthesising.

(0) Call for the different phasis. The phases (1), (2), ...,,(6) are called successively.

(1) Reading of the source-program. The source-program is read character by character and is transformed into a string of characters. The blanks at the head of the program are suppressed and any other spacing is reduced to a single blank. The characters ".", "U", " ", "(", ")" renamed respectively DOT, BLANK, STAR, LBRACK, RBRACK.

(2) Pretreating of the source-program. The string of characters is transformed (by a small metamorphosis grammar) into a string of units. Each unit is either a basic symbol (begin, end, +, -, ...), or an identifier capped by the functionnal symbol ID, or by an integer capped by the functionnal symbol IN.

(3) Analysis of the source-program. The string of units is transformed into a tree which is the normalised form of the program. This is done by means of a metamorphosis grammar derived directly from the definition of the language. The arithmetical and boolean expressions are treated in a very compact and general way. Here follows the structure of all the normalised program-forms.

```
<normalised forme>  ::=  prog ( <instruction> )
<instruction>  ::=  ( sequ . instructions ) |
                    ( assign . <identifier> . <arithmetical exp> ) |
                    (while . <boolean exp> . <instruction> ) |
                    ( repea . <boolean exp> . <instruction> ) |
                    ( read . <identifier> ) |
                    ( write .<arithmetical exp> ) |
                    ( goto . <identifier> ) |
                    ( if1 . <boolean exp> . <instruction> ) |
                    ( if2 . <boolean exp> . <instruction> . <instruction> ) |
                    ( label . <identifier> . <instruction> ) |
<instructions>  ::=  nil | ( <instruction> . <instructions> )
<arithmetical exp>  ::= in ( <integer> ) | <identifier> |
                    ( <+ - mult> .<arithmetical exp> . <arithmetical exp> )
```

```
<boolean exp>  ::= ( <relation> . <arithmetical exp> . <arithmetical exp> ) |
                   ( <and or> . <boolean exp> . <boolean exp> ) |
                   ( not . <boolean exp> )
<+ - mult> ::= + | - | mult
<and or>  ::=  and | or
<relation> , <integer>  and  <identifier>  are defined at para  4.1.
```

(4) Synthesis of the machine-code. A metamorphosis grammar transforms the normalised form of the program into a string of elementary instructions. Each elementary instruction is either an instruction of which the address-part is a prolog-variable, the all capped by the functionnal symbol CODE, or a prolog-variable representing an address capped by the symbol LAB (for label).

The last parameter of the non-terminal INS represents three tables. Each of these is composed of a sequence of doublets (object, prolog-variable representing the address where it is to be found). The first table associates an address to each identifier representing a label. The second table associates an address to each integer or identifier representing an integer. The third table associates an address to each supplementary memory necessary to compute an arithmetical expression. These table which, at the start, are represented by prolog-variables, are constantly updated and consulted by the predicat ADR(x,e,v) which gives the adress e of the object x recorded in the table v .

The code of the boolean expressions is generated by means of the non-terminal IFGO (b,e,d) which means : "if the boolean expression b is true then goto e" (d represents the three preceding tables). This code is optimised so as to minimise the evaluations of relations at run-time.

The code of arithmetical expressions is optimised in the sense that in an operation where the second operand is simple no supplementary memory is used. So as not to complicate the compiler we make no transformation (by playing on associativity, commutativity,...) in order to render this case as commun as possible.

(5) Assembling of the machine-code. All the addresses represented by prolog variables are replaced by integers and some minor transformations allow us to obtain the final result.

(6) Final printing. The final result is printed, each instruction being numbered.

(7) Printing of intermediate results. The call for TRACE provokes the printing of intermediate results. Recalling TRACE suppresses this printing. A second recalling provokes printing anew, etc...

CHAPTER 5

AN INTELLIGENT SYSTEM CONVERSING IN FRENCH

5.1 DESCRIPTION OF THE SYSTEM

We propose to write a system allowing us to hold an "intelligent" conversation in French with the computer. The conversation will concern relations of friendship and parenthood between different persons. The user of this system will be able :

- to communicate information to the computer by means of affirmative and negative sentences (and possibly by replying "yes" or "no" to certain questions) ;

- to suppress information (volontarily or involontarily) by negative or affirmative sentences contradicting facts previously stated ;

- to ask questions of the type "qui est..." ("who is....") or "qui n'est pas..." ("who is not...") to which the computer will attempt to reply by making a certain number of deductions ;

- to ask questions of the type "pourquoi..." ("why...") to which the computer will reply retracing the sequence of deductions which allows him to reach the conclusion ;

- to ask the computer to write or not to write intermediate results instrumental in his understanding of sentences and in his reasoning ;

- to stop the system by saying "au revoir !" ("good bye !").

Here is the set of all the sentences ("phrases" in French) which form the subset of French in which the interlocutor must address the computer.

<phrase> ::= AU REVOIR ! | DES DETAILS ! | PAS DE DETAILS ! | OUI ! |
NON ! | QUI <ne> <est> <pas> <sn> ?
POURQUOI EST-CE <que> <sn> <ne> <est> <pas> <sn> ? |
<sn> <ne> <est> <pas> <sn>.

<sn> ::= <art> <nom> <de> <sn> | TOUT LE MONDE | PERSONNE |
QUELQU'UN | JE | <nom propre>

<art> <nom> DE JE ::= <mon> <nom>

<art> ::= AUCUN | AUCUNE | CHAQUE | L' | LA | LE | UN | UNE

<de> LE ::= DU <de> ::= d' | de

<est> ::= SUIS | EST

<mon> ::= MON | MA

<ne> ::= <vide> | N' | NE

<nom> ::= AMI | AMIE | FEMME | FILLE | FILS | FRERE | MARI | MERE |
NEVEU | NIECE | ONCLE | PERE | SOEUR | TANTE

<nom propre > ::= "any word"

<pas> ::= <vide> | PAS

<que> ::= QU ' | QUE

<vide> ::=

Here now is the list of all the replies ("réponses" in French) which can be produced by the computer.

<réponse> ::= <réponse à : qui...> | <réponse à : pourquoi...> |
<rejet d'une phrase> | <demande d'information>

<réponse à : qui...> ::= TOUT LE MONDE ! | TOUTE FEMME ! | VOUS ! |
TOUT HOMME | <nom propre> !

<réponse à : pourquoi...> ::= PARCE QUE JE SAIS RAISONNER. <et que>

<et que> ::= <vide> | ET QUE VOUS M'AVEZ DIT ' <phrase> ' <et que>

<rejet d'une phrase> ::= JE NE COMPRENDS PAS CETTE PHRASE. |
C'EST TROP COMPLIQUE. |
JE NE COMPRENDS PAS TRES BIEN. IL Y A UN PROBLEME DE SEXE.
VOUS VOUS CONTREDISEZ. J'OUBLIE QUE VOUS M'AVEZ DIT :
' <phrase> '

<demande d'information> ::= VOUS ETES BIEN DE SEXE MASCULIN ? |
<nom propre> EST BIEN DE SEXE MASCULIN ? |
OUI ! OU NON !

5.2 PROGRAM AND EXPLANATION

Here is the whole of the program prolog which realises the system.

```
-AJOP("ET",1,"X£(X£X)")!
-AJOP("IMPLIQUE",1,"X£(X£X)")!
-AJOP("NON",2,"£X")!
-AJOP("/",3,"X£(X£X)")!
-AJOP(".",4,"X£(X£X)")!
-AJOP("-",5,"(0£X)£X")!
```

** (0) IMBRICATION DES DIFFERENTES PHASES.

```
+BAVARDONS -ECHANGES(1) -IMPASSE.

+ECHANGES(*N) -PHRASELUE(*P) -AJOUTER(+(PHRASE(*N,*P)).NIL).
+ECHANGES(*N) -PHRASE(*N,*P) -PRETRAITEMENT(*P,*Q)
   -ANALYSE(*Q,*R) -ENONCE(*R,*S,*N) -AJOUTER(*S).
+ECHANGES(*N) -HALTE -MESSAGE("BONSOIR!") -/.
+ECHANGES(*N) -ABSURDE(*R) -SORTIR(*R) -ELAGUER(*R,*S,*M,*P)
   -REPONSE(*N.*S,*M,*P).
+ECHANGES(*N) -QUESTION -AJOUTER(+(KO(*N)).NIL).
+ECHANGES(*N) -PLUS(*N,1,*M) -ECHANGES(*M).

+ELAGUER(NIL,*S,10000,*P) -/.
+ELAGUER(*I-*U.*R,*S,*K,*P) -/ -OK(*I) -DANS(*I,*S)
   -ELAGUER(*R,*S,*J,*P) -MIN(*I,*J,*K).
+ELAGUER(INDIVIDU(*X).*R,*S,*K,*P) -/ -CONFIRMATION(*X)
   -ELAGUER(*R,*S,*K,*P).
+ELAGUER(*P.*R,*S,*K,*P) -ELAGUER(*R,*S,*K,*P).

+MIN(*I,*J,*I) -INF(*I,*J) -/.  +MIN(*I,*J,*J).

+REPONSE(*S,*N,NIL) -/ -AJOUTER(+(KO(*N)).NIL) -PHRASE(*N,*P)
   -MESSAGE("VOUS VOUS CONTREDISEZ. J'OUBLIE QUE VOUS M'AVEZ DIT:")
   -DIRE("'".*P."'") -LIGNE.
+REPONSE(*S,*N,QUI(*X)) -/ -VALR(*X,*P) -MESSAGE(*P."!").
+REPONSE(*M.*S,*N,POURQUOI) -MESSAGE("PARCE QUE JE SAIS RAISONNER.")
   -ETQUE(*M,*S).

+VALR(NIL-IN(NIL),"TOUT LE MONDE") -/.
+VALR(F-IN(NIL),"TOUTE FEMME") -/.
+VALR(M-IN(NIL),"TOUT HOMME") -/.
+VALR(*G-JE,"VOUS") -/.          +VALR(*G-IN(*A),*P) -UNIV(*A,*P).

+ETQUE(*N,NIL) -/.               +ETQUE(*N,*N.*S) -/ -ETQUE(*N,*S).
+ETQUE(*N,*M.*S) -PHRASE(*M,*P)
   -DIRE("ET QUE VOUS M'AVEZ DIT: "."'".*P."'") -LIGNE -ETQUE(*N,*S).
```

** (1) DEMANDE D'INFORMATION SUPPLEMENTAIRE.

```
+CONFIRMATION(*G-*I) -VAR(*G) -/.
+CONFIRMATION(*G-*I) -NOMPROPRE(*H-*I) -/ -PAREILS(*G,*H).
+CONFIRMATION(*G-*I) -RECONNU(*H-*I) -AJOUTER(+(NOMPROPRE(*H-*I)).NIL)
   -PAREILS(*G,*H).

+RECONNU(*G-JE) -/
   -MESSAGE("VOUS ETES BIEN DE SEXE MASCULIN?") -REPONSELUE(*G).
+RECONNU(*G-IN(*A)) -UNIV(*A,*U)
   -MESSAGE(*U." EST BIEN DE SEXE MASCULIN?") -REPONSELUE(*G).
```

```
+REPONSELUE(*G) -PHRASELUE(*P) -RESULTAT(*P,*G).

+RESULTAT("OUI!",M) -/.          +RESULTAT("NON!",F) -/.
+RESULTAT(*P,*G) -MESSAGE("OUI! OU NON!") -REPONSELUE(*G).


** (2) PRETRAITEMENT DE LA PHRASE.


+PRETRAITEMENT(*U,*V) -SYN(UNITES(*V).NIL,*U).

:UNITES(*U.*X) == :UNITE(*U) -/ :ESPACE :UNITES(*X).
:UNITES(NIL) ==.

:ESPACE == £BLANC -/ :ESPACE.    :ESPACE == £' -/ :ESPACE.
:ESPACE == £TRAIT -/ :ESPACE.    :ESPACE ==.

:UNITE(*X) == £*K -LETTRE(*K) -/ :LETTRES(*U) -UNIV(*X,(*K.*U).NIL).
:UNITE(*K) == £*K.

:LETTRES(*K.*U) == £*K -LETTRE(*K) -/ :LETTRES(*U).
:LETTRES(NIL) ==.


** (3) ANALYSE DU FRANCAIS.


+ANALYSE(*P,*Q) -SYN(PH(*Q).NIL,*P) -/ -SORTIR(*Q).
+ANALYSE(*P,*Q) -MESSAGE("JE NE COMPRENDS PAS CETTE PHRASE.")
   -IMPASSE.

:PH(*U.HALTE) == £AU £REVOIR £! -/.
:PH(*U.DETAILS(*U)) == £DES £DETAILS £! -/.
:PH(NON *U.DETAILS(*U)) == £PAS £DE £DETAILS £! -/.
:PH(NON(*Q ET *U.DANS(QUI(*X),*U)) ET *V.QUESTION) == £QUI -/
   :NE :EST :PAS(*P.*Q) :CO(*X.*P) £?.
:PH(NON(*R ET *U.DANS(POURQUOI,*U)) ET *V.QUESTION) == £POURQUOI
   £EST £CE -/ :QUE :SN(*X.*P.*Q) :NE :EST :PAS(*Q.*R) :CO(*X.*P) £?.
:PH(*R) == :SN(*X.*P.*Q) :NE :EST :PAS(*Q.*R) :CO(*X.*P) £POINT.

:CO(*X.*Q) == :ART(*X.*P.*Q.ILYA(*I,*P ET *Q)) -/ :NOM(*X.*Y.*P) :DE
   :SN(*Y.*P.*Q).
:CO(*X.*Q) == :SN(*Y.(*U.EGAL(*X,*Y,*U)).*Q).

:SN(*X.*Q.*S) == :ART(*X.*P.*Q.*R) :NOM(*X.*Y.*P) -/ :DE
   :SN(*Y.*R.*S).
:SN(*G-*I.*P.TOUT(*G,TOUT(*I,*P))) == £TOUT £LE £MONDE -/.
:SN(*G-*I.*P.(NON ILYA(*G,ILYA(*I,*P)))) == £PERSONNE -/.
:SN(*G-*I.*P.ILYA(*G,ILYA(*I,*P))) == £QUELQU £UN -/.
:SN(*G-JE.*P.LE(*G,*U.NOMPROPRE(*G-JE),*P)) == £JE -/.
:SN(*G-IN(*A).*P.LE(*G,*U.NOMPROPRE(*G-IN(*A)),*P)) == £*A.

:ART(*XPQR) == £*M -VAL(*M,ART(*XPQR)) -/.
:ART(*G-*I.*P.*Q.ILYA(*I,*P ET *Q)) £*M £DE £JE == :MON(*G-*I) £*M.

:NOM(*XYP) == £*M -VAL(*M,NOM(*XYP)).

:DE == £DE -/.                   :DE £LE == £DU -/.
:DE == £D.
```

```
:EST == £SUIS -/.                    :EST == £EST.
:MON(M-*I) == £MON -/.               :MON(F-*I) == £MA.
:NE == £NE -/.                       :NE == £N -/.
:NE ==.
:PAS(*P.(NON *P)) == £PAS -/.        :PAS(*P.*P) ==.
:QUE == £QUE -/.                     :QUE == £QU.

+VAL(*M,*V) -UNIV(*M,*A.NIL) -UNIV(*N,*A.*V.NIL) -*N.
```

** (4) DICTIONNAIRE.

```
+AMI(NOM(M-*I.*Y.*U.AMY(M-*I,*Y,*U))).
+AMIE(NOM(F-*I.*Y.*U.AMY(F-*I,*Y,*U))).
+AUCUN(ART(M-*I.*P.*Q.TOUT(*I,*P IMPLIQUE NON *Q))).
+AUCUNE(ART(F-*I.*P.*Q.TOUT(*I,*P IMPLIQUE NON *Q))).
+CHAQUE(ART(*G-*I.*P.*Q.TOUT(*I,*P IMPLIQUE *Q))).
+FEMME(NOM(F-*I.M-*J.*U.EPOUX(M-*J,F-*I,*U))).
+FILLE(NOM(F-*I.*P)) -ENFAN(F-*I.*P).
+FILS(NOM(M-*I.*P)) -ENFAN(M-*I.*P).
+FRERE(NOM(M-*I.*P)) -FREUR(M-*I.*P).
+L(ART(*G-*I.*P.*Q.ILYA(*I,*P ET *Q))).
+LA(ART(F-*I.*P.*Q.ILYA(*I,*P ET *Q))).
+LE(ART(M-*I.*P.*Q.ILYA(*I,*P ET *Q))).
+MARI(NOM(M-*I.F-*J.*U.EPOUX(M-*I,F-*J,*U))).
+MERE(NOM(F-*I.*Y.*P)) -ENFAN(*Y.F-*I.*P).
+NEVEU(NOM(M-*I.*Y.*P)) -ONTE(*Y.M-*I.*P).
+NIECE(NOM(F-*I.*Y.*P)) -ONTE(*Y.F-*I.*P).
+ONCLE(NOM(M-*I.*Y.*P)) -ONTE(M-*I.*Y.*P).
+PERE(NOM(M-*I.*Y.*P)) -ENFAN(*Y.M-*I.*P).
+SOEUR(NOM(F-*I.*P)) -FREUR(F-*I.*P).
+TANTE(NOM(F-*I.*Y.*P)) -ONTE(F-*I.*Y.*P).
+UN(ART(M-*I.*P.*Q.ILYA(*I,*P ET *Q))).
+UNE(ART(F-*I.*P.*Q.ILYA(*I,*P ET *Q))).

+ENFAN(*X.*G-*I.*U.EGAL(*G-PAR(*G,*X),*G-*I,*U)).
+FREUR(*X.*Y.(*U.EGAL(*G-PAR(*G,*X),*G-PAR(*G,*Y),*U) ET
    NON *V.EGAL(*X,*Y,*V))).
+ONTE(*X.*Y.ILYA(*G,ILYA(*I,*P ET *Q))) -FREUR(*X.*G-*I.*P)
    -ENFAN(*Y.*G-*I.*Q).
```

** (5) CREATION D'ENONCES ELEMENTAIRES.

```
+ENONCE(*R,+(*A).-VALIDE(*N-*V,*U).*C,*N)
    -SYN(ONA(*R,*N/*V/*U.*A).NIL,*C).

:ONA(NON NON *P,*S) == -/ :ONA(*P,*S).
:ONA(NON(*P ET *Q),*S) == -/ :ONA(*P IMPLIQUE NON *Q,*S).
:ONA(NON(*P IMPLIQUE *Q),*S) == -/ :ONA(*P ET NON *Q,*S).
:ONA(NON TOUT(*I,*P),*S) == -/ :ONA(ILYA(*I,NON *P),*S).
:ONA(NON ILYA(*I,*P),*S) == -/ :ONA(TOUT(*I,NON *P),*S).
:ONA(NON LE(*I,*P,*Q),*S) == -/ :ONA(LE(*I,*P,NON *Q),*S).
:ONA(NON *U.NOMPROPRE(*X),*N/1/*U.ABSURDE(*U)) == -/ :SEXE(*X,*U).
:ONA(NON (1.*U).*P,*N/1/*U.ABSURDE(*U)) == £-(*P) -/.
:ONA(*P ET *Q,*N/*I-O/*R) == :ONA(*P,G(*N)/*I/*R).
:ONA(*P ET *Q,*N/O-*I/*R) == -/ :ONA(*Q,D(*N)/*I/*R).
:ONA(*P IMPLIQUE *Q,*N/*I-*J/*T) == -/ :ONA(NON *P,G(*N)/*I/*R)
```

```
    :ONA(*Q,D(*N)/*J/*S) -COMBINAISON(*R,*S,*T).
:ONA(TOUT(*I,*P),*N/*S) == -/ :ONA(*P,*I-*N/*S).
:ONA(ILYA(SK(*N),*P),*N/*S) == -/ :ONA(*P,D(*N)/*S).
:ONA(ILYA(*I,*P),*S) == -/ :ONA(*P,*S).
:ONA(LE(*I,*P,*Q),*S) == -/ :ONA(TOUT(*I,*P IMPLIQUE *Q),*S).
:ONA((2.*U).*P,*N/1/*U.*P) ==.

+COMBINAISON(*U.*P,*U.ABSURDE(*U),*U.*P) -/ .
+COMBINAISON(*U.ABSURDE(*U),*U.*P,*U.*P) -/.
+COMBINAISON(*P,*Q,*R) -MESSAGE("C'EST TROP COMPLIQUE.") -IMPASSE.

:SEXE(*X,*U) == -NOMPROPRE(*X) -/.
:SEXE(*G-*I,*U) == -NOMPROPRE(*H-*I) -/
   -MESSAGE("IL Y A UN PROBLEME DE SEXE.") -IMPASSE.
:SEXE(*G-*I,*U) == £-(DANS(INDIVIDU(*G-*I),*U)) -VAR(*G) -/.
:SEXE(*X,*U) == -AJOUTER(+(NOMPROPRE(*X)).NIL).
```

** (6) REGLES DE RAISONNEMENT.

```
+VALIDE(*N-*U,*V) -OK(*N) -NOUVEAU(*N-*U,*V).

+OK(*N) -KO(*N) -/ -IMPASSE.    +OK(*N).

+NOUVEAU(*A,*B.*U) -VAR(*B) -/ -PAREILS(*A,*B).
+NOUVEAU(*A,*A.*U) -/ -IMPASSE.
+NOUVEAU(*A,*B.*U) -NOUVEAU(*A,*U).

+DANS(INDIVIDU(*X),*U) -NOMPROPRE(*X) -/.
+DANS(INDIVIDU(*G-*I),*U) -NOMPROPRE(*H-*I) -/ -IMPASSE.
+DANS(*X,*X.*U) -/.                 +DANS(*X,*Y.*U) -DANS(*X,*U).

+ABSURDE(*U) -EGAL(*G-IN(*A),*G-IN(*B),1.*U) -PASPAREILS(*A,*B).
+ABSURDE(*U) -EGAL(M-*I,F-*J,1.*U).

+EGAL(*X,*X,1.*U).
+EGAL(*X,*Y,1.*U) -EGAL(*X,*Z,2.*U) -EGAL(*Z,*Y,1.*U).
+EGAL(*X,*Y,1.*U) -EGAL(*Z,*X,2.*U) -EGAL(*Z,*Y,1.*U).

+AMY(*X,*Y,1.*U) -EGAL(*X,*R,1.*U) -EGAL(*Y,*S,1.*U)
   -AMYBIS(*R,*S,*U).
+AMYBIS(*X,*Y,*U) -AMY(*X,*Y,2.*U).
+AMYBIS(*X,*Y,*U) -AMY(*Y,*X,2.*U).

+EPOUX(*X,*Y,1.*U) -EGAL(*X,*R,1.*U) -EGAL(*Y,*S,1.*U)
   -EPOUX(*R,*S,2.*U).

+DETAILS(1.*U) -DETAILS(2.*U).

+PASPAREILS(*X,*Y) -PAREILS(*X,*Y) -/ -IMPASSE.
+PASPAREILS(*X,*Y).

+PAREILS(*A,*A).
```

** (7) LECTURES ET ECRITURES.

```
+PHRASELUE(*L.*U) -/ -LIGNE -DIRE("MOI. -") -LIGNE -LUB(*K)
```

```
   -TR(*K.NIL,*L) -SUITELIRE(*L,*U).

+SUITELIRE(POINT,NIL) -/.        +SUITELIRE(!,NIL) -/.
+SUITELIRE(?,NIL) -/.
+SUITELIRE(*K,*M.*U) -LU(*L) -TR(*L.NIL,*M) -SUITELIRE(*M,*U).

+AJOUTER(*P) -DETAILS(1.*U) -/ -AJOUT(*P) -MESSAGE("J'ENREGISTRE:")
   -SORC(*P) -LIGNE.
+AJOUTER(*P) -AJOUT(*P).

+SORTIR(*U) -DETAILS(1.*V) -/ -MESSAGE("JE TROUVE:") -SORT(*U)
   -LIGNE.
+SORTIR(*U).

+MESSAGE(*U) -LIGNE -DIRE("LA MACHINE. - ") -DIRE(*U) -LIGNE.

+DIRE(NIL) -/.                   +DIRE(*U.*V) -/ -DIRE(*U) -DIRE(*V).
+DIRE(*U) -TR(*V.NIL,*U) -ECRIT(*V).

+TR(".",POINT) -/.               +TR(" ",BLANC) -/.
+TR("-",TRAIT) -/.               +TR(*X.NIL,*X).
```

The program is composed of 8 parts. Here is the explanation relative to each of them.

(0) Imbrication of the different phasis (imbrication des différentes phases). The system functions by executing a series of exchanges. Each exchange consists principally : in reading a sentence and recording it, in transforming it into a sequence of elementary statements (which are regular clauses) and retaining them, in starting a proof from the litteral -ABSURDE(*R), in computing from *R a possibly reply and possibly in suppressing certain clauses which render the recorded information absurd. In this last case, it suppresses the clauses deriving from the oldest sentences.

(1) Request for information (demande d'information). The system manages by itself the dictionnary of proper nouns and of their genders. In certain cases when it has not been able to determine the gender of a proper noun and needs it in its deductions, it requests directly this information from the interlocutor.

(2) Pretreating of the sentence (prétraitement de la phrase). After reading a sentence presented in the form of a sequence of characters, the system eliminates some of them and produces a sequence of words and punctuation marks. This is done by means of a small metamorphis grammar.

(3) Analysis of French (analyse du français). The analysis of each sentence is effected by means of a metamorphosis grammar directly modelled on the formal definition of our subset of French. Each deep structure obtained is a formula of the following type :

```
<formule>   ::=  ( NON <formule> ) | ( <formule> ET <formule> ) |
                 ( <formule> IMPLIQUE <formule> ) |
                 ILYA      ( <indice> , <formule> ) | TOUT ( <indice>,<formule> ) |
                 LE ( <indice> ,<formule>,<formule> ) |
                 <variable> . <formule élémentaire>

<formule élémentaire>  ::=  AMY ( <personne> , <personne> , <variable> ) |
                            DANS ( POURQUOI , <variable> ) |
                            DANS ( QUI (<personne> ) , <variable> ) |
                            DETAILS ( <variable> ) |
                            EGAL ( <personne> , <personne> , <variable> ) |
                            EPOUX ( <personne> , <personne> , <variable> ) |
                            HALTE | NOMPROPRE  ( <personne> ) | QUESTION
```

<indice> ::= <variable> | F | M
<personne> ::= <genre> - <nom>
<genre> ::= F | M | <variable>
<nom> ::= <nom propre> | PAR (<genre> , <personne>) | <variable>
<variable> ::= " variable PROLOG "

(4) Dictionary (dictionnaire). The dictionary associates to each article and each noun a "syntactical-semantic" formula. All the relations of parenthood are expressed in function of the relation EPOUX (spouse), EGAL (equal) by introducing the term PAR(*G,*X) which represents the parent of sex *G of the individual *X .

(5) Creation of elementary statements (créations d'énoncés élémentaires). A metamorphosis grammar permits the transformation of each deep structure into a set of elementary statements. This is essentially an algorithm of the "skolemisation" type which also produces regular clauses. The positive litteral is always placed at the head ; if there is none we create the litteral +ABSURDE(*U), if there are several, the machine emits the message "C'EST TROP COMPLIQUE" (it's too complicated). Moreover, the litteral -VALIDE(*N-*T,*U) is systematically inserted after the first litteral : it permits the control of deductions and allows us to simulate the suppression of a clause. In this litteral *N designates the number of the sentence from which the clauses comes ; *T is a term permitting differentiation between several clauses coming from the same sentence, *U is a variable appearing in all the litterals and which, in the course of a demonstration, permits the cumulation of certain results and in particular the listing of all the clauses instrumental in this demonstration.

(6) Rules of reasoning (règles de raisonnement). In order to reason, the machine knows axioms of equality, it supposes that a person can have only one name and only one sex, and that, it a is the friend of b , then b is the friend of a .

(7) Reading and writing (lectures et écritures). This concerns the management of the input-output device.

5.3 EXAMPLE OF CONVERSATION

Here now is an example of a conversation. When the machine prints intermediates results, it gives all the clauses it is recording, the deep structure of each sentence and the result of the deductions from which it produces its replies.

-BAVARDONS!

MOI. -
DIEU EST L'AMI DE TOUT LE MONDE.

MOI. -
DIEU EST L'AMIE DE TOUT LE MONDE.

LA MACHINE. - IL Y A UN PROBLEME DE SEXE.

MOI. -
DES DETAILS!

MOI. -
JE SUIS HORACE.

LA MACHINE. - J'ENREGISTRE:
+PHRASE(4,J.E.BLANC.S.U.I.S.BLANC.H.O.R.A.C.E.POINT.NIL).

LA MACHINE. - JE TROUVE:
LE(*X0,*X1.NOMPROPRE(*X0-JE),LE(*X2,*X3.NOMPROPRE(*X2-IN(HORACE)),*X4
.EGAL(*X0-JE,*X2-IN(HORACE),*X4)))

LA MACHINE. - J'ENREGISTRE:
+EGAL(*X0-JE,*X1-IN(HORACE),2.*X2)-VALIDE(4-(1-(1-1)),*X2)-DANS(INDIV
IDU(*X0-JE),*X2)-DANS(INDIVIDU(*X1-IN(HORACE)),*X2).

LA MACHINE. - JE TROUVE:
4-(1-(1-1)).INDIVIDU(M-JE).INDIVIDU(F-IN(HORACE)).*X0

LA MACHINE. - VOUS ETES BIEN DE SEXE MASCULIN?

MOI. -
OUI!

LA MACHINE. - J'ENREGISTRE:
+NOMPROPRE(M-JE).

LA MACHINE. - HORACE EST BIEN DE SEXE MASCULIN?

MOI. -
OUI!

LA MACHINE. - J'ENREGISTRE:
+NOMPROPRE(M-IN(HORACE)).

MOI. -
PAS DE DETAILS!

LA MACHINE. - J'ENREGISTRE:
+PHRASE(5,P.A.S.BLANC.D.E.BLANC.D.E.T.A.I.L.S.!.NIL).

LA MACHINE. - JE TROUVE:
NON *X0.DETAILS(*X0)

LA MACHINE. - J'ENREGISTRE:
+ABSURDE(*X0)-VALIDE(5-1,*X0)-DETAILS(1.*X0).

LA MACHINE. - JE TROUVE:
5-1.3-1.*X0

LA MACHINE. - J'ENREGISTRE:
+KO(3).

LA MACHINE. - VOUS VOUS CONTREDISEZ. J'OUBLIE QUE VOUS M'AVEZ DIT:
'DES DETAILS!'

MOI. -
POURQUOI EST-CE QUE JE NE SUIS PAS DIEU?

LA MACHINE. - PARCE QUE JE SAIS RAISONNER.
ET QUE VOUS M'AVEZ DIT: 'JE SUIS HORACE.'

LA MACHINE. - PARCE QUE JE SAIS RAISONNER.
ET QUE VOUS M'AVEZ DIT: 'JE SUIS HORACE.'

MOI. -
L'AMI DE MA SOEUR EST CURIACE.

LA MACHINE. - CURIACE EST BIEN DE SEXE MASCULIN?

MOI.
ZOZO EST MON FILS.

LA MACHINE. - OUI! OU NON!

MOI. -
OUI!

MOI. -
ZOZO EST MON FILS.

MOI. -
QUI EST L'AMI DE LA TANTE AU ZOZO.

LA MACHINE. - JE NE COMPRENDS PAS CETTE PHRASE.

MOI. -
QUI EST L'AMI DE LA TANTE DE ZOZO?

LA MACHINE. - DIEU!

LA MACHINE. - CURIACE!

LA MACHINE. - DIEU!

LA MACHINE. - CURIACE!

LA MACHINE. - DIEU!

LA MACHINE. - CURIACE!

MOI. -
POURQUOI EST-CE QUE CURIACE EST L'AMI DE LA TANTE DE ZOZO?

LA MACHINE. - PARCE QUE JE SAIS RAISONNER.
ET QUE VOUS M'AVEZ DIT: 'L'AMI DE MA SOEUR EST CURIACE.'
ET QUE VOUS M'AVEZ DIT: 'ZOZO EST MON FILS.'

LA MACHINE. - PARCE QUE JE SAIS RAISONNER.
ET QUE VOUS M'AVEZ DIT: 'L'AMI DE MA SOEUR EST CURIACE.'
ET QUE VOUS M'AVEZ DIT: 'ZOZO EST MON FILS.'

LA MACHINE. - PARCE QUE JE SAIS RAISONNER.
ET QUE VOUS M'AVEZ DIT: 'JE SUIS HORACE.'
ET QUE VOUS M'AVEZ DIT: 'L'AMI DE MA SOEUR EST CURIACE.'
ET QUE VOUS M'AVEZ DIT: 'ZOZO EST MON FILS.'

MOI. -
SATAN EST MON AMI.

MOI. -
QUI EST L'AMI DE DIEU?

LA MACHINE. - DIEU!

LA MACHINE. - TOUT HOMME!

LA MACHINE. - VOUS!

LA MACHINE. - VOUS!

LA MACHINE. - CURIACE!

LA MACHINE. - HORACE!

LA MACHINE. - HORACE!

MOI. -

SATAN N'EST L'AMI DE PERSONNE.

LA MACHINE. - VOUS VOUS CONTREDISEZ. J'OUBLIE QUE VOUS M'AVEZ DIT:
'SATAN EST MON AMI.'

LA MACHINE. - VOUS VOUS CONTREDISEZ. J'OUBLIE QUE VOUS M'AVEZ DIT:
'DIEU EST L'AMI DE TOUT LE MONDE.'

MOI. -
QUI N'EST PAS MON AMI?

LA MACHINE. - SATAN!

LA MACHINE. - SATAN!

LA MACHINE. - SATAN!

MOI. -
L'AMI DE LA SOEUR DE MA NIECE N'EST PAS MON AMI.

LA MACHINE. - C'EST TROP COMPLIQUE.

MOI. -
AU REVOIR!

LA MACHINE. - BONSOIR!

BIBLIOGRAPHY

(1) BATTANI G. et MELONI H., Interpréteur du langage de programmation PROLOG, Rapport de DEA, Groupe d'Intelligence Artificielle, UER de LUMINY, Université d'AIX-MARSEILLE, September 1973.

(2) BATTANI G. et MELONI H., Mise en oeuvre des contraintes phonologiques, syntaxiques et sémantiques dans un système de compréhension automatique de la parole, Thèse de 3ème cycle, Groupe d'Intelligence Artificielle, UER de LUMINY, Université d'AIX-MARSEILLE, June 1975.

(3) BERGMAN M. et KANOUI H., Sycophante : Système de calcul formel et d'intégration symbolique sur ordinateur, Rapport de recherche, Groupe d'Intelligence Artificielle, UER de LUMINY, Université d'AIX-MARSEILLE, October 1975.

(4) COLMERAUER A., les systèmes-q ou un formalisme pour analyser et synthétiser des phrases sur ordinateur, publication interne n° 43, Département d'Informatique, Université de MONTREAL, September 1970.

(5) COLMERAUER A., DANSEREAU J., HARRIS B. et KITTREDGE, TAUM 71, Rapport annuel du projet de traduction automatique de l'Université de MONTREAL, Januar 1971.

(6) COLMERAUER A., KANOUI H., PASERO R. et ROUSSEL Ph., Un système de communication homme-machine en français, Rapport de recherche, Groupe d'Intelligence Artificielle, UER de LUMINY, Université d'AIX-MARSEILLE, June 1973.

(7) PASERO R., Représentation du français en logique du 1er ordre, en vue de dialoguer avec un ordinateur, Thèse de 3ème cycle, Groupe d'Intelligence Artificielle, UER de LUMINY, Université d'AIX-MARSEILLE, October 1972.

(8) KOWALSKI R. et KUEHNER D., Linear resolution with selection function, Artificial Intelligence 2, 1971.

(9) KOWALSKI R. et VAN EMDEN M., The semantic of predicate logic as programming language, JACM, 23, n° 4, pp. 733-743, October 1976.

(10) ROBINSON J.A., A machine-oriented logic based on the resolution principle, JACM 12, n°1, pp. 227-234, December 1965.

(11) ROUSSEL Ph., PROLOG, Manuel d'utilisation, Rapport interne, Groupe d'Intelligence Artificielle, UER de LUMINY, Université d'AIX-MARSEILLE, September 1975.

(12) WARREN D., WARPLAN : A system for generating, plans, Memo n° 76, Department of computational logic, School of Artificial Intelligence, Université d'EDIMBOURG, June 1974.

METAMORPHOSIS GRAMMARS

CONTENTS

THE THEORY AND PRACTICE OF AUGMENTED TRANSITION NETWORK GRAMMARS

Madeleine Bates
Boston University Mathematics Department
Boston, Massachusetts 02115 / USA
and Bolt Beranek and Newman Inc.
Cambridge, Mass. 02138 / USA

1. INTRODUCTION

For the last eight years augmented transition network (ATN) grammars have been used in natural language understanding systems and question answering systems for both text and speech. They have proved to be flexible, easy to write and debug, able to handle a wide variety of syntactic constructions, and easy to interface to other components of a total system. They provide a useful way to give an account of linguistic structures which can be easily communicated to both humans and computers, and they may be (partially) presented by easily visualized diagrams. One does not need to know how to program a computer in order to write or use an ATN grammar. This fact makes it easy for linguists to learn about ATNs. Even linguists without access to a computer have found ATNs useful in the description of several languages [Grimes, 1975]. Although ATN grammars can be written for languages other than English, English will be used for examples throughout this paper; most of the techniques presented will be useful for other languages as well.

Augmented transition network grammars were developed by William Woods [Woods, 1969, 1970, 1973; Woods et al, 1972], although similar but less well developed models appeared independently in earlier work [Thorne et al, 1968; Bobrow and Fraser, 1969]. The advantages of ATNs may be summarized as 1) perspicuity, 2) generative power, 3) efficiency of representation, 4) the ability to capture linguistic regularities and generalities, and 5) efficiency of operation.

Much has been written about both the ATN formalism and various applications, but unfortunately many of these sources are not widely available. This paper attempts to bring together the primary content of those sources and to provide the reader with examples of several styles of ATN grammars. It is intended to be a guide for those who wish to learn enough about ATNs to implement their own. I have attempted to describe not only the basic mechanism but also recent advances and applications and unsolved problems. I have also tried to indicate time/space/clarity tradeoffs since no one grammar or style of grammar is suitable for all purposes.

The following section introduces the ATN formalism and discusses several types of parsers for ATN grammars. The first part may be skipped by readers familiar with the presentation of ATNs given in [Woods, 1970] and the second may be skipped by those not interested in the details of parser implementation. There follows a discussion of some of the issues and tradeoffs involved in writing ATN grammars for a variety of purposes and illustrations of how some of the syntactic constructions of English may be handled. The paper concludes with a suggested procedure to follow in order to formulate an ATN grammar.

2. THE ATN FORMALISM

A _basic_ transition network (BTN) grammar looks like a collection of finite state transition diagrams; each is a directed graph with labeled states and labeled arcs, a distinguished start state, and a set of distinguished final states. The label on an arc indicates the type (usually the syntactic category, i.e., part of speech) of input which will allow the transition to be made to the next state. A input sequence is said to be accepted by the network if, beginning in the start state, some path (sequence of arcs) can be followed which terminates on a final state.

The network differs from a finite state automaton in that it permits recursion by allowing the label on some arcs to be a nonterminal rather than a terminal symbol. That is, the label on some arcs may call not for a word of input but for a constituent which is found by recursively re-applying the network beginning with an indicated new start state. When such a recursive arc is encountered, the current computation is pushed onto a stack and a new process is begun to look for the desired constituent. When a final state in this lower level is reached, the stack is popped and the suspended computation is continued. The input pointer, in the meantime, will have been moved to a later point in the sentence (just after the accepted constituent) by the lower level process. An attempt to pop an empty stack when the input pointer is at the end of the input means that the sentence has been found acceptable.

Figure 1 illustrates such a basic transition network with two levels. In it and in all subsequent diagrams in this paper the following conventions are used. States are written as circles or ovals around the name (label) of the state. Start states are indicated by double circles (the initial state for the entire grammar is usually obvious, most likely the first one on the page) and final states are shown by the presence of an arc labeled POP which does not terminate on any other state. The arc types will be described in detail later; in Figure 1 JUMP indicates that a transition may be made without processing any input, CAT means that the current word in the input string must be of the indicated syntactic category (and is "consumed" as the arc is taken), and PUSH means that a recursive call is to be made beginning in the indicated state.

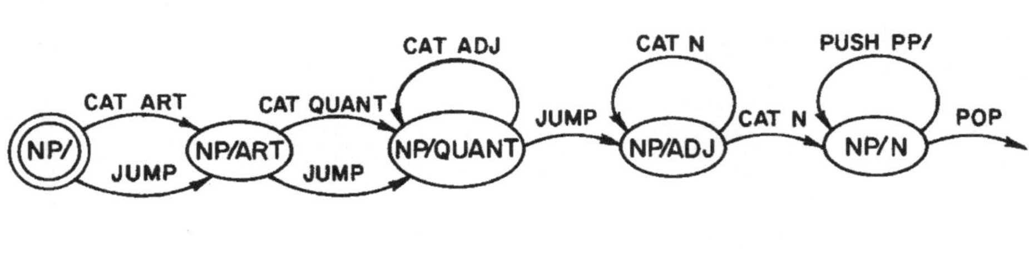

Figure 1: A Small Grammar for Noun Phrases

The convention followed in this paper for labeling states is that state names will generally composed of two parts separated by a slash.

The first part indicates the type of constituent being processed (a noun phrase, for example); the second part indicates either how far through the constituent the parse has proceeded or the sort of construction which may occur next. For example, in a hypothetical grammar: S/IMP may mean that in parsing a sentence it has been discovered to be imperative; NP/ADJ that in a noun phrase either an adjective has been found or we have gotten past the place where an adjective could occur; NP/CONJ? that in a noun phrase we are at a point where a conjunction may be expected; S/S that an entire sentence has been processed (a name like S/POP is also used in this situation to indicate that a POP, the termination of one level of the network, is about to be done). It is crucially important to remember that the state names have meaning <u>only</u> to the writer of the grammar; the parsing system does <u>not</u> use them as anything but unique identifiers for the set of arcs coming from them. Thus the states could just as well be named A, B, C, D, ... instead of S/, NP/HEAD, REL/PRO, ... without changing the operation of the parser. A grammar writer will discover, however, that the the use of mneumonically accurate state names (by the above convention or any other) will greatly clarify the grammar for human use and will simplify the writing and debugging of the grammar.

A BTN grammar as described above is weakly equivalent to a context free grammar or a pushdown store automaton. It differs from strong equivalence only in its inability to characterize unbounded branching, as in

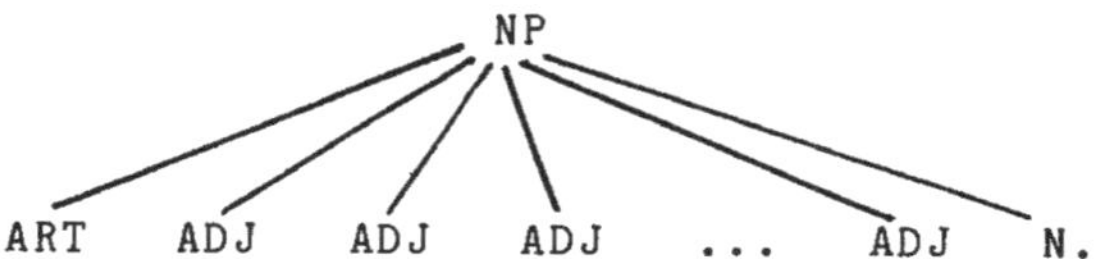

The grammar of Figure 1 corresponds to the following context free grammar (which uses empty productions):

```
NP --> ART? QUANT? ADJS? NMODS? N PPS?
ART? -->      ¦ the ¦ an ¦ a ¦ ...
QUANT? -->     ¦ all ¦ some ¦ ...
AJDS? -->     ¦ ADJ ADJS
ADJ --> pretty ¦ red ¦ ...
NMODS? -->     ¦ N NMODS
N --> dog ¦ girl ¦ love ¦ ...
PPS? -->     ¦ PP PPS?
PP --> PREP NP
PREP --> of ¦ in ¦ with ¦ by ¦ ...
```

Both grammars can produce and can be used to accept sentences such as

The new red law books.
Each beautiful picture in the recent exhibit.
Men with wives in professional careers. (ambiguous)
The tallest boy in a group of students.

One can look at a BTN as a model of a context free grammar in regular expression form. Thus a regular expression rule [Woods, 1969] such as X -> (A) B C* D can be represented by the BTN shown in Figure 2.

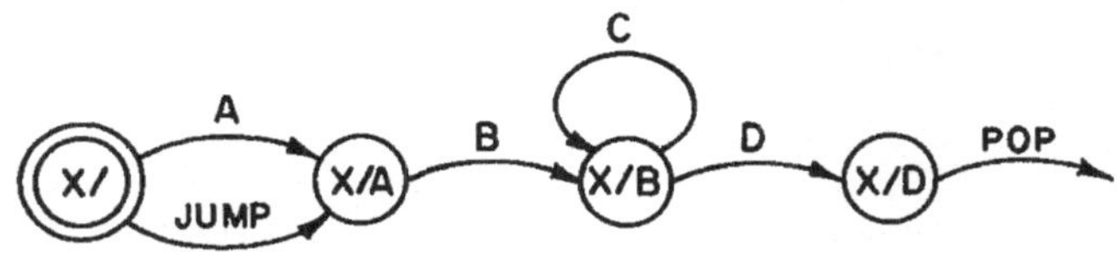

Figure 2: Another Simple Network

But it is well known that context free grammars are not adequate for English. In addition, the basic grammar we have described is capable only of accepting or rejecting input strings; it cannot produce a structure which shows something about the relationships among the words.

To make a more powerful model, each arc is provided with a test and a sequence of actions, thus producing an augmented transition network. The test associated with an arc must be satisfied (in addition to the label) for the arc to be taken, and the actions are executed as the arc is traversed. The actions construct pieces of structure (tree structures, case structures, etc.) and keep them in registers, which may be thought of in programming terms as variables local to the level of the grammar where they are set. Registers and their contents are available on subsequent arcs and can be combined, copied, changed, or added to as more of the input is processed.

The arrangement of states and arcs reflects the surface structure of acceptable input sentences, and the actions permit rearrangements and embeddings to create a structure which may be quite different from the surface structure. This very general mechanism provides a transformational capability which can produce deep structures of the same sort as those of a transformational grammar, and it makes the ATN formalism equivalent in power to a Turing machine.

We now describe in detail the format and operation of the arcs of an ATN grammar. An arc is represented as a parenthesized list of elements which may themselves be words or lists. There are seven types of arcs as shown by the schemas in Table 1. (Capitalized words are actual elements, lower case words in brackets are descriptions of elements which will be defined below, and * is the Kleene star operator which indicates zero or more occurrences of the previous element.)

The first element of each arc indicates its type. The interpretation of the second element depends on the type of the arc and will be explained below. The third element is an arbitrary test which must be satisfied in order for the arc to be taken. Actions, which may occur in any number on all arcs except POP arcs, generally manipulate information that is stored in registers. The register contents are either constants (often used as flags to be tested on later arcs) or pieces of structure. The structures are built using previous register contents and/or the current item of input and/or the features of the current item which are found in the dictionary. The last element of every arc type except JUMP an POP indicates which state of the grammar is to be considered next.

(CAT <category> <test> <action>* (TO nextstate>))

(WRD <word> <test> <action>* (TO nextstate>))

(MEM <list> <test> <action>* (TO nextstate>))

(PUSH <state> <test> <pre-action>* <action>* (TO <nextstate>))

(VIR <constit-type> <test> <action>* (TO <nextstate>))

(JUMP <nextstate> <test> <action>*)

(POP <form> <test>)

Table 1: The Form of Arcs of an ATN Grammar

A CAT arc may be taken if the current input word is of the (syntactic) category specified by the second element of the arc. A WRD arc specifies the exact word of input which is required, rather than a category, and a MEM arc is exactly like a WRD arc except that the input word must be one of the list of words which is the second element of the arc. (Some implementations eliminate MEM arcs but allow the second element of a WRD arc to be a list of words.) All three of these arcs "consume" input when they are taken, that is, they cause the input pointer to be advanced to the next word.

A JUMP arc specifies the state to which a transition is to be made without "consuming" anything from the input string. A VIR arc checks to see whether a constituent of the named type has been placed on the HOLD list by a HOLD action of some previous arc (see below).

A PUSH arc initiates a new, perhaps recursive, call to the network which begins in the indicated state and which looks for a constituent. A POP arc, which has no destination state, marks the state that it leaves as a terminal state for some level of the network; its second element indicates the form (usually some sort of syntactic structure) which is to be returned as the result of the analysis of the portion of input parsed by the current level of the network. The POP causes control to return to the PUSH arc which caused the process at it's level to be invoked. See Figure 3 for an example of the order in which the arcs of a path involving a PUSH and POP are traversed.

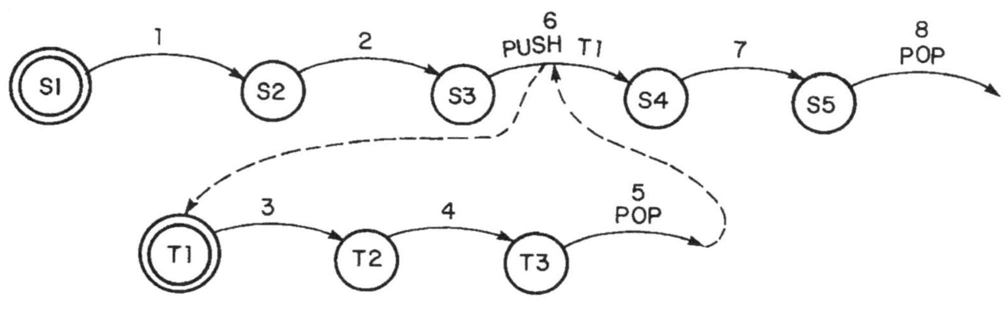

Figure 3: The Operation of PUSH and POP Arcs

When the parser is operating, a number of registers are active. Whenever a PUSH occurs, this register list, along with other information, is saved on a stack while the parser recursively operates on the new (lower) level beginning with an empty register list. When a POP arc is taken, the stack is popped, wiping out the current (lower level) register list and restoring the register list which was current before the last PUSH. The constituent which was POPed (the value of the second element of the POP arc) then becomes the current input item for the rest of the PUSH arc.

In most of the examples given in this paper, the type of structure produced is a parse tree like the deep structure trees of transformational grammar theory. To represent a tree structure in linear form, it is written as a list of elements surrounded by parentheses; the first element is the root of the tree and the subsequent elements are the sons of the root which may be either terminal leaves or subtrees. Figure 4 shows both a standard tree and a linear representation which has been formatted for further clarity.

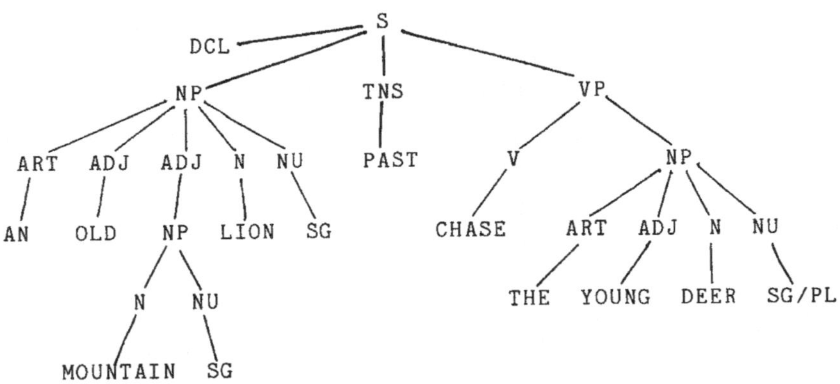


```
(S DCL
   (NP (ART AN)
       (ADJ OLD)
       (ADJ (NP (N MOUNTAIN)
                (NU SG)))
       (N LION)
       (NU SG))
    (TNS PAST)
    (VP (V CHASE)
        (NP (ART THE)
            (ADJ YOUNG)
            (N DEER)
            (NU SG/PL))))
```

Figure 4: Two Representations of a Parse Tree

Other structures can be produced just as easily, for example, case representations:

```
((ACT: HIDE)
 (ACTOR: JOHN)
 (OBJECT: MONEY)
 (TIME: PAST)
 (LOCATION: FLOWER-POT))
```

tagmemic representations [modified from Grimes, 1975 p.169]:

```
(NP ,ANIM (DET:ART,DEF:THE)
          (MOD:ADJ:PLEASANT)
          (HEAD:NW,ANIM_PL
                    (NUC:STEM,ANIM:BOY)
                    (PER:SFX,PL:S)))
```

semantic representations:

```
(FOR: ALL X1 / (FINDQ: TRIP
                    (DESTINATION CHICAGO)
                    (TRAVELER BILL))
   ; (EXPENSIVE X1) : (OUTPUT: (TIMEOF: X1)))
```

dependency structures, stratificational analyses, and many others as well.

Figure 5 shows the details of the arcs which are needed to make the grammar of Figure 1 an ATN. It is a slightly edited listing of a computer file containing the grammar. Because ATN grammars were developed using the LISP language [Weisman, 1967; Teitelman, 1974] they were written in the LISP form shown below. Each state is represented as a list whose first element is the state name and whose other elements are the arcs emanating from that state. Comments are in upper and lower case and begin with a *. (Readers not familiar with LISP should read Appendix I at this point.) It should be emphasized that ATN parsers and grammars may be written in a variety of programming languages, and that if one other than LISP is chosen it may be advisable to modify the notation.

The actions SETR, SENDR, and LIFTR are the basic actions of an ATN grammar, but implementors may extend this set. Here are descriptions of a number of actions which have been found convenient.

(SETR <reg> <form>) This causes the indicated <u>register</u> to be set to the value of the <u>form</u>.

(SETRQ <reg> <value>) This is like SETR except that the last element is not evaluated. It is equivalent to (SETR <reg> (QUOTE <value>)). Thus (SETR HEAD (NPCLAUSE)) sets a register named HEAD to the value returned by the function NPCLAUSE; (SETRQ HEAD

```
(NP/
   (CAT ART T (* T is a predicate which is always true)
       (SETR ART (BUILDQ ((ART *))))
       (TO NP/ART))
   (JUMP NP/ART T))

(NP/ADJ
   (CAT N T
       (SETR N *)
       (SETR NU (GETF NUMBER))
       (TO NP/N))
   (CAT N T
       (ADDL ADJS (BUILDQ (ADJ (NP (N *) (NU #)))
                          (GETF NUMBER)))
       (TO NP/ADJ)))

(NP/ART
   (CAT QUANT T
       (SETR QUANT (BUILDQ ((QUANT *))))
       (TO NP/QUANT))
   (JUMP NP/QUANT T))

(NP/QUANT
   (CAT ADJ T
       (ADDR ADJS (BUILDQ (@ (ADJ) # (*))
                          (GETF DEGREE)))
       (* This will add the form (ADJ SUPERLATIVE root) for words
             like BIGGEST and the form (ADJ word) if uninflected.)
       (TO NP/QUANT))
   (JUMP NP/ADJ T))

(NP/N
   (PUSH PP/ (PPSTART)
       (* the test checks that the next word is a preposition)
       (ADDL NMODS *)
       (TO NP/N))
   (POP (BUILDQ (@ (NP) + + + ((N +)) ((NU +)) +)
                ART QUANT ADJS N NU NMODS)
       (DETAGREE)
       (* the predicate DETAGREE tests for agreement between the ART
          and N registers to screen out "a books", "an table")))

(PP/
   (CAT PREP T
       (SETR PREP *)
       (TO PP/PREP)))

(PP/PREP
   (PUSH NP/ (NPSTART)
       (* predicate fails if the next word cannot begin a NP)
       (SETR NP *)
       (TO PP/NP)))

(PP/NP
   (POP (BUILDQ (PP (PREP +) +)
                PREP NP)
       T))
```

Figure 5: Details of the Noun Phrase Grammar

(NPCLAUSE)) sets the register to a list which has one element, the word NPCLAUSE.

(ADDL <reg> <form>) This action takes the previous contents (which is expected to be a list) of the named register, adds the value of the form to the left end of the list, and sets the register to this new list. If the register has not been previously set, ADDL sets it to a list which contains the value of the form. It is equivalent to (SETR <reg> (CONS (EVAL <form>) (GETR <reg>))).

(ADDR <reg> <form>) This action is exactly like ADDL except that it adds elements to the right of the previous list. It is equivalent to (SETR <reg> (APPEND (GETR <reg>) (LIST (EVAL <form>)))). ADDL and ADDR are useful for accumulating things like adjectives and conjuncts.

(SENDR <reg> <form>) This is a pre-action which is only used on PUSH arcs. It causes the register to be set to the value of form at the lower level of recursion about to be initialized by the PUSH. This, in effect, allows the lower level network to be like a subroutine to which parameters can be passed via SENDRs.

(SENDRQ <reg> <value>) This is to SENDR as SETRQ is to SETR.

(LIFTR <reg> <form>) This is the inverse of SENDR in that it sets the register to the value of the form at the level just above the current level.

(HOLD <constit-type> <form>) This places the indicated form on the HOLD list as a constituent of constit-type. The HOLD list is a global list which is accessible at all levels. This action together with VIR arcs constitute a mechanism for dealing with the phenomenon called left extraposition in transformational grammar theory. Examples of this will be given below.

(VERIFY <form>) Sometimes it is useful to have a second test on an arc. VERIFY evaluates its form as if it were a predicate. If the form fails, the arc is aborted just as if the condition on the arc had failed. (If this action is implemented, one may do away with the test component on arcs.)

A number of different <form>s may be used within an action. The basic ones are the variables * and LEX and the functions GETR, GETF, and BUILDQ, but others may be included. (In a LISP implementation it is useful to allow any LISP form.) These forms are evaluated as follows:

LEX is always set to the current word of input as it appears before any morphological analysis has been performed on it.

* refers to the current item of input. On a JUMP, POP, WRD, or MEM arc it has the same value as LEX. On a CAT arc it is the root form of the word; thus if LEX = "stopped", * = "stop". On a PUSH arc, * is the current input word for the test and pre-actions, but on subsequent actions on the arc it is the value returned from the lower level computation which was initiated by the PUSH arc.

(GETR <reg>) returns the current contents of the indicated <u>reg</u>ister. If the <u>reg</u>ister has never been set, it returns the value NIL but does not cause an error.

(GETF <feature> <word>) checks the dictionary entry of the <u>word</u> and returns the value of the indicated <u>feature</u>. If the <u>word</u> is omitted, the current word of input is assumed. Thus (GETF NUMBER) may return SG or PL. It may also be used as a predicate for features without values; e.g., (GETF PASSIVE) will return true or false depending on whether or not the current word has the feature PASSIVE. It may be used without its second argument only on a CAT arc, where features are dependent on the syntactic category involved.

(BUILDQ <template> <form>*) is a constructor that takes a <u>template</u> (an arbitrary fragment of structure containing constants and special marks) and a series of <u>forms</u>. It returns a piece of structure that results from substituting the values of the <u>forms</u> for the special marks in the <u>template</u>. The special marks are as follows:

+ expects the corresponding <u>form</u> to be a register name and causes the contents of the register to be substituted for the +.

causes the corresponding <u>form</u> to be evaluated as a LISP form and substitutes the value for the #.

* causes the value of * to be substituted. It does not need a corresponding *form*.

@ appears in the form (@ x x ... x) and causes the lists which follow it to be appended together. It does not take a corresponding *form*.

As an example, if the DET register contained the list (DET THE) and the current word of input on a CAT arc were "books" then the form (BUILDQ (NP + (N *) (NU #)) DET (GETF NUMBER)) would return the structure (NP (DET THE) (N BOOK) (NU PL)). If in addition to the registers just mentioned the ADJS register were set to ((ADJ OLD)(ADJ DUSTY)(ADJ RED)) then the form (BUILDQ (@ (NP +) + ((N *) (NU #))) DET ADJS (GETF NUMBER)) would produce the structure (NP (DET THE) (ADJ OLD) (ADJ DUSTY) (ADJ RED) (N BOOK) (NU PL)).

(ABORT) is a form which causes the arc to fail just as if the test on the arc had failed. It is useful in conditional expressions used as actions.

```
(COND (<pred1> <e11> <e12> ... <e1n>)
      (<pred2> <e21> <e22> ...<e2m>)
       ...
      (<predi> <ei1> <ei2> ... <eij>))
```

This is the LISP way of writing a nested conditional statement. The <e>s may be either actions or forms. See Appendix I for details.

(QUOTE <value>) This is a LISP function which keeps *value* from being evaluated. See SETRQ above for an example.

It is probably useful to mention a few of the predicates which may be used as tests on the arcs (or in VERIFY or COND forms). The most common predicates are NULLR and the Boolean functions AND, OR, NOT, and EQUAL, but the user will be even more likely to develop his own tests than to invent new actions and forms. Some useful ones follow.

(NULLR <reg>) is true if the *register* has never been set or if it has been set to NIL.

(CHECKF <feature> <value>) succeeds if the value of feature for the current word is the indicated value; e.g., (CHECKF ROLE OBJ) is equivalent to (EQUAL (GETF ROLE) (QUOTE OBJ)).

(CATCHECK <word> <cat>) tests whether word is of the lexical category cat. It is useful to test words in registers, as in (CATCHECK (GETR V) (QUOTE MODAL)).

(ENDOFSENTENCE) succeeds only if there are no more words in the input string.

(x-AGREE <form> <form>) represents a family of predicates to check some sort of agreement between the forms, e.g., DET-N-AGREE, SUBJ-V-AGREE, etc.

(x-START) represents a set of "look-ahead predicates" which are useful on JUMP and PUSH arcs. For example, IMP-START could be used on a JUMP arc from the initial state of the grammar to test whether there were an untensed verb at the beginning of the sentence; similarly QSTART could be used to see if the input began with a question word.

NIL is a LISP consant which means false. this does not appear by itself as the test on an arc (since the arc would never be taken), but it is the value returned by a predicate function which fails.

T is a LISP constant which is used to represent true; however, since any non-NIL value in LISP is interpreted as true in a Boolean context, any function may be used as a predicate. For example, (GETR SUBJ) can be used not only in a form which uses the contents of the SUBJ register but also as a predicate which tests whether or not the SUBJ register has been set.

To test his understanding, the reader may wish to modify the grammar of Figures 1 and 5 to include pronouns, proper nouns, and/or possessives.

2a. A Detailed Example

In this section we present a more complex grammar and describe the processing of an actual sentence. Figures 6 and 7 show a grammar which, together with the noun phrase and prepositional phrase levels of Figures 1 and 5, can handle a large number of fairly complex English sentences. (This grammar is an elaboration of that given in [Woods, 1970].) Some of the sentences it can parse are:

The girl on the red bus was wanted in several countries by the police.
Will a boy scout help an old woman to cross the street?
The mayor would not have wanted to be elected to the position of dog-catcher.
The money was believed to have been hidden by a thief.
Was the fire engine trying to get to the fire?
A forest fire had been burning in western Colorado for several weeks.

The diagram of the grammar is fairly straightforward, but the details probably look very confusing to those readers new to ATNs. For this reason we will take the time to examine this grammar in detail. It is hoped that the reader will not just skim this section but will take pencil in hand and put as much effort into understanding the following explanation as was put into writing it.

Let us consider the parsing of the sentence "The mayor would not have wanted to be elected to the position of dog-catcher." We will give an overview of the purpose of all the arcs in the grammar, with special attention to the ones used in the parse of this sentence.

Beginning in state S/ we look for a noun phrase to serve, perhaps temporarily, as the subject of the sentence. If one is found, we assume the sentence is declarative. (This is reasonable since our current noun phrase grammar does not accept question determiners like "what" or "which".) If we cannot find a noun phrase at the beginning of the sentence, we assume that we are in a question. We will not give the details of the parse through the NP/ level (it would be a good exercise for the reader) but we assert that the PUSH arc succeeds and that the structure (NP (DET THE)(N MAYOR)(NU SG)) is returned from the lower level and is put in the SUBJ register. The TYPE register is

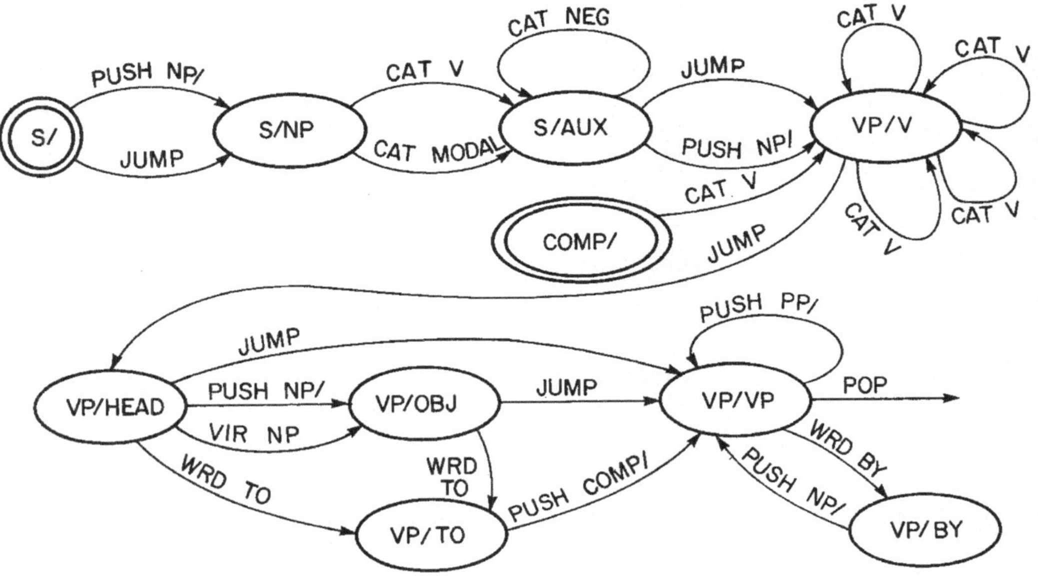

Figure 6: A Grammar for Sentences

set to the constant DCL to indicate that the sentence is declarative, and control moves to S/NP.

In state S/NP the CAT V arc cannot be taken with the word "would" in the input, but the CAT MODAL arc succeeds. The MODAL register is set to the form ((MODAL WILL)), using the root form of "would." (The need for the extra parentheses will be clear later.) The tense is recorded in the TNS register in the form (TNS PAST).

In state S/AUX we pick up the negative. The test on this arc ensures that the arc has not been taken before, thus making double negatives unacceptable. The NEG register is being used both as a flag for the test and as a piece of structure to be later incorporated in the parse structure. The test for "do" in the verb register is necessary to undo the effect of do-support in sentences like "Didn't I meet you in Pango-Pango?" If we were not permitted to have such a conditional action it would be necessary to have two CAT NEG arcs, one with the test for "do" and an unconditional action removing it from the V register and one with a condition that "do" not be in the V register.

```
(S/
   (PUSH NP/ T
       (SETR SUBJ *)
       (SETRQ TYPE DCL)
       (TO S/NP))
   (JUMP S/NP T
       (SETRQ TYPE Q)))

(S/NP
   (CAT V (GETF TNS)
       (SETR V *)
       (SETR TNS (BUILDQ (TNS #)
                         (GETF TENSE)))
       (SETR PNCODE (GETF PNCODE))
       (TO S/AUX))
   (CAT MODAL T
       (SETR MODAL (BUILDQ ((MODAL *))))
       (SETR TNS (BUILDQ (TNS #)
                         (GETF TENSE)))
       (TO S/AUX)))

(S/AUX
   (CAT NEG (NULLR NEG)
       (SETRQ NEG (NEG))
       (COND ((EQUAL (GETR V) (QUOTE DO))
              (SETRQ V NIL)))
       (TO S/AUX))
   (JUMP VP/V (AND (GETR SUBJ)
                   (AGREE (GETR SUBJ) (GETR PNCODE))))
   (PUSH NP/ (NULLR SUBJ)
       (COND ((NOT (AGREE * (GETR PNCODE)))
              (ABORT)))
       (SETR SUBJ *)
       (TO VP/V)))

(VP/V
   (CAT V (AND (GETF PASTPART)
               (EQUAL (GETR V) (QUOTE BE)))
       (HOLD (QUOTE NP) (GETR SUBJ))
       (SETRQ SUBJ (NP (PRO SOMEONE)))
       (SETR AGFLAG T)
       (SETR V *)
       (TO VP/V))
   (CAT V (AND (GETF PASTPART)
               (EQUAL (GETR V) (QUOTE HAVE)))
       (ADDR TNS (QUOTE PERFECT))
       (SETR V *)
       (TO VP/V))
   (CAT V (AND (GETF UNTENSED)
               (GETR MODAL)
               (NULLR V))
       (SETR V *)
       (TO VP/V))
   (CAT V (AND (GETF PRESPART)
               (EQUAL (GETR V) (QUOTE BE)
       (ADDR TNS (QUOTE PROGRESSIVE))
       (SETR V *)
       (TO VP/V))
   (JUMP VP/HEAD T
       (COND ((OR (GETR MODAL) (GETR NEG))
              (SETR AUX (BUILDQ ((@ (AUX) + +))
                                      MODAL NEG))))))
```

```
(VP/HEAD
   (JUMP VP/VP (GETF INTRANS (GETR V)))
   (PUSH NP/ (GETF TRANS (GETR V))
       (SETR OBJ *)
       (TO VP/OBJ))
   (VIR NP (GETF TRANS (GETR V))
       (SETR OBJ *)
       (TO VP/OBJ))
   (WRD TO (AND (GETF SCOMP (GETR V))
                (NULLR AGFLAG))
       (SETR SPECIALSUBJ (GETR SUBJ))
       (TO VP/TO)))

(VP/OBJ
   (JUMP VP/VP T)
   (WRD TO (GETF SCOMP (GETR V))
       (SETR SPECIALSUBJ (GETR OBJ))
       (TO VP/TO)))

(VP/VP
   (PUSH PP/ T
       (ADDR VMODS *)
       (TO VP/VP))
   (WRD BY (GETR AGFLAG)
       (SETR AGFLAG NIL)
       (TO VP/BY))
   (POP (COND ((GETR OBJ)
               (BUILDQ (S + + + (@ + (VP (V +) +) +))
                       TYPE SUBJ TNS AUX V OBJ VMODS))
              (T (BUILDQ (S + + + (@ + (VP (V +)) +))
                         TYPE SUBJ TNS AUX V VMODS)))
       T))

(VP/BY
   (PUSH NP/ T
       (SETR SUBJ *)
       (TO VP/VP)))

(VP/TO
   (PUSH VP/ T
       (SENDR SUBJ (GETR SPECIALSUBJ))
       (SENDR TNS (TENSEOF (GETR TNS)))
       (SENDRQ TYPE COMP)
       (SETR OBJ *)
       (TO VP/VP)))

(COMP/
   (CAT V (GETF UNTENSED)
       (SETR V *)
       (TO VP/V)))
```

Figure 7: Details of the Grammar for Sentences

Going back to our analysis, we find ourselves again in state S/AUX with the input pointer positioned at the word "wanted". Since we have something in the SUBJ register which agrees with the verb, we can follow the JUMP arc to state VP/V. If we had had no subject, the PUSH NP/ arc would try to find one, as in "Will the clock strike thirteen?"

Whatever the sentence, by the time state VP/V is reached the first verb (or modal) has been processed. In this state all the rest of the complex verb auxiliary structure is processed. All four CAT V arcs are self loops, implying that they may be taken multiple times in any order unless the conditions on the arcs make this impossible. The first arc may be taken only if the previous verb were some form of "be" and if the current verb may be passivized ("The promise was broken," "Would he have been killed?"); it places what we thought was the subject on a special HOLD list as a NP so it can be picked up later, probably as the object. We invent a dummy subject "someone" to put in the SUBJ register. This may not be correct, so we set a flag, AGFLAG, to indicate that if an agent is found in a by-phrase later in the sentence ("Juliet was loved by Romeo.") it should replace the dummy. This ability to put information in registers and later remove it on the basis of subsequent context is one of the best features of ATN grammars. Although this looks like we are making and later reversing a decision about the role of a portion of input, it can also be thought of as postponing a decision until the differential point is reached.

The second CAT V arc in state VP/V requires that the previous verb be a form of "have" and that the current one be a past participle, as in "may have been killed" or "has surprised." It remembers the effect of the "have" by appending an indicator, PERFECT, to the TNS register and replaces the "have" in the V register by the current verb.

The third CAT V arc may be taken only if the current word is untensed and is preceded by only a modal, as in "Can I go to Washington?" and "He will emulate his superiors." The final CAT V arc handles present participles which are preceded by a form of "be," as in "He will be going to school" and "Was the clown crying?" It adds a PROGRESSIVE indicator to the TNS register and remembers the current verb. (For a sentence like "Has the gambler been losing?" the TNS register would now be (TNS PRESENT PERFECT PROGRESSIVE).)

Note that it would be possible to collapse all four CAT V arcs into one arc which had a T test and a complicated conditional action. That would be slightly more efficient for time and space but would be less clear. This method of processing verb sequences may seem complex, but it is simpler than a set of context free rules to express the same constraints.

For our sample sentence, the third and second arcs would be taken, resulting in the following register settings:

```
SUBJ:  (NP (DET THE) (N MAYOR) (NU SG))
TYPE:  DCL
MODAL: ((MODAL WILL))
NEG:   (NEG)
TNS:   (TNS PAST PERFECT)
V:     WANT
```

Finally only the JUMP arc to state VP/HEAD may be taken. This arc creates an AUX register if either the MODAL or NEG registers are set, so for our sample sentence we get ((AUX (MODAL WILL) NEG)) in the AUX register. (This is a good example of the use of @ in a BUILDQ.)

In state VP/HEAD we know that the head verb of the sentence is in the V register. If the verb is intransitive we jump directly to VP/OBJ. We can look for an object if it is transitive. There are two ways to get an object: by pushing for a noun phrase directly ("I lost my mittens.") or by picking up on the VIR arc the noun phrase which was placed on the HOLD list in VP/V when we discovered that the sentence was passive ("The seed was sown."). None of those three arcs can be taken in our example, but we will postpone discussion of the last arc while describing the rest of the network.

When we get to VP/OBJ, either with or without a direct object, we either jump directly to VP/VP or find the word "to" and go to VP/TO. In state VP/VP we can, if the AGFLAG was set to indicate that the sentence is passive, look for the real agent of the action. If we find it, it is put in the SUBJ register (wiping out the dummy "someone") and the AGFLAG is reset to prevent finding another agent. We can also pick up any number of prepositional phrases modifying the verb. The agent may be interspersed with the prepositional phrases. We now postpone discussion of the POP arc and return to the place we left off above.

Returning to our sample sentence in state VP/HEAD, we find the word "to" in the input string. Since the verb "want" in the V register is marked in the dictionary with the feature SCOMP, meaning it can take a sentential complement and since we are not in a passive sentence, we can take the WRD TO arc to VP/TO. A new register, SPECIALSUBJ, holds the subject; the word "to" is not placed in any register since it does not need to appear in our final tree. A complement of the type we are looking for looks like a declarative sentence beginning with an untensed verb which has no subject in the surface structure. However the deep structure subject of the embedded clause may be the subject of the upper level, e.g. "The sword swallower liked to eat greasy food". After the first verb, we may have anything in the rest of the complement which could occur in the verb phrase of a sentence, hence it is convenient to merge the end of the complement network with the end of the sentence network as shown

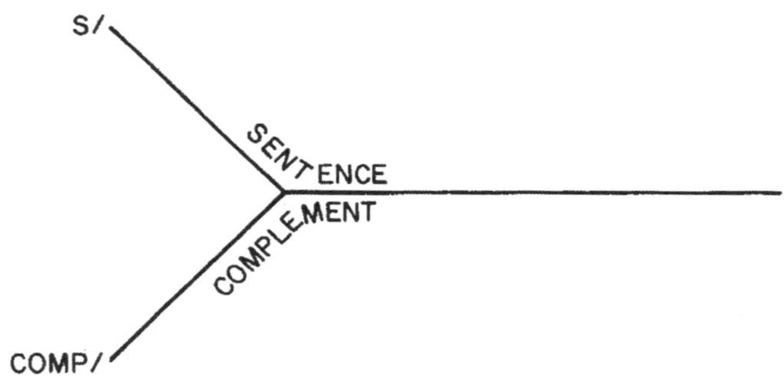

Figure 8: Merging Networks

abstractly in Figure 8. In order for this double use of a portion of the network to work correctly, we must be sure that the registers which are used in the tail of the paths are set on both initial portions. To accomplish this, the PUSH COMP/ arc from VP/TO has three pre-actions which initialize the SUBJ, TNS, and TYPE registers at the lower level with values from the current level. On the path of our example, the SUBJ register is initialized with the contents of SPECIALSUBJ, which is the old subject. If we had reached this state via the WRD TO arc from VP/OBJ, we would be sending down the object to become the lower level subject ("Alice wanted the parrot to speak," "The prodigy was expected to win the prize." Notice the movement of "the prodigy" from the SUBJ to OBJ registers and then to SUBJ at a lower level!). TENSEOF is a function which will extract the tense, leaving behind the mood and aspect, if any.

Thus we find ourselves in a lower level computation in state COMP/ with three registers set; the registers which existed before the PUSH are hidden on the stack and are completely inaccessible. Taking the CAT V arc from COMP/ (since "be" is untensed) results in a transition to VP/V with the following registers set:

```
SUBJ: (NP (ART THE) (N MAYOR) (NU SG))
TYPE: COMP
TNS:  (TNS PAST)
V:    BE
```

Now the first CAT V arc may be taken. We put the mayor on the HOLD list and replace the SUBJ register by the dummy (NP (PRO SOMEONE)). Then the AGFLAG register is set, and we take the JUMP arc to VP/HEAD without setting the AUX register. Here the VIR arc removes the mayor from the HOLD list and puts him in the OBJ register. NOTE: we did not really need to use the HOLD list here. We could have put the mayor into another register, say EXTRANP, in state VP/V and had a (JUMP VP/VP (GETR EXTRANP)(SETR OBJ (GETR EXTRANP))) arc in place of the VIR arc. The real power of the HOLD list is in holding constituents which must be picked up at an even lower level, e.g. "What painter did he want to have his portrait painted by?"

In VP/VP we push for the prepositional phrase "to the position of dog-catcher" (details left to the reader) and place the resulting structure into the VMODS register. Thus the registers are:

```
SUBJ:   (NP (PRO SOMEONE))
TYPE:   COMP
TNS:    (TNS PAST)
AGFLAG: T
V:      ELECT
OBJ:    (NP (ART THE) (N MAYOR) (NU SG))
VMODS:  ((PP (PREP TO) (NP ...)))
```

Finally the POP arc in state VP/VP is taken. The BUILDQ creates the structure

```
(S COMP
   (NP (PRO SOMEONE))
   (TNS PAST)
   (VP (V ELECT)
       (NP (ART THE)
            (N MAYOR)
            (NU SG))
         (PP (PREP TO)
             (NP (ART THE)
                 (N POSITION)
                 (NU SG)
                 (PP (PREP OF)
                     (NP (N DOG-CATCHER)
                         (NU SG))))))).
```

This structure is returned to the configuration we were in at the time of the PUSH from state VP/TO, and the remaining actions on that arc place the structure in the OBJ register. Since there are no more words in the input string, the PUSH PP/ and WRD BY arcs cannot be taken, so the POP arc creates the following structure to return as the value of the successful parse:

```
(S DCL
   (NP (ART THE)
       (N MAYOR)
       (NU SG))
   (TNS PAST PERFECT)
   (AUX (MODAL WILL)
        NEG)
   (VP (V WANT)
       (S COMP
          (NP (PRO SOMEONE))
          (TNS PAST)
          (VP (V ELECT)
              (NP (ART THE)
                  (N MAYOR)
                  (NU SG))
              (PP (PREP TO)
                   (NP ...))))))
```

which in tree form is:

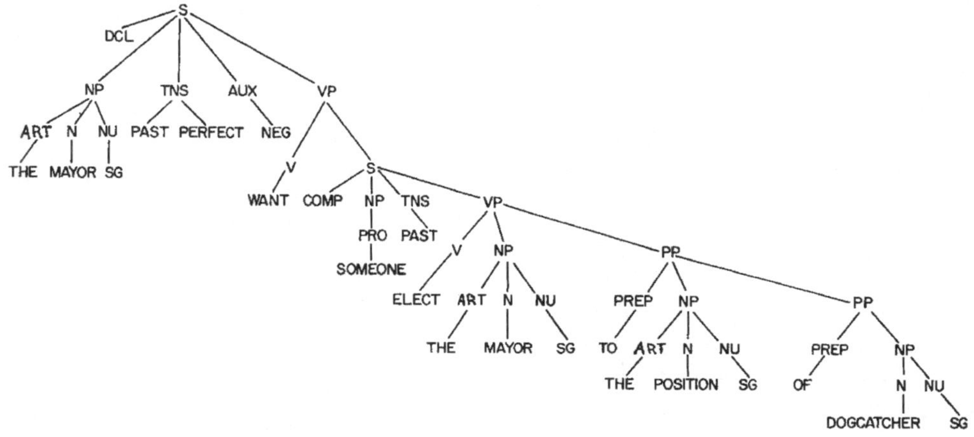

In this discussion we have been viewing the parsing process as a top down, non-deterministic process where, at any state, any arc whose label and test are satisfied may be taken. Of course, for purposes of illustration, the correct choice was made at every state. The next section will discuss other parsing algorithms which may be used with ATN grammars.

A few comments are in order about the inadequacies of the sample grammar just presented. For passive sentences, there is no check that the NP picked up in a by-phrase can really be the deep structure subject. This is not a check which can be made strictly on syntactic grounds. (Consider, for example, "Caesar was killed by Brutus" and

"They will be married by the time the clock strikes ten.") If a semantic check were made on the head of the NP to see whether it could be the subject of the verb, the incorrect parsing could be ruled out. Similarly, the dummy subject should be "something," not "someone" in cases like "The mountains were worn down (by the wind)." Again, a call to a function outside the parser could determine which form to use.

The complement structure in this grammar is also limited to the simplest cases. Some verbs should cause their subject rather than their object to be sent down:

John told his friend to leave. (obj)
John promised his friend to leave. (subj)

This feature, if noted in the dictionary, may be tested on the WRD TO arc in VP/OBJ to determine which NP to send down. This grammar will also accept various badly formed sentences, for example, "The house has have painted." Additional tests could be added to screen out these ill-formed strings, but only at the cost of complicating the grammar more than is desired for this introduction.

To show how large, and yet understandable, ATN grammars can grow, Figure 9 shows a diagram of the grammar which was used for the LUNAR question answering system [Woods et al, 1972]. This grammar can handle some forms of anaphoric reference, some ellipsis, several types of complements, reduced and unreduced relative clauses, parenthetical expressions, comparatives, passives, and a number of other syntactic constructions.

ATN grammars large enough to be really useful are too large to be included in a paper such as this. Readers who are interested in seeing complete listings of large ATN grammars should consult other references. The final report of the LUNAR question answering system [Woods et al, 1972] contains a listing of the grammar shown in Figure 9 together with descriptions of many of the functions used in tests and actions on the arcs. Leal [Leal, 1975] gives a grammar based on tagmemic theory that is written in a semi-LISP notation which is particularly easy for non-LISP-users to follow. Bates gives a listing of the large syntactic grammar used in the BBN speech understanding system in [Bates, 1975] and diagrams of a portion of the semantic grammar for the same system in [Woods et al., 1976]. Anyone who knows

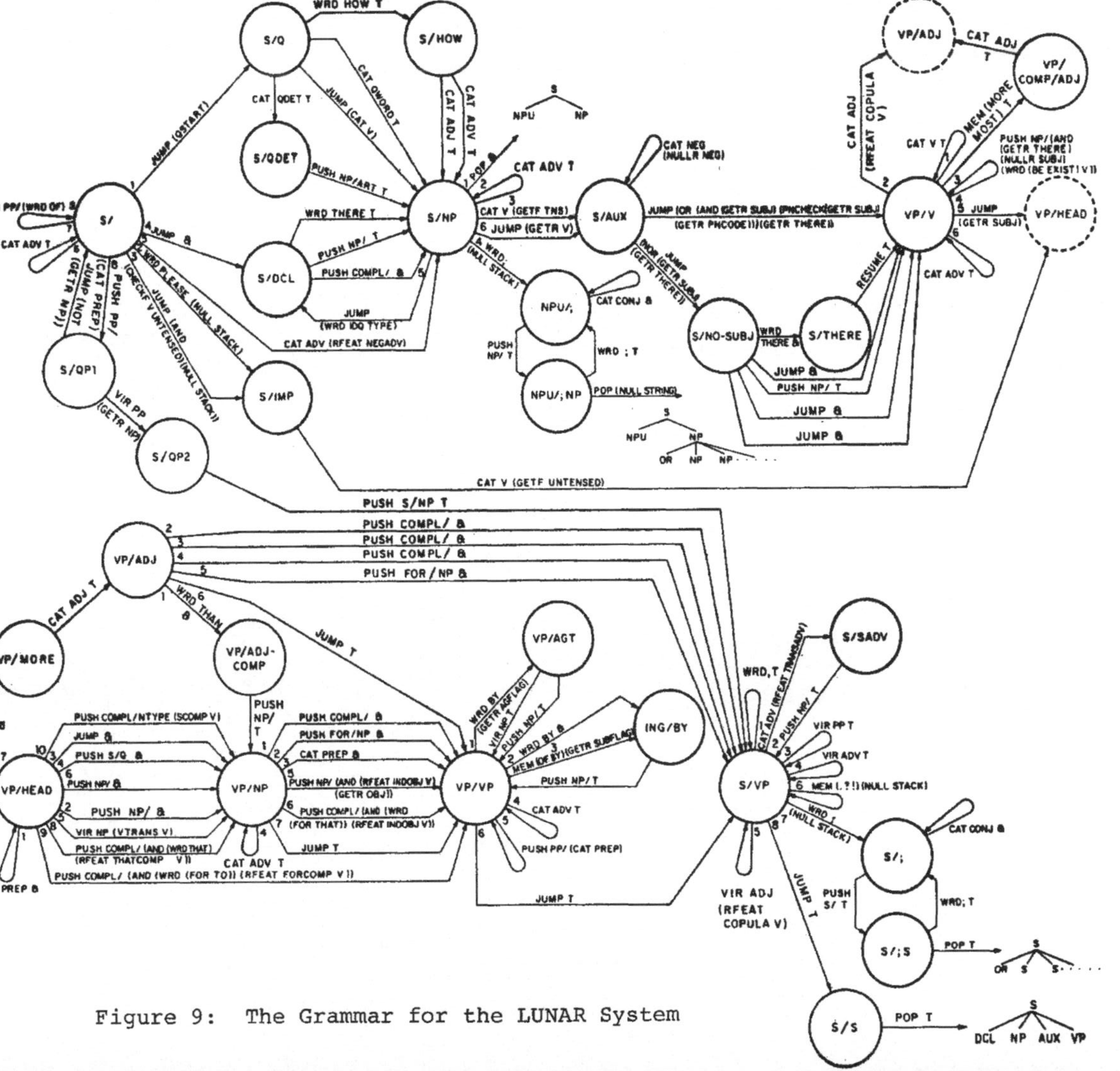

Figure 9: The Grammar for the LUNAR System

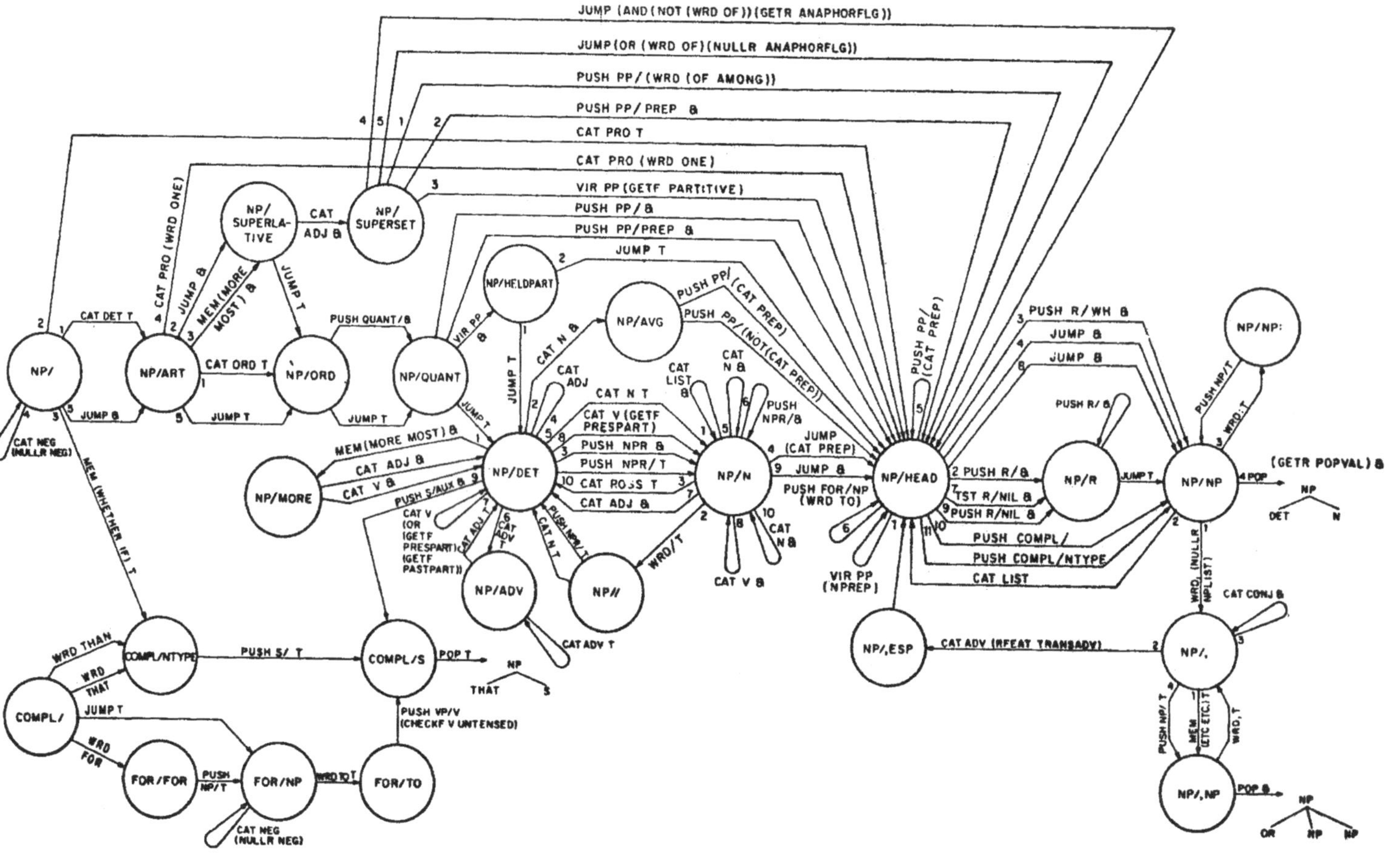

Figure 9 (con't): The Grammar for the LUNAR System

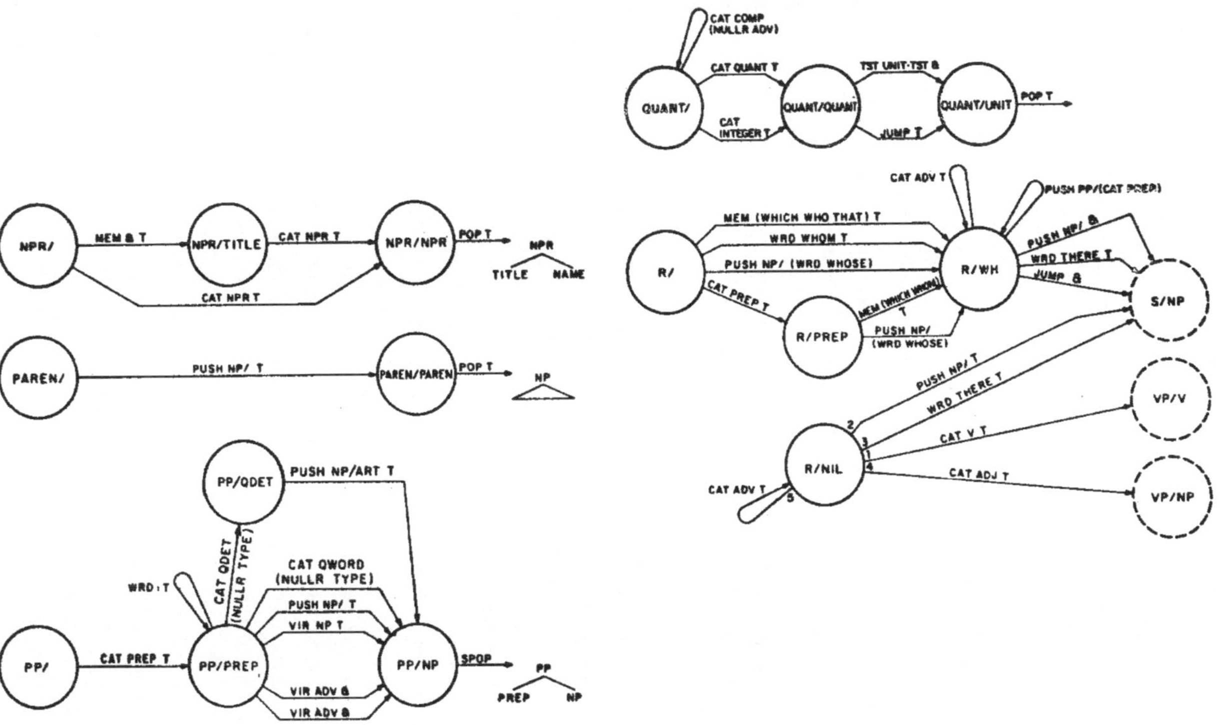

Figure 9 (con't): The Grammar for the LUNAR System

Lamnsok (a Benue-Congo language spoken in part of the United Republic of Cameroun) will be interested in the verb cluster grammar given in [Grebe, 1975]. Grimes [Grimes, 1975] gives an ATN diagram followed by two sets of arcs and actions: one produces tagmemic structures and the other regular parse trees.

2b. Formal Properties of ATNs

It can be shown that the ATN formalism described above is equivalent in power to a Turing Machine. However, so are many unwieldy and inefficient formal systems. It has also been shown [Woods, 1969] that it is possible to eliminate direct left and right recursion and to optimize an ATN network using finite state optimization techniques.

Earley's algorithm for context free recognition [Earley, 1970] follows all alternatives in parallel, using a particularly clever method of merging parse paths. It can parse strings in an amount of time bounded by Kn↑3 where n is the length of the input string and K is a constant of proportionality which is dependent on the grammar (but not on the input); for linear grammars the recognition time is bounded by n↑2, and for LR(k) grammars the bound is n.

There are two interesting things to note about Earley's algorithm. First, it works for context free grammars in any form (not in just a normalized form) and it automatically achieves the smaller bounds for the linear or LR(k) grammars (without having to be told that the grammar is so restricted). Second, an ATN grammar can be recognized by a modification of Earley's algorithm which maintains the time bounds. That is, removing recursion from an ATN causes the upper time bound to be reduced from n↑3 to n↑2 or even to n. Simple finite state optimization may be used to reduce the constant of proportionality in the n↑3 case.

2c. Modifications to the Grammar Formalism

For particular applications, changes may easily be made in the grammar formalism (necessitating corresponding changes in the parser).

The following changes have been incorporated in various ATN grammars.

1. Weights on arcs. A number can be placed on every arc, just after the test, to indicate either how likely the arc is to be taken from that state or how much information is likely to be gained from taking the arc. The parser can use this information to score alternative paths in order to pursue the best ones first. A variation of this would be to have an action on the arc which calculates (using all context available) a score for the parser to incorporate in its paths.

2. Actions on POP arcs. Such actions could be used to lift register contents to the next level or to ready registers for building the final structure.
If actions are not permitted here, they may have to be duplicated on each arc entering the final state.

3. Factorization of tests. For the BBN speech parser [Bates, 1975b, 1976] each arc test was split into two tests; one was context free (testing only features of the current word) and the other was context-sensitive (involving register contents).

4. Grouping of arcs. The Burton grammar-compiler (see below) allows a subset of the arcs from any state to be grouped in a list which means that whenever one arc from that set is taken the others will necessarily fail, so they do not have to be examined even if the parse should back up over the arc which was originally taken. For example, a set of mutually exclusive WRD arcs should be so grouped. This is purely an efficiency measure.

5. New actions. Because of the EVAL feature of LISP, any LISP form can be used as an action on an arc. If this feature is not available, a fixed set of actions must be known to the interpreter, but the designer of the parser/grammar combination still has the freedom to specify actions particular to his domain before implementation. If the parser is to be interfaced with another program, say a semantic interpretation routine, it is convenient to be able to call that program by an action on an arc. In that way the results of the interpretation (or whatever) may be used to guide the further parsing.

3. PARSERS FOR ATN GRAMMARS

Because an ATN grammar is separate from its parser, a number of different parsing algorithms can be used, just as there exist top down, bottom up, table driven, and other types of parsers for context-free grammars. In fact, almost any classical context free parsing algorithms could be adapted to ATNs by providing a mechanism to carry along register contents and to perform the tests and actions on arcs of the grammar. Parsers can be tailored for speed, debugging aids, or special requirements of the application for which they will be used.

Although all the parsers described below have been implemented in LISP, there is no reason why one could not be written in a high level language such as PL/1, ALGOL, PASCAL, or BCPL, or even in an assembler language. The language should be recursive or at least able to simulate recursion, and the ability to evaluate a portion of the grammar as if it were a part of a program is a very desirable, though not absolutely necessary, feature.

3a. ATN Interpreters

The first parsers which were written for ATNs (and the easiest to reproduce) act like interpreters for the grammar-language, using the input string and dictionary as data. The simplest ATN parser to build is a top down, depth first interpreter of the grammar similar to a parser for a context free grammar. In this model the arcs from each state are tried in the order in which they are written. This allows the grammar writer to deliberately order the arcs so that the most likely ones come first and thus gain control over the order in which alternative paths are tried. Such a parser may be written using less than 5000 LISP cells.

The original ATN parser [Woods, 1970. 1973] is more versatile than the parser just described. It is based on a list of alternatives, each of which contains all the information necessary to restart the parser at the point at which the alternative was created. This implies that alternatives can be done in any order, not just depth first. An alternative consists of the current input string, the current state of the grammar, the arcs remaining to be tried at that state, the register list, and the stack. If the HOLD list is used, it must be remembered as part of an alternative too, and it is often useful to remember the path of arcs which have been taken at the current level. Alternatives may be created at several different times during the parsing process. The most common one remembers the arcs remaining to be tried after one arc from the state is followed. Resuming this alternative "backs up" to that state and looks for another arc to try. Another type of alternative may be created when there is ambiguity about the part of speech of a word. Another is created (by a function called LEXIC) when there is ambiguity about the next word of input. (This happens in cases where there are compound words like "common market" which possibly should be collapsed.

One may think of the parsing process as one of moving from one configuration to another, where a configuration is a snapshot of the current state of the parse (i.e., the current input state, stack and register list). When processing one word of input the parser may follow just one path or may try to follow several in parallel. The process of creating a path is exactly the process of creating one or more configurations from a given configuration. To make this a little more concrete, let us look at the main functions of the parser for the LUNAR system.

The function PARSER is called with the input string as its argument. It sets up an initial configuration (initial state, empty register list and stack). It calls the function LEXIC to perform lexical analysis of the string to determine the next word. This may involve expanding contractions, compressing compound words, making substitutions according to dictionary information, etc. Then PARSER calls STEP to compute a new set of configurations from each currently active configuration.

STEP, which may be given either a configuration or an alternative (usually as a result of backup), uses its argument to restore the state of the parse and attempts to follow an arc, thus creating a new configuration. If no more arcs may be taken from the current state, STEP returns NIL. The functions PARSER, LEXIC, and STEP are shown in flowchart form in Figure 10. (These flowcharts are from [Woods et al, 1972]).

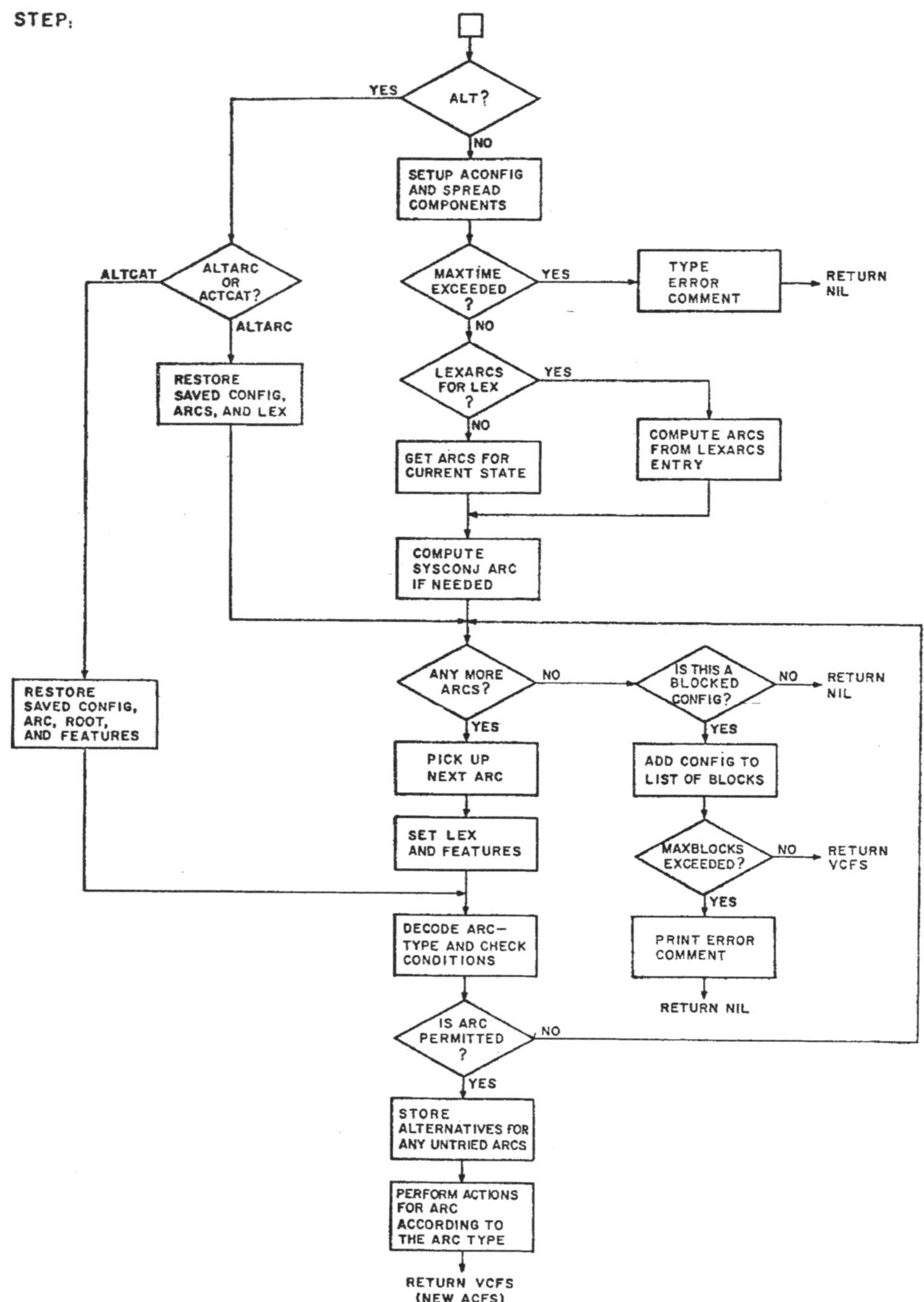

Figure 10c: The Function STEP

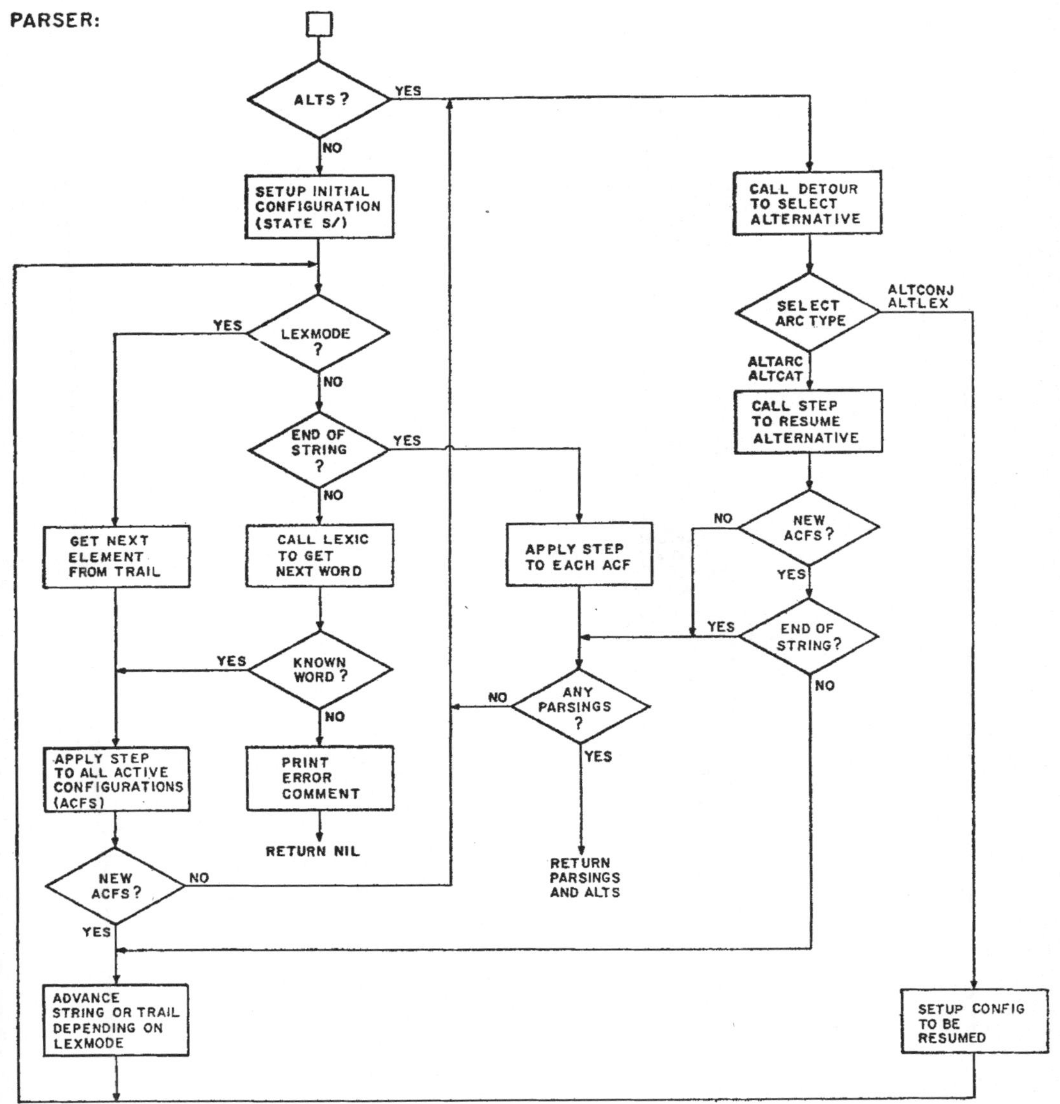

Figure 10a: The Function PARSER

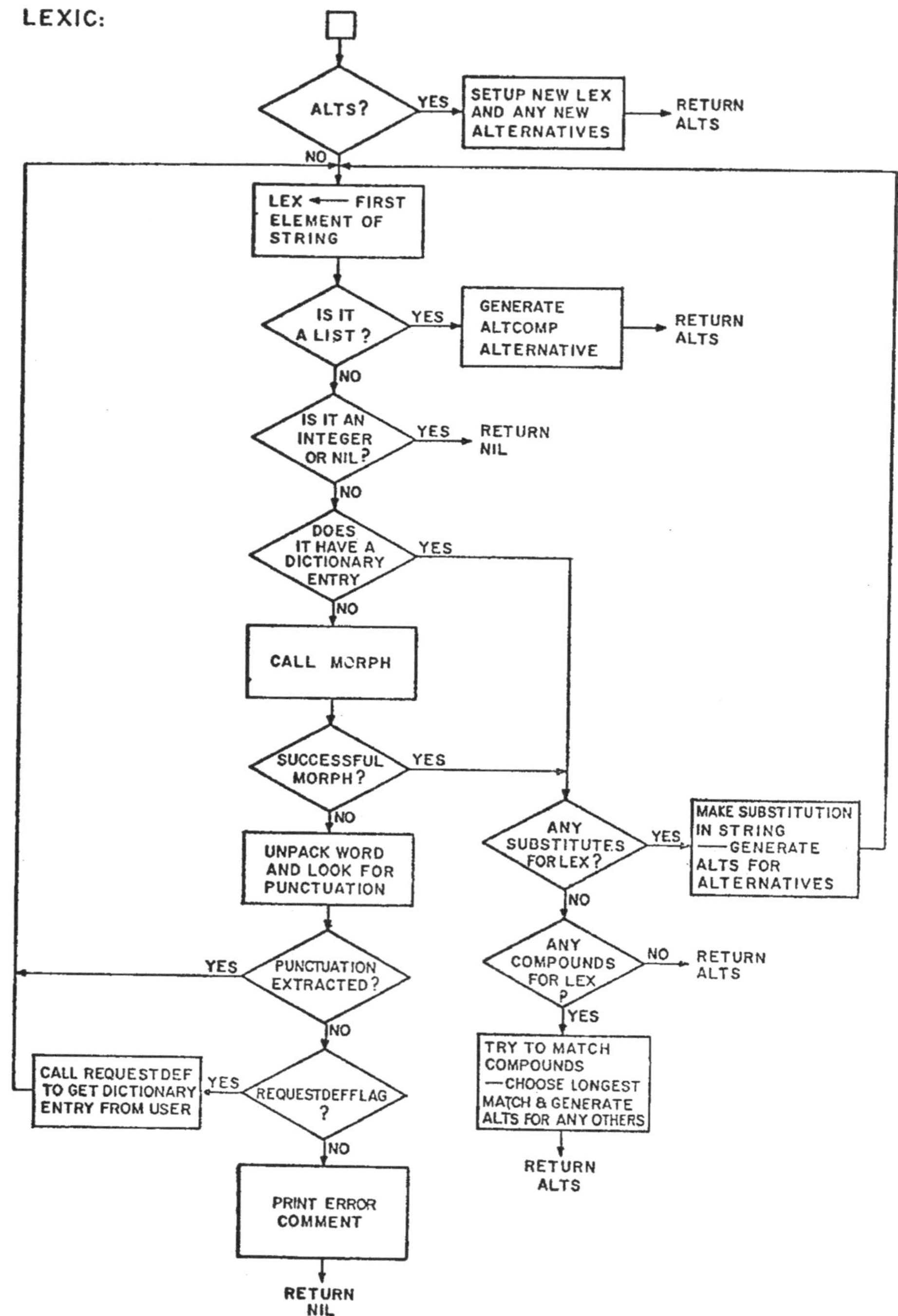

Figure 10b: The Function LEXIC

When PARSER runs out of active configurations which can be STEPed, a function called DETOUR is used to select the next alternative to be tried. If nothing special has been done to give the alternatives special weights, DETOUR will pickup alternatives in the usual backup order.

This parser has the advantage of allowing actions on the arcs to influence the order in which alternatives are chosen. This means that it is not necessary to completely exhaust the search space by following all possible parse paths; by careful ordering of the alternatives, the most likely parsing can be found first, leaving the others to be found later if necessary. Because many sentences and many partial sentences are ambiguous, any natural alnguage parser must be able to cope with alternatives. The ability to order them, together with the alternatives implicit in the factoring and merging of the grammar, help to reduce the number of alternatives which must be considered during a parse.

This parser has also proved to be a flexible testbed for modifications and special features (for examples, see the sections on conjunction and selective modifier placement below.) This parser (compiled in LISP) using the grammar of Figure 9 could parse 8 word sentences in about 2 seconds of cpu time on a PDP-10.

Several important efficiency issues for both parsers should be mentioned. The first is the problem of storing register contents in a space-conserving yet easily accessible manner. Although only a few registers are likely to be used on any one arc, the total number of registers used in the grammar may be quite large. A representation which fixes this number or which requires large numbers of unchanged registers to be copied would be wasteful of both space and time. This problem can be solved by representing a register list as a list of name/value pairs. The function GETR searches the list from front to back for the first occurrence of the named register and returns the associated value. SETR does not change the name/value pair in the current list but instead adds to the front a new name/value pair. This new pair will effectively hide from GETR any old pair with the same name. Thus to preserve the entire register list at a particular point, only a pointer to the current front of the list need be remembered. Other processes can add new information to the list and remember only their new front pointer. Thus the register lists resemble a tree structure with much information on commonly shared branches; any one process is only able to see its unique path from leaf to root. This makes setting a register much faster than accessing one, but registers are generally set more often than they are retrieved for structure building.

Another way to speed up the parsing process, particularly in cases where a lot of backup is likely to be done, is the use of a well-formed-substring table (WFST). At every POP, the constituent just found together with the portion of input it spans is placed in the WFST. Then whenever a PUSH is encountered, the WFST is checked to see whether a constituent of the desired type has been found at the current place in the input. If so, the constituent may be used directly from the WFST instead of redoing the parsing at the lower level. (The use of the HOLD list complicates the WFST slightly, since a constituent can be taken from it only if the current HOLD list matches the one which was current when the constituent was originally parsed. A similar situation holds for the use of SENDRs.)

3b. Inside-Out Parsers

Two parsers have been developed for an experimental speech understanding system which are quite different from the preceding parsers. They illustrate the extraordinary flexibility of ATNs with respect to the environment where they are applied.

Current and all forseeable acoustic processors cannot uniquely identify all words in an acoustic signal. This is due to problems with homonyms (bear, bare), disputable word boundaries (tea meeting, team meeting, team eating), phonological effects (why choose, white shoes), incomplete pronunciation of most function words in context (of, have, a, the), low energy at the beginning and end of an utterance, and errors induced by the acoustic analysis and word matching process. Thus it is not necessarily the case that a speech understanding system should attempt to process an utterance left to right; it may be better to begin in the middle with a reliably identified long content word and work from the inside of the sentence out to the ends. In this way, the grammar can also provide predictions about what can be adjacent to a portion of the sentence already processed, and these expectations can be used by the rest of the system in its analysis of subsequent (or previous) portions of the utterance.

With these constraints in mind, a parser was developed [Bates, 1975a and b, 1976] which could start parsing anywhere in the input stream and could parse despite the lack of certainty as to the exact nature of the words at each point in the input. As partial parse paths were built up, their pieces were stored in tables so that any other parse that could use them did not need to reparse common sections of input. (This is like a WFST for partial paths rather than complete constituents.) Using the grammar, the parser could make predictions about the words of lexical classes that could be used to extend a sequence of words either to the right or to the left. If a gap between words was small enough to contain just one word, the parser could predict just the class or classes of words to fill the gap. The control structure of the parser could be modified fairly easily to allow experimentation with various combinations of backup, sequential, and parallel search. It used a combination of depth-first and breadth-first techniques, usually following a single path but splitting into parallel paths when desirable. Care was taken to allow the parser to interact frequently and easily with other components of the system (notably semantics) in order to receive guidance and to verify completed constituents.

As part of its initialization, the parser set up an index into the grammar so that, for example, all arcs which consume nouns could be easily located. Then, if a noun in the middle of the utterance were presented to the parser, it would retrieve those arcs and set up a partial parse path for each of them. By adding onto these paths as new words were added (and by using the grammar to make predictions to the right and the grammar index to make predictions to the left) the "island" of words could be grown until it spanned the entire utterance. Careful use of a well-formed-substring table and the maintenance of numerous alternate possible partial paths allowed a very general middle-out parsing algorithm.

A second, faster, more efficient parser was later built for the same system [Woods et al, 1976]. It too was designed for an island driven strategy. It did less interpretation of the grammar while parsing than the previous system because it pre-processed the grammar to obtain a set of useful relations between states. (For example, the relation (S1 J S2) holds if there is a path made up exclusively of JUMP arcs from state S1 to S2.) The pre-processor created arrays which described the grammar in a bi-directional way rather than the in the inherently left-to-right way it is written. The sets of relations were used by the parser in a way similar to the L set in Earley's algorithm for context free grammars [Earley, 1970] and a technique similar to Earley's for eliminating the stack and performing indirect PUSHes was used.

This parser had the advantage of being able to follow efficiently all possible partial paths in parallel, thus eliminating the need to try to calculate which paths were most likely to be correct. It could also do more context sensitive checking and register setting, thus allowing very good predictions to be made at the ends of islands. These predictions could also be tightened as more information was added to the utterance.

The only accommodation that the grammar writer needed to make to this system was to mark actions which used register contents with the state or states where the original setting could have taken place. (These "scope" declarations were used to determine when sufficient context is present to perform a test or to do an action.) This was a small price to pay for the speed and accuracy of the parser's predictions.

3c. A Grammar-Compiler

A system has been written by R. Burton [Burton, 1976; Burton and Woods, 1976] which produces an extremely fast ATN parser by a two step process. In the first phase, an interpreter converts (compiles) the ATN grammar into a single LISP function. The second phase is to compile this function, thus producing a compiled program which is the parser/grammar combination. This process is schematically illustrated in Figure 11. The operation of the resulting program is shown in Figure 12. (Both figures are from [Burton, 1976].)

The LISP function which is produced by the first phase is a PROG in which the state names of the grammar become labels and the tests and actions are the "statements". The function looks like this:

```
(LAMBDA (ACF)
   (PROG (special variables like STATE, STACK, REGS, HOLD,  , LEX)
     SPREAD-ACF  (code to set up current configuration)
```

```
              (GO EVAL-ARC)
    NEXTLEX   (if (another word?) then (advance input)
                                       (GO EVAL-ARC))
    DETOUR    (if (another alternative?) then (ACF-alt)
                                              (GO SPREAD-ACF)
                                         else (RETURN failure))
    EVAL-ARC  (BRANCH STATE arclabel1 arclabel2 ... arclabeln)
    arclabel1 (code for arc)
    arclabel2 (code for arc)
    ...
    arclabeln (code for arc))).
```

The arc code for JUMP, WRD, CAT, and VIR arcs generally looks like:

```
  (if (arctype and test satisfied?)
      then (create alternative for remaining arcs)
           (do actions)
           (DOTO nextstate)
           (GO nextstate-arclabel1))
```

The function DOTO changes the state and advances the input. If the arctype or test is not satisfied, the function "falls through" to the next arclabel, which is the following arc. The arc code for the last arc of a state must have a "else (GO DETOUR)" clause.

PUSH arcs generate arc code to recursively invoke the grammar:

```
  label  (if (test satisfied?)
             then (create alternatives for remaining arcs)
                  (DOPUSH pushstate remaining-actions-label)
                  (GO pushstate))

  remaining-actions-label
         (do actions on PUSH arc)
         (DOPTO nextstate)
         (GO nextstate-1starclabel)
```

The function DOPUSH saves the current configuration (with the remaining-actions-label as the current state) on the stack and does any pre-actions to initialize registers. The lower level is started

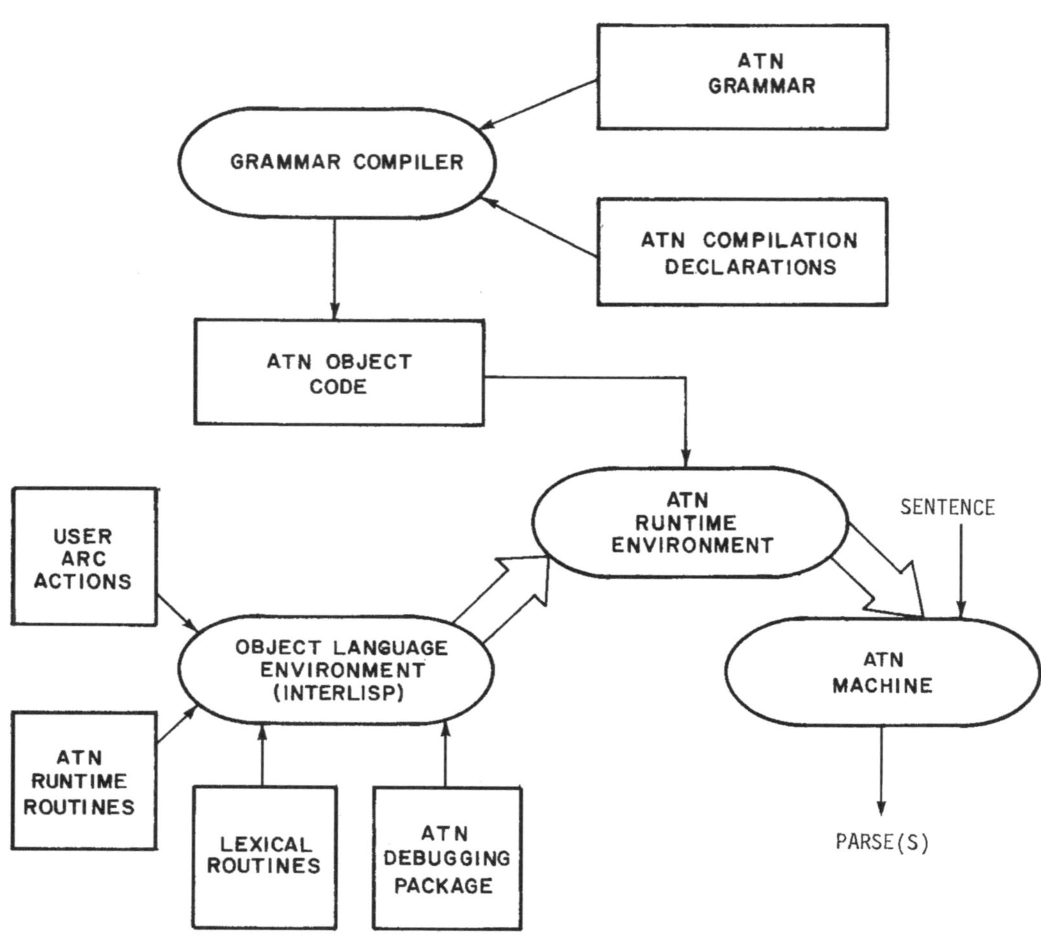

Figure 11: The Operation of a Grammar-Compiler

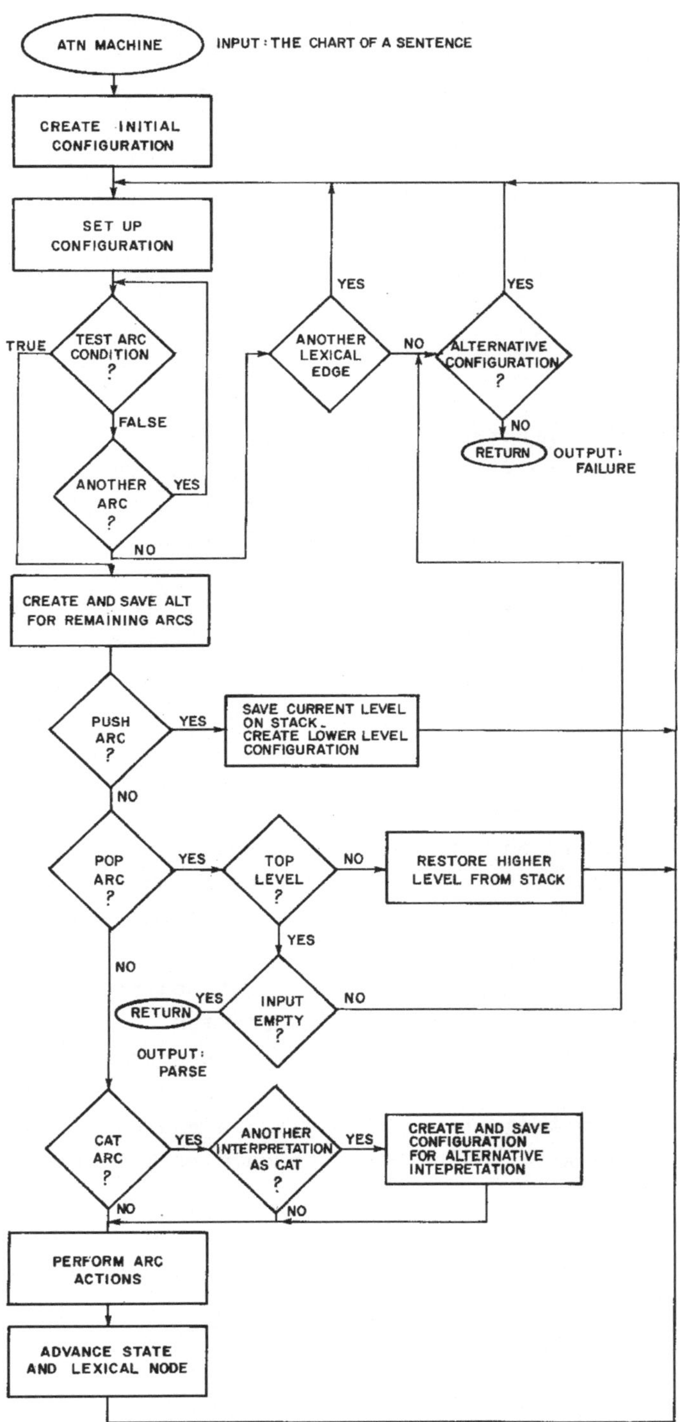

Figure 12: The Operation of an ATN Parser

by the GO to the arc label of the state. When and if the lower level finishes, control will transfer to remaining-actions-label where the actions are performed, the state (but not the input) changed by DOPTO, and the next state is begun.

POP arcs produce code like:

```
(if (test satisfied?)
    then (create alternative for remaining arcs)
         (DOPOP form)
         (GO EVAL-ARC))
```

DOPOP builds the structure to be returned, restores the higher level by getting information from the configuration on the top of the stack, and sets to the value of form. The branch at EVAL-ARC activates the state which was saved (remaining-actions-label).

This "parser" executes very much faster than the previously described methods, about 10 times faster than the compiled version of the LUNAR parser with the same grammar, parsing 8-12 word sentences in about 150 milliseconds.

For production programs where speed is essential, this method is extremely good. The compiler can check, for example, whether the test on an arc is T and if so it can omit the generation of code to evaluate the test; this sort of checking eliminates much inefficiency. The compiler allows unused features of the ATN formalism (recursion, WFST, alternate lexical interpretations, etc.) to be removed, thus improving the efficiency even more. It has the disadvantage that whenever a change is to be made to the grammar both phases of the compiler must be redone -- a time consuming process, especially if the grammar is large. There are also few tracing or debugging aids in the final version. A method similar to this one could be used to write an ATN system in a language which does not have an EVAL function.

4. VARIOUS TYPES OF ATN GRAMMARS

In this section we explore some of the tradeoffs and decisions which must be made by someone who wants to write an ATN grammar for a particular purpose. As was noted earlier, there is no one grammar or style of grammar which suits every purpose. The linguist who is interested in testing a theory of language will write a very different grammar from a systems programmer who needs a small, fast natural language front end for a programming system, and both of those will differ from a grammar written for instructional purposes. Here are some of the issues involved.

4a. Parsing vs. Generation

Computational linguists and those who want to build a "natural language front end" for a system tend to think of a grammar as something which will be used exclusively for analysis, i.e. parsing. However there are many cases where it is useful to generate English text, as in some question answering systems and computer assisted instruction programs. It is not at all clear whether the same grammar can or should suffice for both analysis and generation, but because an ATN grammar is written separately from its parser, it can be thought of as a form which is independent of analysis or production.

A generator (rather than a parser) may be written which takes an ATN grammar and a dictionary as data and produces sentences. Beginning with the initial state of the grammar, the generator can randomly select an arc from that state to be followed. The following of PUSH, POP, VIR, and JUMP arcs would be nearly the same as in a parser, but WRD and CAT arcs would try to select a word from the dictionary which satisfies the conditions on the arc.

Of course, the method just outlined will produce random sentences since it is in no way guided by intentions or concepts. It may be useful, however, to test grammars which are supposed to be "tight" in the sense of being able to identify and reject incorrect input. Such a generator was written to help debug the ATN grammar for the BBN speech understanding system and was very helpful in the discovery of sentences which would (erroneously) have been accepted by the grammar.

One generation scheme [Simmons, 1973; Simmons and Slocum, 1972] has been proposed which is driven by a semantic network and a grammar very similar to a BTN grammar. A similar but more general system [Shapiro, 1975] uses an ATN grammar whose input is a node of a semantic network and whose output is a linear string, a sentence describing the node.

If a grammar is to be written exclusively for parsing, one can usually make the assumption that the input will be correct according to the common rules of English syntax. (This may not always be the case, for example, in a computer assisted instruction system which is supposed to check and correct input from students or in a system which is expected to parse a naturally spoken dialog or transcript of such a dialog as opposed to written text.) If one can make the assumption of correct input then in many places the grammar can be simplified by allowing it to accept incorrect input which it will not encounter in practice. A grammar which is written to generate English must contain a great many checks to eliminate incorrect combinations. A grammar which is designed to help choose among many conflicting possible inputs must make extensive tests to screen out the incorrect input.

4b. Competence vs. Performance

Linguists have long made a distinction between language as people actually use it (performance) and language as one may ideally abstract it (competence). As an example, it is in the realm of competence that one knows that a reduced relative clause may be used in a noun phrase, but it is a fact of performance that this embedding is usually performed only once and in the subject position:

The girl the man kissed screamed.
The girl the man the mugger robbed kissed screamed.

Competence tells us that the verb of a sentence must agree in number with the subject and sometimes with the object, yet sentences such as the following are often spoken:

The boys in the band plays at the football game.
That's them!

There is a rule (competence) which says that a particle associated with a verb (as in "call up") may be moved beyond the object of the verb, yet if the object is very long or complex most people would say the sentence is bad.

I called up my neighbor.
I called my neighbor up.
?I called my neighbor in the town where I used to live before financial problems forced me to move to Chicago last month up.

Most systems must deal with some aspects of performance which are outside the formal competence model. For this reason, the term "ungrammatical" becomes ambiguous when referring to the input of a parsing system. A sentence may be conventionally ungrammatical ("A apples falls") but may still be accepted by the grammar, or it may be conventionally correct yet be rejected by the grammar.

4c. Syntactic vs. "Semantic" Grammars

For many particular applications, one can take advantage of key words or classes of words and the small range of likely syntactic constructions by restricting the grammar to accept sequences which are correct not only syntactically but also semantically and pragmatically.

It is possible to use a dictionary which classifies words not (or not only) by their syntactic parts of speech but also by relevant semantic groupings. For example, in a system to parse sentences about people at a zoo, lexical classes such as ANIMAL, PEOPLE, ANIMAL-ADJ, and PEOPLE-ADJ could be used. They would contain words like (bear, goat, lion), (boy, father, woman), (hungry, caged, fierce), and (hungry, naughty, educated, vain) respectively.

Figure 13 shows portions of two different semantic grammars. Of course, a grammar may blend syntactic and semantic categories to any desired extent.

A purely syntactic grammar would be confined to the usual parts of speech and would accept a large number of syntactic constructions which were meaningless ("Colorless green ideas speep furiously"). In a limited domain of discourse where the input can be assumed to be meaningful, a semantic grammar is a very efficient solution to the parsing problem. It is also useful for the generation of meaningful sentences. See [Burton, 1976] for the description of a very efficient system using such a grammar.

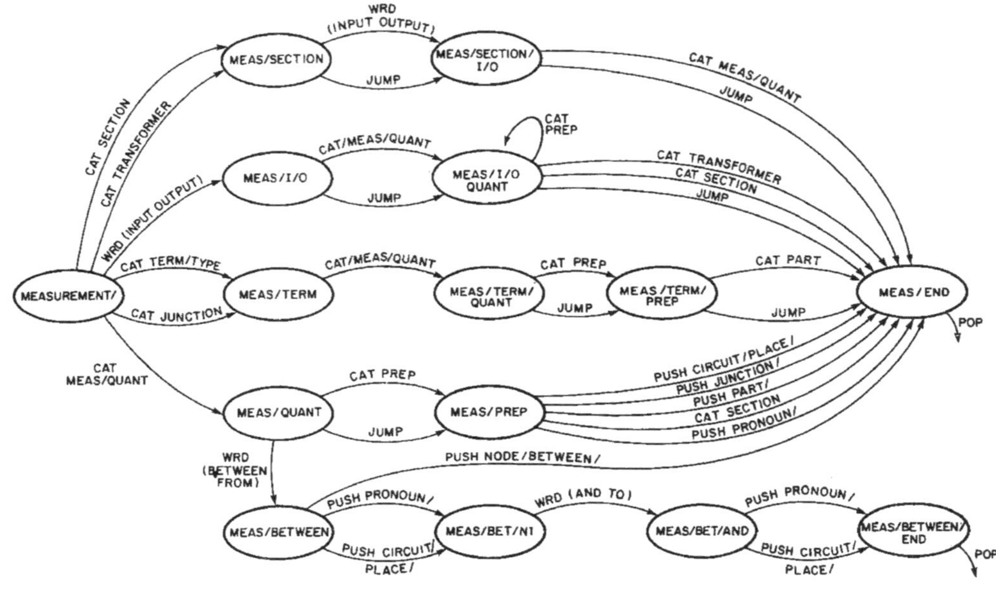

Figure 13a: A Semantic Grammar for Circuit Measurements

Semantic grammars tend to be much larger than syntactic grammars which accept the same set of sentences. The largest ATN grammar this author knows of is one she wrote for the BBN speech understanding system [Bates, 1975]; it contained 448 states, 881 arcs, and 2280 actions but was more limited in the variety of constructions it could accept than a 83 state, 202 arc, 386 action syntactic grammar for the same system. Another drawback to a semantic grammar is that it must be written anew if the domain of discourse is changed, and it would be extremely impractical to attempt to write such a grammar for anything but a limited application area.

4d. Semantics, Pragmatics, and Prosodics

Because syntax, semantics, and pragmatics interact in a very complex way in natural languages, it is desirable to attempt a similar fusion when modeling linguistic processing.

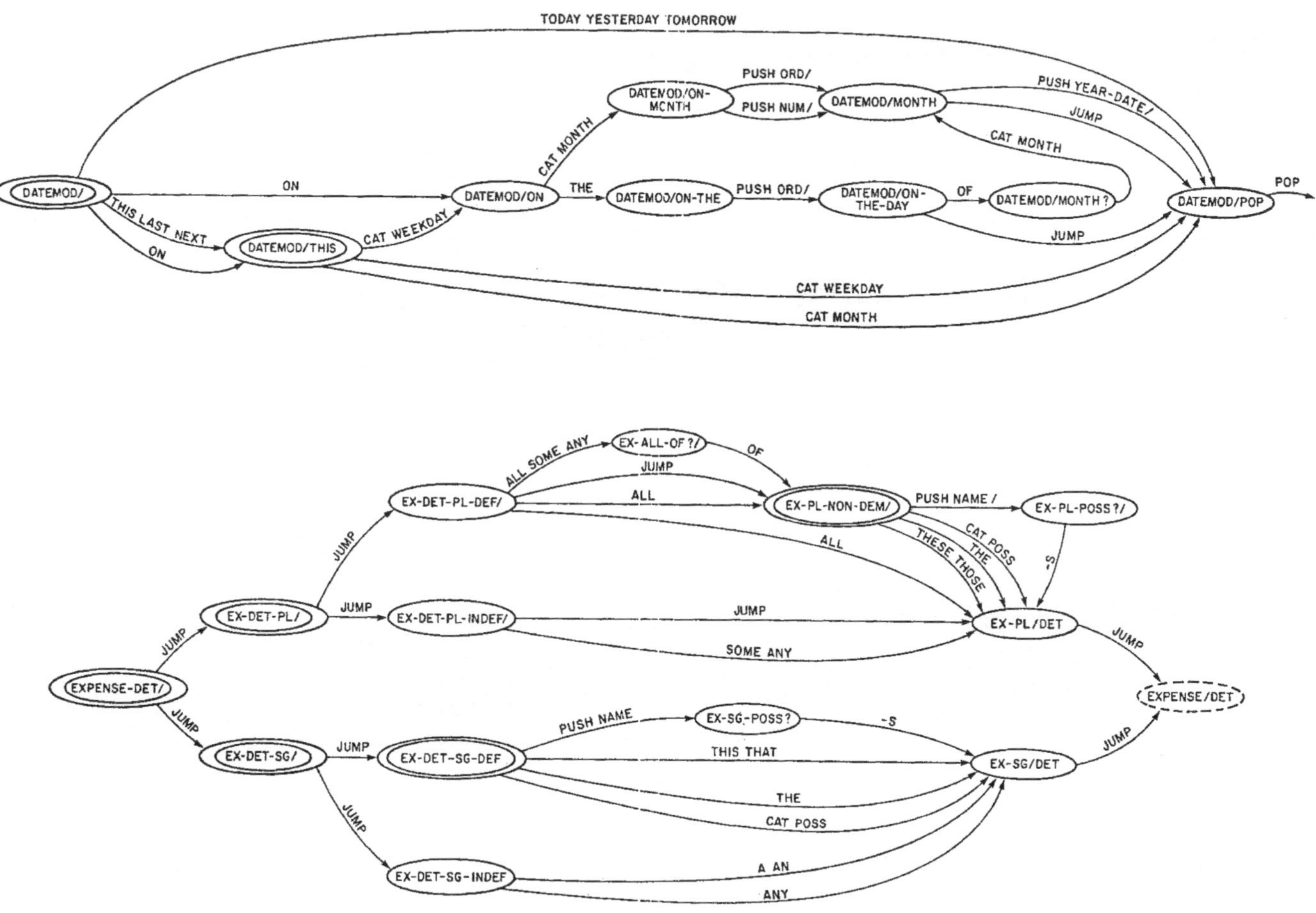

Figure 13b: A Semantic Grammar for Dates and Travel Expenses

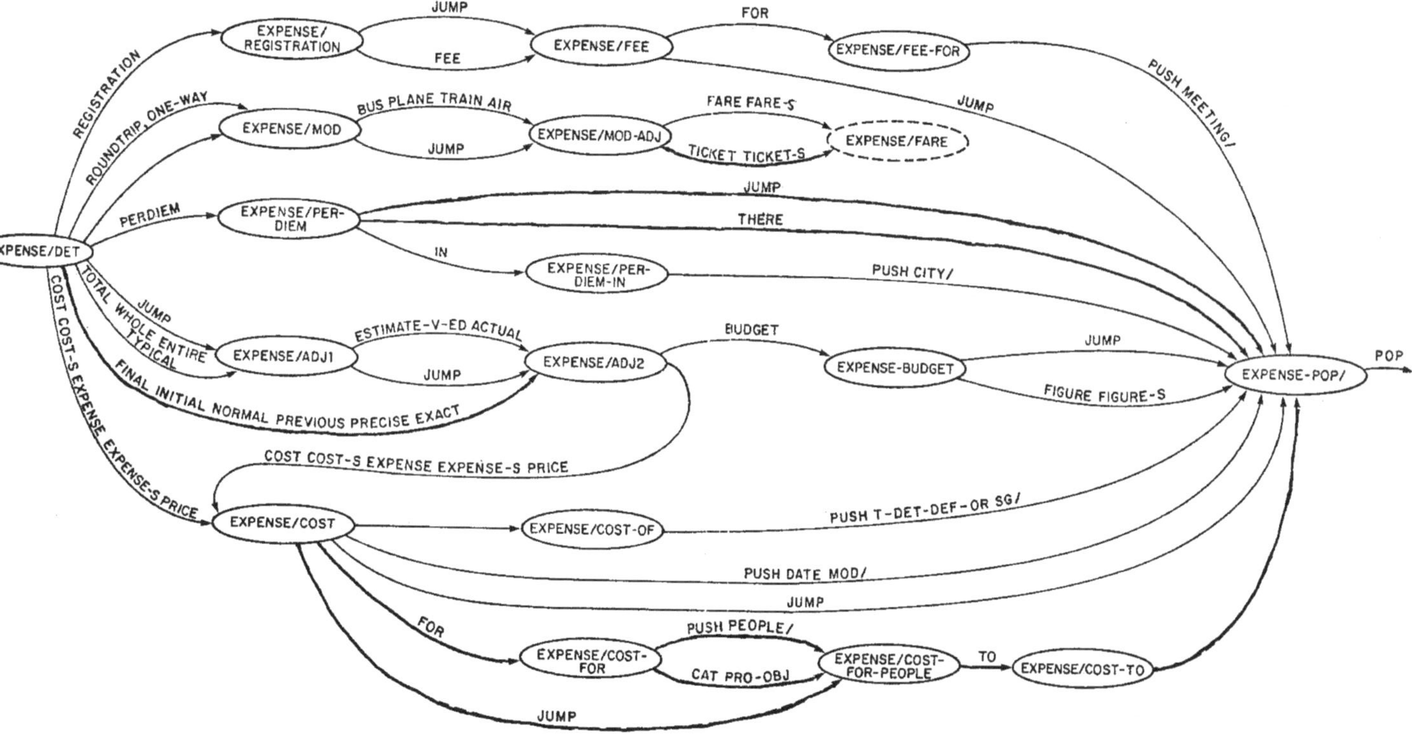

Figure 13b (con't): A Semantic Grammar for Travel Expenses

As was described above, it is possible to place semantic constraints on the grammar by using semantic lexical categories, but this is not the only way to achieve the desired synthesis. Tests and actions on arcs may call semantic routines to check any number of constraints such as the ordering of adjectives within a noun phrase and the agreement between modifiers and the things they modify. The parser may also be modified to call a semantic verification routine to test the completeness or meaningfulness of each constituent as it is produced by a POP arc.

If the parser is structured to allow the order of alternatives to be modified, the semantic functions called on the arcs can be used to effect the modification. Similar functions may be used to detect prosodic features in speech, punctuation in text, and even non-linguistic events (e.g., body actions) in an appropriate environment.

Weischedel [Weischedel, 1976] demonstrates an ATN to compute the presuppositions and entailments of fairly complex sentences. Consider the following sentences:

a. The professor doubted that John managed to translate an assignment.
b. The professor is human.
c. The professor believed that John attempted to translate some assignment.
d. The professor believed that it is not the case that John translated some assignment.

Sentences b and c are presupposed by a, while a entails d. Since presuppositions and entailments are determined by both the meaning of certain words and the syntactic constructs used, it is necessary to have special entries in the lexicon as well as an ATN which can accept the relevant structures.

For systems dealing with speech input, prosodic information is very important. In the BBN speech understanding system [Woods et al, 1976] a special pseudo action called PBDRY was placed on arcs which consumed words before which a prosodic boundary was expected. This function would in effect change the score of the process depending upon whether or not a prosodic boundary was actually detected in the expected location. Prosodic information provides good clues (for humans) about syntactic boundaries, sentence type (for example imperative vs. a yes-no question), pronominal reference, and other things, but very little is currently known about how to automatically detect and use such information.

It is not always necessary to have a tradeoff between the efficiency of a semantic grammar and the compactness and generality of a syntactic one. A system [Bobrow and Bates, 1977] is currently being built which uses a very general syntactic ATN grammar together with a case-oriented dictionary (that also contains semantic interpretation rules). The grammar uses case information to help guide the parsing, and semantic interpretations can be done as soon as a constituent is complete. This grammar is of moderate size (75 states, 153 arcs) but, using Burton's grammar-compiler, has parsed and interpreted 20-word sentences in under one second.

5. LINGUISTIC ISSUES

There are a number of syntactic structures which have been studied in varying degrees of depth by linguists. The current paradigm of linguistic theory, transformational grammar, is not very suitable for either theoretical or applied computational purposes. ATNs provide a model which captures many of the ideas of transformational grammar in a computationally efficient and theoretically interesting way. While it is not necessary for every ATN grammar to account for all the structures which may be used in a natural language, and in fact most grammars written for practical use will have to include ad hoc methods to deal with those which have not been studied linguistically, it is important to khow that many of the generalizations captured by the theory of transformational grammar can be handled smoothly by an ATN grammar. The following are some such issues.

5a. Extraposition

In many English sentences, a constituent may be moved from its deep structure position up and to the left, out of its original subtree to a place in a dominating tree. The following sentences are examples:

This is the cat that I was afraid someone was going to try to steal.
The man in the red shirt is the one who John wanted to speak to.

The problem with this construction is that the constituent when found during parsing cannot just be put in a register to be picked up and used later because the place at which it is likely to be needed is one or more levels down; by the time that the proper place in the input is reached, the constituent is hidden and inaccessible on the stack.

The HOLD action and VIR arcs may be used to handle this problem in an efficient, uncomplicated way. The HOLD action associates a constituent with a name and places this pair on a special list called the HOLD list. The HOLD list is in effect a global variable which is accessible at all lower levels. A VIR arc on the original level or at any lower level may remove a constituent from the HOLD list and use it just as if it had actually occurred at the current position in the input string. To insure that held constituents are used in constructions dominated by the one in which they are found, the parser must be modified so that every POP arc has an implicit test which will make the arc fail if any constituents which were placed on the HOLD list at the current level remain on it.

The HOLD-VIR mechanism is not absolutely necessary to deal with left extraposition. It would be possible to put the extraposed constituent in a register which was then sent down every time a PUSH were done. JUMP arcs could then test for that register and insert the constituent in its proper place. Every POP arc would have to lift an indication of whether or not the constituent had been used. This is a complicated, error-prone procedure which does not have the clairty of the previous mechanism.

Another way to avoid using the HOLD-VIR mechanism is to use in place of VIR arcs JUMP arcs which put an identifiable "dummy node" into the constituent which is being built. A tree with such a dummy node is given in Figure 14. At a higher level (on the PUSH arc on the level where the HOLD action would have been done) a copy of the structure returned from the lower level can be made, substituting the appropriate structure for the dummy node. An advantage of this method over the one just described is that the constituent with the dummy node may be placed in the WFST for use by other paths, which may want to substitute a different structure for the dummy. However, there are numerous disadvantages compared to the HOLD method; an explicit test must be made to avoid returning a constituent with a dummy node from a level where it should have been replaced, much time may be wasted constructing constituents with dummy nodes which cannot be replaced at higher levels, and it is more difficult to do agreement tests between the extraposed portion and the rest of the constituent.

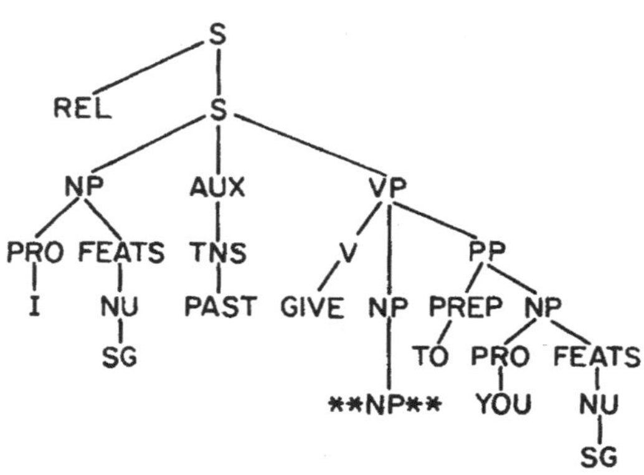

Figure 14: A Relative Clause Tree with a Dummy Node

Extraposition may happen to the right as well as the left. In sentences like

The resort I went to which was on the Mediterranean was pleasant.
How many chickens were there which crossed the road?

a complete constituent is moved out of another constituent (which is still completely well-formed despite the loss) to a position farther to the right and above the original constituent.

To handle this right extraposition, two new actions are used. The action (RESUMETAG <state>) creates a marker combining the current register list with the named state at which parsing could continue at some later time. Then at some later time, if the action (RESUME) is encountered on an arc, the marker is retrieved and the configuration the parser was in when the RESUMETAG was executed is re-established.

The extraposed text can be parsed as usual, and when a POP is done the completed constituent is used as the current input item on the arc containing the RESUME.

5b. Conjunction

Conjunction in English (and many other languages) is a problem for both the theoretical linguist and the applied computational linguist. In its simplest form, two complete constituents are conjoined; at its most complex, numerous constituents can be conjoined in an overlapping manner. The following sentences illustrate the range of complexity.

The quick brown fox and the lazy dog are famous.
Enclose this message with the red, orange and blue packages.
Will you plant the roses or cut the grass?
I groomed and brushed my cat.
The easy homework and exams made the course hard to fail.
She often fought with, later married, and soon divorced the boy next door.

If only complete constituents could be conjoined (either by a single conjunction, a list with commas having the conjunction before the last conjunct, or a list with the conjunction between all conjuncts) then any type of constituent X could be made conjoinable by having a new level of the grammar called XLIST. XLIST/ would be PUSHed to by all the arcs which formerly PUSHed to X/. The XLIST/ level would simply PUSH to X/, accumulate the result in a register, and either POP or find a conjunction (or comma). In the latter case control would transfer to XLIST/ to look for the next conjunct. If more general conjunction is allowed, for example, "and," "or," and "not" with different precedence, then a more complex grammar would be required.

However, general conjunction which can violate constituent boundaries cannot be conveniently handled this way. It is possible to add a facility to the ATN parser which provides some insight into the general process. This facility, called SYSCONJ in [Woods, 1973] handles reduced conjunctions and constructs the appropriate unreduced deep structures without requiring any changes to the grammar.

The most general kind of conjunction is the reduced conjunction as seen in "John seldom talked about and tried to forget the war." In this case the conjoined fragments "... seldom talked about" and "tried to forget ..." are not constituents, nor are they similar at either their beginning or their end. There is, however, a great deal of structure to conjunctions of this type. There is a place in the first conjunct (after "seldom") where the parser could begin parsing the second conjunct, and there is a place in the second (after "forget") where the parser is in the same state it was in at the end of the first.

Because of this regularity, the SYSCONJ facility may be built into the parser to intercept a conjunction before the grammar processes it. At this point the parser has available to it the entire history of the parse up to that time in the form of configurations on the path and stack. SYSCONJ selects one of these configurations (how it decides which one can be a deterministic, non-deterministic, or semantically motivated decision) and restarts it using the string following the conjunction. The configuration which the parser was in when the conjunction was encountered is saved. The restarted configuration will allow the parser to proceed until it reaches some portion of the input which is shared with the suspended configuration. Then the paths can be combined and the constituent completed. If the restarted configuration cannot find a point at which the suspended configuration can join it, it is an indication that the original selection of a restart configuration was in error, and another one may be tried.

This method is potentially very combinatorially explosive, but it may be guided by some syntactic heuristics such as restarting just before a word which is identical to or of the same category as the word after the conjunction (e.g., "The dogs in the yard, on the porch, and in the house barked"). Semantic guidance may be useful also, but this has not been investigated in depth. It also will not work for embedded complex structures. Further study and experimentation with this feature are necessary to show the limits of this approach to the problem.

5c. Punctuation and Contraction

Usually punctuation is an aid to parsing because it can be used to delimit the scope of constituents, as in

John, the plumber, fixed it.
He eats fried eggs, over-ripe bananas, and soft custard.

It is useful to have a prepass to scan the input to separate punctuation from the preceding word. Then an arc like WRD , or WRD ; or CAT PUNCT may be put in the grammar.

It is tempting to separate endings like "n't," "'ve," and "'s" and turn them into the separate words "not," "have," and "is" in the prepass, but here the problem is more complex. For example, "'s" can be a contraction for "is" or it can be the possessive morpheme ("Helen's jewelry"), and "n't" can change the form of its predecessor ("won't" -> "will not"). There are also restrictions on where contraction can occur ("Mary's eating and Joe is too," but not "Mary's eating and Joe's too"), so information useful to the grammar may be lost by expanding the contraction out of context. One way to handle the latter problem is to attach a feature CONTRACTED to words which have been so expanded.

5d. Modifier Placement

One of the most common sources of syntactic ambiguity in English is the problem of what head is modified by a modifier. This is particularly true of a series of prepositional phrases, and it also occurs with adverbs. Often, but not always, semantics determines the correct attachment:

I saw the man in the {park / dark suit} with {a telescope. / pigeons.}

Paul borrowed the book that {belonged to / mentions} Jane on Friday.

The orchestra performed the music Walter {wrote / likes} recently.

Woods' parser [Woods, 1973] incorporated a selective modifier placement facility that was invoked by a special type of POP arc called SPOP. When an SPOP arc was encountered, the parser would search the stack for other configurations that could use the constituent about to be SPOPed. For the second sentence shown above, an SPOP arc at the end of the PP/ network would find configurations PUSHing for a prepositional phrase (after "Jane"), for a relative clause (after "book"), and for a noun phrase (after "borrowed"). At the configuration for the most recent PUSH, the SPOP process determines that a POP could have been done instead of the PUSH. Then it finds out that the next higher level (the PUSH for a relative clause) could also PUSH for a prepositional phrase. This means that the configuration PUSHing for a relative clause is a candidate for the prepositional modifier.

Continuing up the stack in the same way, a list of candidate configurations is made. Then semantic information associated with the head of the level represented by the candidates is examined to see which ones may be associated with the semantic head of the modifier. (This semantic information may come from the dictionary or from special-purpose functions.) Checks which may be made include: heads which forbid modifiers of that type ("sincerity on the table") heads which require modifiers of that type to make sense ("consort with criminals"), and heads which may use such a modifier ("see with a telescope"). The chosen configuration is the closest one which needs the modifier most. Alternatives are created for other placements (in case of backup or to ensure the eventual production of the less likely ambiguities), and the prefered one is continued.

6. DEVELOPING AN ATN GRAMMAR

This final section is designed for those who wish to write an ATN grammar. Remember that it is not necessary to have a parser in order to effectively use an ATN grammar. One can learn a lot about the structure of a language (even a restricted subset) by going through the exercise of expressing the language in an ATN form. Careful hand simulation of parses is usually sufficient for testing portions of the grammar.

The first step in writing a grammar is to have a clear idea in mind of the types of sentences one would like to handle. What aspects of competence must be handled? Of performance? Is the grammar going to be used to generate or to parse? Make a list of ten or twenty sample sentences. Then decide on the general type of grammar which is desired, for example, decide on a syntactic grammar which will produce stratificational structures.

Next, sketch an ATN diagram of the most common constructions which you find in your sample sentences. After the surface structure has been drawn, add a few tests and actions. It is a good idea to use carefully chosen state and register names and to record on every arc (as a comment) its purpose together with a sample phrase or two which will use the arc. Like completely commenting a computer program as it is being written, this is almost never actually done, but the closer one can come to this ideal the easier it will be to debug and modify the grammar later.

Look for portions of the diagram which are identical. There are two ways to consolidate these: merging by loops and making a new level to be reached by PUSH arcs. Every grammar writer is eventually faced with the choice of whether to create a new level of the network to PUSH to or to use a longer, more complex set of arcs in the original net.

For inexperienced grammar writers, deciding where to separate a grammar into levels can be a problem. It seems natural to say that a noun phrase is a constituent, but what about a verb phrase? a determiner? an auxilary? a reduced relative clause?

Some linguists have fairly fixed ideas about what constitutes a constituent. To them it is a convenient grouping of words which can be moved as a whole (but not in part unless the part is also a constituent) to another place in the sentence and which obeys certain rules with respect to transformational rules. This definition is not very helpful to writers of ATN grammars for applications, however, except that it does indicate that certain groups of words may appear in several places in a sentence. It is more efficient to have a single level of the grammar to process such units rather than to repeat the arcs and nodes comprising them. Sometimes a PUSH is required by the nature of the structure to be parsed, as in noun phrases which may contain prepositional phrases which must contain noun phrases. In other cases a PUSH may be used merely for convenience when a section of input can be processed relatively independently of any information preceding it.

Now look for parts of the network which are very similar, but not quite identical. Again, there are two alternatives: either merge the nets using registers and tests to keep track of which path is being followed, or make a new level to be reached by PUSHs which use SENDRs to convey the necessary information about the differences. Merging similar networks by using tests is usually desirable since it cleanly and concisely expresses some generalization about the language. If this method is carried to extremes, however, the clarity is lost in the complexity of the tests. One could merge an entire network into one arc with a huge number of conditional tests, but this would not express very much about the language!

The merging of common portions of the network does more than permit a more compact representation; it eliminates the necessity of redundant processing when parsing. When two rules have common parts, by matching (or even attempting to match) the first, one has already performed some of the tests required for the matching of the second. Thus one can take advantage of this information to avoid redoing the work when trying the second rule.

Next, for each of the sample sentences decide on the structure which you want the parser to return. Try to sketch the structure of the major constituents within the sentence. Add more actions to the grammar to produce those structures. When conflicts arise, use a conditional action or use two arcs of the same type but with different tests and actions.

Try to consolidate the network by using self loop arcs with tests to prevent them from being taken more than once. For example, the grammar fragment in Figure 15 may be reduced by one state and one arc if it is represented as it was in Figure 6.

The use of "look-ahead" tests on PUSH arcs is a great time saver, since a lot of work is wasted if a recursive call is set up but fails before it consumes any input.

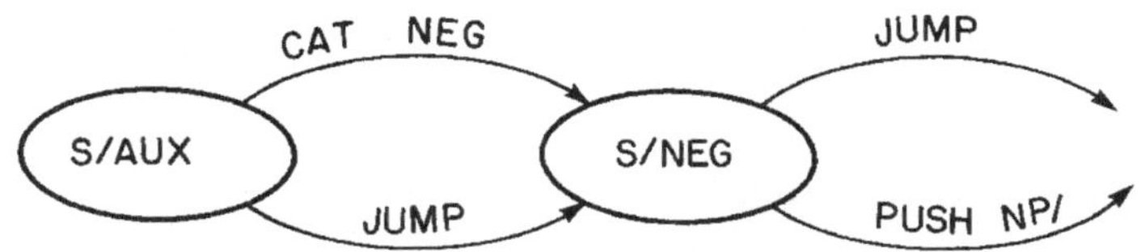

Figure 15: A Grammar Fragment Which May be Reduced

The best way to debug a grammar is to parse a number of sentences and examine the opertion of the parser on those which fail. It is extremely useful to have a tracing facility in the parser which will print out each state entered, each arc taken (not the whole arc, just enough to identify it), each register set, each structure POPed, and each state which blocks.

The trace is useful not only to debug sentences which didn't parse or which parsed and returned the wrong structure, but also to find inefficiencies in the processing of correct sentences. If a sentence parses correctly but requires much backup, there are several things to look for between the point where the parser started down the wrong path and the point where it blocked: Can a test be made at the beginning of the erroneous path that would prevent the arc from being taken? Should the arcs be reordered so that the correct one is taken first? Can the right and wrong paths be merged?

The overriding consideration in a decision among several adequate but different network representations should be the clarity of the method. After all, the ultimate purpose of writing a grammar is to communicate something about the structure of language to other human beings. A grammar writer who always sacrifices clarity for the sake of efficiency will waste extraordinary amounts of time modifying and explaining his work. The programmer's maxim, "Make it work, _then_ make it fast," should be heeded.

One portion of the grammar interacts with many others, so as the grammar gets large it becomes harder to keep track of (or even to discover) the implications of additions or changes. This is where copious commenting of the grammar pays off. It is also a good idea to keep a list of sentences which thoroughly exercise all parts of the grammar. Add to the list whenever new capabilities are added to the grammar and occasionally parse the entire list, just to be sure that what used to parse still does.

As the grammar grows, the dictionary will probably grow at the same time. It is important to keep track of what features the grammar will be testing and how to decide whether a word is to get that feature or not. See Appendix II for a description of the information which may be kept in the dictionary.

The reader who has carefully studied the concepts presented here should now be able to design an ATN grammar and/or parser with which to experiment. It is a rewarding experience to use such a simple yet powerful mechanism. The author would greatly appreciate receiving comments, suggestions, and reports of others' experiences with ATN grammars.

I would like to express appreciation to William A. Woods for his reading of a draft of this paper; the responsibility for errors is my own.

References

Bates, M. "The Use of Syntax in a Speech Understanding System," IEEE Transactions on Speech and Signal Processing, Vol. ASSP-23, No. 1, Feb. 1975, pp. 112-117.

Bates, M. "Syntactic Analysis in a Speech Understanding System," BBN Report No. 3116, Bolt Beranek and Newman Inc., Cambridge, Ma., 1975.

Bates, M. "Syntax in Automatic Speech Understanding," American Journal of Computational Linguistics, Microfiche 45, 1976.

Bobrow, D.G. and Fraser, J.B. "An Augmented State Transition Network Analysis Procedure." Proc. IJCAI, 557-567, 1969.

Bobrow, R. and Bates, M. "The Efficient Integration of Syntactic Processing with Case-Oriented Semantic Interpretation," submitted to the Annual Meeting of the Association for Computational Linguistics, Georgetown University, Washington D.C., March 1977.

Burton, R.R. "Semantic Grammar: An Engineering Technique for Constructing Natural Language Understanding Systems." BBN Report No. 3453, Bolt Beranek and Newman Inc., Cambridge, Ma., December 1976.

Burton, R.R. and Woods, W.A. "A Compiling System for Augmented Transition Networks," presented at the International Conference on Computational Linguistics, Ottawa, Canada, June 1976.

Earley, J. "An Efficient Context-Free Parsing Algorithm." _Communications of the ACM_. 13, 1970, 94-102.

Grebe, K. "Verb Clusters of Lamnsok," in _Network Grammars_, Grimes, J., ed., 1975.

Grimes, J. "Transition Network Grammars: A Guide," in _Network Grammars_, Grimes, J., ed., 1975.

Grimes, J., ed. _Network Grammars_, a publication of the Summer Institute of Linguistics of the University of Oklahoma, 1975.

Leal, W.M. "Transition Network Grammars as a Notation Scheme for Tagmemics," in _Network Grammars_, Grimes, J., ed., 1975.

Rustin, R., ed. _Natural Language Processing_. Algorithmics Press, N.Y., 1973.

Shapiro, Stuart C., "Generation as Parsing from a Network into a Linear String," American Journal of Computational Linguistics, Microfiche 33, 1975.

Simmons, R.F. "Semantic Networks: Their Computation and Use for Understanding English." in _Computer Models of Thought and Language_. Eds. R.C. Schank and K.M. Colby. San Francisco: W.H. Freeman and Company. 1973.

Simmons, R. and Slocum, J. "Generating English Discourse from Semantic Networks," CACM, 15:10 (Oct. 1972) pp. 891-905.

Teitelman, W. INTERLISP Reference Manual. Xerox Palo Alto Research Center, Palo Alto, California, 1974.

Thorne, J.P., Bratley, P., and Dewar, H. "The Syntactic Analysis of English by Machine," in Michie, Machine Intelligence 3, pp. 281-309, 1968.

Weischedel, R.M. "A New Semantic Computation While Parsing: Presupposition and Entailment." Technical Report 76, Department of Information and Computer Science, University of California, Irvine, California, 1976.

Weissman, C. LISP 1.5 Primer, Dickenson Publishing Co, Belmont, Calif., 1967.

Woods, W.A. "Augmented Transition Networks for Natural Language Analysis." Harvard Computation Laboratory Report No. CS-1, Harvard University, Cambridge, Ma., 1969. (Available from the National Technical Information Service 5285 Port Royal Rd., Arlington, Va., 22209, USA, as Microfiche PB-203-527; also available from ERIC, PO Box O, Bethesda, Md., 20014, USA as publication ED-037-733)

Woods, W.A. "Transition Network Grammars for Natural Language Analysis." Communications of the ACM. 13(1970), 591-606.

Woods, W.A. "An Experimental Parsing System for Transition Network Grammars." Natural Language Processing, Randall Rustin, ed., New York: Algorithmics Press, 1973.

Woods, W.A., R.M. Kaplan, and B. Nash-Webber, "The Lunar Sciences Natural Language Information System: Final Report." BBN Report No. 2378, Bolt Beranek and Newman Inc., Cambridge, Ma., 1972. (available from the National Technical Information Service as publication N72-28984)

Woods, W.A. et al, "Speech Understanding Systems, Final Report Vol. IV (Syntax and Semantics)," BBN Report No. 3438, Bolt Beranek and Newman Inc., Cambridge, Ma., 1976.

APPENDIX I

SOME COMMENTS ON LISP

For those readers not familiar with LISP, a brief explanation may be necessary to make the text of the ATN grammar fragments intelligible.

Since programs and data are interchangeable in LISP, we will speak of either of them as "forms." Forms in LISP are either atoms (alphanumeric sequences like NOUN, COND, 23, and MOD4) or lists of forms like (NOUNTYPE ABSTRACT), (NP (N MILK)), and (JUMP X T).

A form which is a function call is written as a list whose first element is the name of the function and whose subsequent elements are the arguments. Thus (EQUAL (LENGTH FOO) 7) is the function call that in some other language might be written as EQUAL(LENGTH(FOO), 7) or as LENGTH(FOO) = 7. In this case FOO must be evaluated before LENGTH is evaluated just as the length of FOO must be calculated before EQUAL can operate. Most functions require their arguments to be evaluated in this way; to pass an argument unevaluated the special function QUOTE is used. Thus the form (LENGTH (QUOTE (FE FI FO FUM))) has the value 4 but (LENGTH (FE FI FO FUM)) assumes that there exists a function named FE which takes three arguments and that FI, FO, and FUM are variables with values.

Some functions have the quality of not evaluating one or more of their arguments (i.e. their arguments are implicitly QUOTEd). Such functions sometimes (but not always) have names ending with the letter Q to remind the user of this property (e.g. SETRQ).

Since all operations in LISP are functions and hence must be called in prefix form, some rather unusual forms result from fairly common operations, for example, conditional expressions. In LISP the form:

```
(COND (p1 e11 e12 e13 .. e1n)
      (p2 e21 e22 .. e2m)
      ...
      (pi ei1 ei2 .. eij)).
```

is equivalent to

```
if p1 then begin e11 e12 ... e1n end
     else if p2 then begin e21 e22 .. e2m end
                else if ...
                        else if pi then begin ei1 ... e1j end.
```

If none of the predicates (p1, p2, ...) are true, then the conditional is simply a no-op. Only one of the expression lists is evaluated, the first one which has a true predicate. The value of the conditional (since it is a function, it has a value) is the value of the last expression e evaluated.

When functions are defined in LISP they are written as Lambda-expressions. This simply means that the defining form is a list which begins with the atom LAMBDA followed by a list of the formal parameters followed by the body of the function. The body is often a PROG form, which is a list beginning with the atom PROG followed by a list of local variables and a sequence of forms to be evaluated. The forms to be evaluated may be prefaced by labels, which are (unevaluated) atoms. Thus the definition of the factorial function in LISP is the following (SETQ is the assignment operator):

```
(LAMBDA (N)
  (PROG  (X)
         (SETQ X 1)
   LOOP  (COND((EQUAL N 1)
                (RETURN X)))
         (SETQ X (TIMES N X))
         (SETQ N (SUBTRACT N 1))
         (GO LOOP)))
```

APPENDIX II

THE DICTIONARY

The dictionary is an important part of any parsing system. It contains information about the lexical categories of words, their features, and perhaps their morphological properties.

Table II shows some of the common syntactic categories of English, and Table III shows a selection of features. Neither of these lists are definitive; many other classification schemes and features may be used.

SYMBOL	MEANING	EXAMPLE
ADJ	adjective	actual, special, nice
ADV	adverb	quickly, again, too
ART/DET	article	a, an, the, this
CONJ	conjunction	and, or, both, either
MODAL	modal	can, could, may, will
N	noun	air, group, stone, year
NEG	negative	not
NPR	proper noun	Jimmy, France, TWA
POSS	possessive	her, my, whose, your
PREP	preposition	by, for, from, in, under
PRO	pronoun	someone, he, it, what, I
QADV	question adverb	when, where, why
QDET	question determiner	what, which, whose
QUANT	quantifier	all, enough, many, much
QWORD	question word	how, what, which, who
V	verb	kiss, want, see, jump

Table II: Typical Syntactic Categories

When the parser asks the dictionary if a particular word is in a particular category (as on a CAT arc or via the function CATCHECK) the answer is not just yes or no. If yes, it is also necessary to return the root form of the word and the set of features which is implied by that morphological form. As examples, the word "tallest" has the root "tall" and the feature SUPERLATIVE; "talks" has the root "talk" and the features (TNS PRESENT), (PNCODE 3SG) when considered as a verb, but as a noun its features are (NUMBER PL).

Feature	Meaning	Sample Words	Sample Sentence
FORCOMP	may take a FOR---TO-- complement	afford,need,plan,want	I'll arrange for him to go.
TOCOMP	may take a TO-- complement	try,begin,continue,need	The boy started to cry.
THATCOMP	may take a THAT--- complement	assume,estimate,show,know	She forgot that the iron was hot.
INDOBJLOW	indirect object may be sent down to lower level	arrange,cost,get	The car cost him $50 to fix.
OBJLOW	direct object may be sent down to lower level	afford,allow,need,send	I planned a trip for John to take.
SUBJLOW	subject may be sent down to lower level	arrange,forget,need	I need to learn to swim.
INDOBJ	may take an indirect object	cost,get,send,show,tell	He gave the dog a bone.
(INDOBJ FOR)	indirect object goes with FOR, not TO	allow,arrange,plan	Find the guests a room.
INTRANS	does not need an object	begin,fly,leave,travel	The snow won't last.
TRANS	may take an object	add,compute,give,know	We finished the work.
PASSIVE	may be passivized	arrange,cancel,do,give	The story was told.
(ROLE OBJ)	may not appear as subject	him,them,us,her	She liked him.
(ROLE SUBJ/OBJ)	may be either subject or object	it,who,you	Who liked it?
(NUMBER SG/PL)	may be singular or plural	deer,you	The deer played.
(PNCODE X13SG)	goes with all except 1st and 3rd person singular	are,were	You are sleepy.
(PNCODE 3SG)	goes with 3rd person singular only	does,goes,is,spends	The child knows a game.

TABLE III: Sample Syntactic Features

A very detailed presentation of the format of the LUNAR dictionary is given in [Woods et al, 1972]. One if its most interesting characteristics was the inclusion of morphological codes with the root forms of regularly inflected words. (Irregular words appeared as separate entries, the root forms of which has a morphological code indicating the irregularity.) Using this code, a function (named MORPH, called from LEXIC) took a word of input and attempted to strip off regular endings in such a way that the remaining root was a word in the dictionary whose morphological code agreed with the endings which had been removed. This mechanism made for considerably more compact dictionaries than if all inflected forms had to be stored.

Unfortunately, for languages with very complex morphological structures this method may not be adequate. It has been suggested [Grimes, 1975] that for such languages the input words be hyphenated and that separate levels of the grammar be written to do the detailed morphological decompositions.

Besides the parts of speech and features, the dictionary may also contain information about substitutions which should be made in the input string or compounds which should be collapsed. For example, the following may be considered equivalent:

United States
United States of America
USA
United-States

If the last form is chosen to be the "standard" one, the first two can be collapsed to it and the third can be expanded to it by either a prepass on the input or by the function LEXIC which gets the next word of input from the string.

SYNTACTIC ANALYSIS OF WRITTEN POLISH

Stanisław Szpakowicz

Institute of Informatics

University of Warsaw

Pałac Kultury i Nauki, pok. 850

00-901 Warszawa, POLAND

Abstract

The aim of the paper is to give an idea of methodology and of technical solutions used in the design of an experimental syntax-oriented program to process Polish texts; the program is currently being developed by the author. A classification of Polish words is presented. It is based on the notion of syntactic category and it covers in principle most of the inflexional and syntactic features of words. Polish syntax is to be described by means of a formal grammar; the description takes into account some newer results concerning the syntactic function of particular word classes. The formalism used to describe syntax is the Colmerauer's metamorphic grammar. The program will be implemented in PROLOG, the powerful programming language in which metamorphic grammars are directly available. The output of the program will be the surface syntactic structure of each sentence. Next, a subset of Polish is specified. The subset consists of sentences to be processed by the program. Finally, some details of the program are given.

1. Introduction

Syntactic analysis may be understood in several ways, depending on the definition or the description of syntax itself and on the task performed by the analysis process, for example by some algorithm (program, system). The analysis may concern texts, or single sentences, or phrases. The results of analysis depend again on the definition of syntactic units and relations between them.

I use the results of Saloni (1976) as the theoretical foundation of my syntax definition; I confine myself to sentences (compound clauses as well as simple clauses); I ignore the interrogative sentences for the time being. Syntax describes formal relations between words. It gives the rules allowing to recognize the syntactic function of each word in the sentence by indicating the possibility of locating it in the abstract syntactic structure of the sentence, e.g. in such units as noun-phrase, verb-phrase, adjective-phrase etc.

Recognition of the relations is based on the occurrence of some required inflexional ending or on another similar formal representation. The syntactic relations consist first of all in matching the values of such grammatical categories as case, gender, number and person; among the matchings of such kind agreement and government are traditionally distinguished. The important problem is also to recognize in the sentence obligatory subordinate constituents, which are syntactically implied by the head of the construction. I do not consider any semantic interdependence of words.

The words are the basic constituents of a sentence. I do not use the notion of morphemes, that is, I do not distinguish stems and affixes. Instead, I assume that each word is supplied with sufficient inflexional and syntactic information. This can be achieved by some dictionary-based preprocessing of the input sentence.

The outcome of syntactic analysis is the sentence representation revealing its structure and the relations between particular words. It might be, for instance, a tree of parsing.

2. The scope of syntactic description of words

Polish is the inflexional language, so the inflexional features of a word determine to some extent its syntactic rôle. The word order is definitely less important from the point of view of Polish syntax, though it has some impact on the stylistic and semantic characteristics of the sentence.

I distinguish seven inflexional categories. They are as follows:

1) Case, assuming six values - nominative, genitive, dative, accusative, instrumental, locative.
2) Gender; it is useful to single out at least six distinct values, which are the following:
   a) masculine-personal (e.g. "chłopiec" - "boy");
   b) masculine-animate ("kogut" - "cock");
   c) masculine-inanimate ("stół" - "table");
   d) feminine ("kobieta", "noga" - "woman", "leg");
   e) neuter ("dziecko", "okno" - "child", "window");
   f) plurale tantum ("rodzeństwo", "drzwi" - "siblings", "door").
3) Number - singular, plural.
4) Person - first, second, third.
5) Degree - positive, comparative, superlative.
6) Mood - indicative, imperative, conditional.
7) Tense; it is sufficient to distinguish only two possible values - past and nonpast (the compound future will be treated at the level of syntax).

Sometimes it is useful to distinguish, besides the values mentioned above, the universal value 0 (i.e. "another value"), for instance: the case 0, realised as an empty word, like in an implied first person subject; the degree 0, which means that an adjective has no comparative and superlative degree.

I assume that words can be gathered into sets called lexemes, which group words differing only in the value of some grammatical category (or values of categories). A lexeme may be thought of as a dictionary entry of the kind used e.g. in the great dictionary of Polish (Doroszewski 1958).

The proper inflexional category of a word is the category that determines some opposition within the lexeme to which the word belongs. It is easiest to define each lexeme by simply listing its elements and indicating which inflexional features are actually relevant. Here are the examples of proper inflexional categories: the case of a noun; the gender of an adjective; the number of a personal verb.

The selective inflexional category is the category which itself does not constitute any opposition. Instead it determines the value of the proper inflexional category of a governed word. For instance: a preposition decides the case of a noun; a noun has the selective category of gender which determines the gender of an adjective connected with the noun. The selective category can coincide with the proper category (e.g. the case of a noun is proper and at same time selective from the point of view of an adjective).

The generalized selective category or the syntactic requirement has to do with syntactic implication. If a word implies, say, an infinitive, I recognize infinitive as the value of the syntactic requirement of this word. A word can require: nothing; an infinitive; an adjective; a noun in a particular case; an adverb or an adverbial modifier; a preposition group; and several combinations of the above. Moreover a subordinate clause can be required, as in "wiem, że..." ("I know that ..."). All mentioned word categories are understood syntactically, that is "an infinitive" stands for every distributive equivalent of an infinitive, for instance for an infinitive modified by an adverb.

I assume for the sake of clarity that no word has more than three different requirements at a time; the assumption seems to be justified in almost all cases.

The inflexional categories (both proper and selective) and the syntactic requirements I treat jointly and I call them syntactic categories.

Below I present the classification of words according to the combinations of relevant syntactic categories. Irrelevant ones are ignored. Basically each class has a unique selection of categories. Several classes are further subdivided. Needless to say, the classification is arbitrary, although relatively well suited to the recent results in the morphology and syntax (Saloni 1974, 1976a); there are also some similarities to the ideas expressed in (Misz 1971) and (Misz, Szupryczyńska 1971).

I use the following abbreviations: c - case, g - gender, n -

number, p - person, d - degree, m - mood, t - tense, r1, r2, r3 - requirements (an absent one may be assigned the value "nothing" for greater consistency). The symbol x_o means that the category x has a fixed value regardless of the values of remaining categories. Proper categories, selective categories and requirements are separated by semicolons, "-" means that the respective group of categories is wholly absent. I omit the selective categories coinciding with some proper ones.

Word class	Categories
1) Noun	$c,n;g,p_o;-$
2) Substantival pronoun (e.g. "ja" - "I")	$c,n_o;g,p;-$
3) Adjective	c,g,n,d;-;
4) Adjectival pronoun ("taki" - "such")	c,g,n;-;-
5) Adverb	d;-;-
6) Adverbial pronoun ("tak" - "so")	-;-;-
7) Numeral	$c,g;n_o;-$
8) Preposition	-;c;-
9) Conjunction	-;-;-
10) Personal verb	g,n,p,m,t;-;r1,r2,r3
This class includes three subclasses for which different sets of proper categories are relevant. These are:	
10.1) Imperative verb	$n,p,m_o,t_o;-;r1,r2,r3$
10.2) Present (or simple future) verb ("idę", "przyjdę" - "I go", "I shall come")	$n,p,m_o,t_o;-;r1,r2,r3$

10.3) Past verb ("znałem" - "I knew") g,n,p,m,t_o;-;r1,r2,r3

11) Impersonal verb ("zrobiono" - "one did" or "it was done") m;-;r1,r2,r3

12) Infinitive -;-;r1,r2,r3

13) Gerund c,n;g_o,p_o;r1,r2,r3

14) Adjectival participle c,n,g;-;r1,r2,r3

This class is further divided into two subclasses with distinct syntactic functions but with identical categories:

14.1) Active participle ("idący" - "going" as in "a going man")

14.2) Passive participle ("bity" - "beaten")

15) Adverbial participle ("idąc" - "going" as in "he slept, going") -;-;r1,r2,r3

16) Auxiliary verb "będę" ("shall", "will") constituting the compound future n,p;-;-

17) Unclassified, i.e. anything else; this class has no syntactic categories.

Remarks:

a) An adjective may have certain requirements which will be taken into account later.

b) At the present stage of research the list of categories of the numeral is still incomplete.

c) Certain characteristics of the conjunction can be categorized, for example affinity to another conjunction, say, "either" to "or", "if" to "then". Such facts will be investigated later.

d) The mood of present verbs is fixed otherwise than that of imperative verbs.

e) The class "unclassified" may be further diversified to include proper names, numbers, abbreviations, scientific symbols, foreign throw-ins etc.

The process of assigning each word in a given sentence a set of values of its syntactic categories I call syntactic preprocessing. A simple search algorithm will suffice if only the search space is properly organized. One approach can consist in writing down all inflexional forms of all words of vocabulary. The dictionary obtained in such a way should also include selective categories and requirements.

I assume that the syntactic preprocessing can be relatively easy to implement or at any rate easy to simulate. It is so because no connections between words need to be analysed. The syntactic categories of a word can be singled out solely on the basis of its appearance. Any possible ambiguities can be solved just by repeating an appropriate dictionary entry as many times (with suitable values of categories) as is needed to account for those ambiguities. Therefore in further considerations I shall use freely all necessary syntactic information.

The above classification and the grammatical characterization of word classes have been already outlined and partially verified in the MARYSIA system (Bień et al. 1973, 1973a, 1973b, 1974; Łukaszewicz, Szpakowicz 1973, 1974, 1976).

3. The method of syntax description

Syntax is described by means of a formal grammar. Syntactically preprocessed words are the terminal symbols of this grammar. The non-terminal symbols (further referred to as syntactic units) are chosen more or less arbitrarily, although according to some linguistic intuitions. The productions, which I call replacement rules, define the structure of syntactic units. The topmost unit, or theaxiom of the grammar, is SENTENCE. At the bottom, nearest to the words, are syntactic units representing any word of a particular class (cf 2). Actually the syntactic units are not listed explicitly, they are instead given implicitly by a set of rules. The words are not listed at all: the set of words is determined by the content of a dictionary.

The task of syntactic analysis consists in mapping an analysed sentence onto an appropriate structure; such mapping need not be unique but it should reflect the fundamental characteristics of a sentence. Within the adopted set of replacement rules one should be able to find (for each sentence of a predefined collection) at least one sequence of rules which constitutes a derivation of a given sentence from the axiom of the grammar. The derivation should comprise every match needed to take into account values of syntactic categories of words which make the sentence. Every syntactic unit has also some syntactic categories due to the word class distributively equivalent to i These are the external categories of a unit which determine its connections, as a whole, with another constituents of a sentence. If a unit includes something more than a single specimen of a word class, then i has its own internal structure expressed by means of suitable category matches. This structure is hidden from above but it must be revealed if the analysis is to be complete.

The structure found out in the course of analysis I call surface syntactic structure. The only considered features of a word are its word class characteristics. Any word of a given class can be substituted for another one provided that both have identical values of all syntactic categories; the resulting surface syntactic structure is the same in both cases. On the other hand, changing order of two different neighbouring units renders a different (however similar) structure, although both structures may differ only at the lowest level.

The surface syntactic structure can be represented by a parsing tree. Every rule used during analysis specifies a parent node and its daughter nodes. The leaves of such a tree are the syntactically preprocessed words. An augmented version of a parsing tree might be a parsing graph, produced from the tree by linking up all pairs of nodes which have some matching category. Every such link would be an arch labelled with name and value of an appropriate category. All syntactic relations observed in a sentence would be thus fully exposed.

Some well known facts should be pointed out. It is practically impossible to describe the natural language in extenso by means of a formal grammar. It would be unrealistic, if at all possible. A reasonably chosen subset of the language can be, however, described in a sufficiently detailed manner. A carefully selected collection of syntactic units makes it possible to write down such a set of rules that is highly plausible as a starting point of some computer-based implementation. The same is valid in case of vocabulary, which should be always considered as specific to some application.

At the present stage of research it is convenient to express syntactic relations by means of context-free rules with parameters. Those parameters stand for syntactic categories. The rule with a parameter can be treated as an abbreviation of a set of rules concerning individual values of the parameter.

The parameter can occur in various units in the same rule; it assumes then the same value. This means that the corresponding syntactic categories have identical value. This is how the matching is realized. If the proper inflexional categories of two units match, then it may be interpreted roughly as agreement (for instance, the connection between the case of a noun and of an adjective can be thus reflected). If the proper category of a unit matches the selective category of another unit, then we can interpret it as government (in this mannner the gender of a noun and of an adjective can be matched). Similarly the syntactic requirement can be matched with an appropriate word class of a required unit. In general, matching the values of syntactic categories enables us to render distributive similarities of different syntactic units, such as noun phrases with different order of complexity.

The motivation underlying the choice of syntactic units is strictly distributive. The word class may be (slightly imprecisely) thought of as including items which are distributively equivalent but have different degree of complexity in some specific sense. It is then convenient to distinguish a number of subclasses of a word class;

they should have approximately the same degree of complexity. I call such subclasses phrases. The phrases can be arranged in a sequence according to their growing complexity. The simplest phrase is just a single word of an appropriate class. The phrase of each next degree consists of some phrases of the previous degree (in particular, of only one). The phrases are linked up by means of conjunctions or, speaking more precisely, by means of constructions syntactically equivalent to conjunctions. The phrase of the lowest degree may be either a single word or (recursively) a highest degree phrase; it is an illustration of the fact that the phrases of all degrees are essentially equivalent from the standpoint of distribution.

The number of degrees is arbitrary. It seems to me, though, that it should conform to the experimentally determined relative frequency of respective constructions in a given text corpus.

In order to attain the greatest possible generality of replacement rules one should always choose the most complicated phrase to stand for an element of a word class: this phrase can be directly replaced by any less complicated one.

As an example, let us consider the sequence of syntactic equivalents of a noun. A "series of noun phrases" (SNP) consists of one or more "noun phrases"; each of those includes, in turn, one or more "single-noun phrases". A single-noun phrase deprived of all adverbial modifiers (that are insignificant from the point of view of fundamental syntactic relations) makes a "trimmed single-noun phrase", which may be one of the following: a substantival pronoun; a noun accompanied by an attribute, which can be, by the way, a fairly complicated adjective phrase; the same plus an SNP in genitive case; one of the mentioned above with numerals involved; moreover the phrase can include subordinate clause.

I introduce the phrases related to the following word classes: noun, verb (classes 10, 11), adjective, adverb, infinitive, numeral. Every member of each of the classes can be located at various levels of the syntactic structure of the sentence, depending on the degree of complexity of a relevant phrase. For instance, "he" in "he fences" is treated as an SNP, in "he and Jack fence" - as a "noun phrase", whereas in "either he and Jack or Jim and Joe fence" - as a "single--noun phrase".

Here are a few examples of rules, connected with the noun-like phrases described above. Let us assume that every such phrase has four parameters: case, number, gender, person. The names of syntactic units and the constant parameters are written in block letters. The sequence number is not the part of a rule.

1) SERNOUNPHR(case,numb,gend,pers) = NOUNPHR(case,numb,gend,pers)

2) SERNOUNPHR(case,PLURAL,gend,pers) = NOUNPHR(case,numb2,gend2,pers2)
CONJUNC SERNOUNPHR(case,numb3,gend3,pers3)

3) NOUNPHR(case,numb,gend,pers) = SNGLNOUNPHR(case,numb,gend,pers)

4) NOUNPHR(case,PLURAL,gend,pers) = SNGLNOUNPHR(case,numb2,gend2,
pers2) CONJUNC NOUNPHR(case,numb3,gend3,pers3)

5) SNGLNOUNPHR(case,numb,gend,pers) = TRIMSNGLNOUNP(case,numb,gend,per

6) TRIMSNGLNOUNP(case,numb,gend,pers) = NOUNATTR(case,numb,gend,pers)

7) TRIMSNGLNOUNP(case,numb,gend,pers) = NOUNATTR(case,numb,gend,pers)
SERNOUNPHR(GENITIVE,numb2,gend2,pers2)

Each rule is applied according to the left-to-right principle. That is, a rule reads: a left side syntactic unit is to be replaced by a sequence of right side units, if the sections of a sentence, corresponding to the right side units, are contiguous. Moreover, all categories supposed to match should actually match.

Note that in case of the rules 2 and 4 an additional procedure ought to be used which adjusts the gender of a left side to the genders of all right sides. Care should be also taken that more subtle rules are used to handle special cases of number and gender adjustment. As an example let us consider the sentence:"Dziecko, koń i kobieta przyszli" ("A child, a horse and a woman have come"). Each of the nouns has different gender, neither is masculine-personal, which is the case with the whole group. Another example: "Jan lub Piotr przyjdzie" ("John or Peter will come"), where the group is to be treated as singular.

4. The tools for describing and analysing syntax

A grammar of the kind described in the previous section can be directly and conveniently expressed as a metamorphic grammar. The metamorphic grammars have been invented by Colmerauer (1975) and already proved in practice as useful means of defining some formal properties of a natural language (Battani, Meloni 1975). Metamorphic grammars are said to be at least as powerful as context-sensitive grammars. It is then presumably even more than is currently needed from the standpoint of surface syntactic analysis of written Polish.

Analysis of words belonging to a language defined by a metamorphic grammar can be easily implemented in the PROLOG programming language. In fact, the grammar rules themselves are translated one-to-one into PROLOG subprograms. (By the way, synthesis of language elements is equally easily available in PROLOG; it is a very appealing property of metamorphic grammars implementation.)

PROLOG has been designed and developed by Colmerauer's team (Roussel 1975). It is an implementation of the idea of programming in predicate calculus, which has been advocated e.g. by Kowalski (197 1974), and it actually exceeds the capabilities of first order logic. Externally it can be viewed as a theorem prover for the facts expressed in clausal form, which is based on the SL-resolution principle (Kowalski, Kuehner 1971). Internally, certain side-effects of a proving process, such as substitutions necessary to unify appropriate literals, result in that PROLOG is a very powerful, concise and elegant programming language. It is not, however, particularly efficient.

The basic data structures in PROLOG are terms, or tree structures. The proof procedure, and therefore control flow, is top-down, depth-first with backtracking in case of failure. A program in PROLOG is made of subprograms, each consisting of a sequence of clauses, and a sequence of invoking clauses which can be interpreted as subprogram calls. The choice of a clause within a subprogram resembles a case statement with a set of parameters as a selector. It is then a kind of pattern-directed procedure invocation where the pattern-matching process is carried out by means of unification.

The metamorphic grammar rules can be straightly incorporated into a PROLOG program. They are in fact treated as a part of the program, since each rule corresponds to a clause. A set of rules can be thus regarded as a predicate calculus version of a language definition. The rules "work" in two directions: they can be used equally well during analysis and during synthesis of elements of a given language. Activation of any of those processes requires a PROLOG command. This command specifies both the direction of a process and the parameters which indicate a particular object submitted to the process.

The metamorphic grammars in PROLOG are especially handy for two reasons. First, one can interpret any parameter of a syntactic unit as another syntactic unit; a distinguished nonterminal NT(x1,...,xn) is interpreted reughly as a nonterminal x1(x2,...,xn). If x1 is a unit name, then the nonterminal x1(x2,...,xn) makes this unit. The second reason is the possibility of inserting in the right side of a rule any number of procedure calls which are called conditions. They are verbatim transmitted to the clause corresponding to a rule and they explicitly condition the use of the rule: the activation of a literal must succeed unless the rule is to be abandoned. Moreover, some useful action may be done, like gender and number adjustment of a noun-like phrase.

5. The specification of a subset of Polish

Here are the properties of a subset of Polish, to be actually processed by a preliminary version of a syntactic analysis and synthesis system which is currently being implemented in PROLOG. For the sake of the system it is useful to determine what is meant by a sentence from the technical point of view: it is each section of an input text terminated by a period or a semicolon. The task of syntax analysis of a sentence consists in examining its syntactic correctness (that is, its accordance with a given set of replacement rules which implicitly define the notion of correctness); every correct sentence should be assigned its surface syntactic structure. Punctuation must be correct too.

The subset of Polish includes then all and only those sentences that conform themselves to the restrictions listed below.

1) Only proper clauses are considered, indicative or conditional. Compound clauses are admissible too. (By a proper clause I mean a clause which has at least one predicate; e.g. a sole noun phrase would not be accepted.)
2) No ellipses are allowed, e.g. "Dali wczoraj." ("They gave yesterday.") is not accepted.
3) The phrases ought to be continuous: no two distinct phrases should interlace, e.g. "Dobrym jest on lekarzem."("He is a good physician.") is not accepted.
4) The word order should be approximately neutral, although permutations of whole phrases are possible.

A finite verb is the pivot of a Polish sentence. It is the verb belonging to word classes 10 and 11. The members of word classes 12-15 play a specific rôle in a sentence too, due to their syntactic requirements. Corresponding items of classes 10-15 have (with few exceptions) identical requirements. These classes have been therefore collected into a superclass of verb derivatives. A new syntactic category has been introduced: it is called derivational discriminant and it applies only to a verb derivative, dividing it into original classes.

I follow here the idea of verb derivatives formulated by Tokarski (1973). It has also (in a specific form) occurred in the MARYSIA system.

A verb derivative is the central syntactic unit of a generalized verbal construction built of the derivative itself and of the units required by it. According to the principle given earlier, each requirement is satisfied by the most complicated phrase which can stand for an element of a required word class. For instance, if a verb derivative requires a noun in dative case, then we refer to a "series of noun phrases" in dative. The verbal construction with a fixed discriminant makes a special case of: verb phrase, adjective phrase, adverb phrase, infinitive phrase. It is then convenient for the technical reason too, as it allows us to limit the number of replacement rules.

The syntactic units which may correspond to single words I regard as elementary units. The elementary units are associated with each of classes 1-16, with five subclasses of classes 10 and 14, and with the superclass of verb derivatives. Every elementary unit is given the parameters that are necessary to stand for all syntactic categories of a suitable class; moreover it has an additional parameter which represents a word form belonging to that class. For instance the elementary unit NOUN has five parameters that correspond to a word form, case, number, gender and person, respectively.

The elementary units are, in some sense, terminal units with respect to the definition of the subset of Polish. That is, within a surface syntactic structure any representative of a word class may be substituted for an elementary unit related to the class, and the structure will remain unchanged (obviously, semantic considerations would be needed to restrict the number of permissible substitutions). As a matter of fact, a description of syntax (in the sense adopted here) should well do without lexical items, since their only features relevant to syntax are their syntactic categories.

6. The organization of an experimental program

The syntactic analysis program has not been implement yet. Below I shall present some technical decisions which will be thoroughly tested soon.

The replacement rules constituting the syntax definition are the global rules. They apply to every sentence of the subset of Polish which has been described above, provided that each word of the sentence is linked to a corresponding elementary unit. This can be accomplished via syntactic preprocessing. If a separate sentence ought to be analysed, then it will be sufficient to complement the global rules with those and only those specific rules which concern this sentence. These rules can be regarded as local (to the sentence). A local rule defines an elementary unit having a specified word form parameter as this particular word form. The form is supplied with pertinent syntactic categories.

The global rules would be the constant part of a PROLOG program. The local rules would be exchangeable: they would vary from one sentence to another. In the current tentative version, though, the arrangement of rules is slightly different, because not only syntactic preprocessing but also the dictionary are simulated as yet. I use the distinguished nonterminal NT (cf 4). There is one global rule for each elementary unit. For example, a rule for the NOUN unit is:

NOUN(form,case,numb,gend,pers) == NT(form,case,numb,gend,pers)

(The double "=" separates left and right sides of a rule.)

For a fixed word form, NT(form,case,numb,gend,pers) corresponds to a nonterminal

form(case,numb,gend,pers)

If the parameter "form" has the value, say, PIŁKĘ ("a ball", accusative), then the nonterminal looks like this:

PIŁKĘ(ACC,SING,FEM,3)

The vocabulary is composed of word forms. Every form has one or more readings with respect to its syntactic categories. There is a rule for each reading, with a nonterminal of the above form at the left side of the rule and with a word form at the right. The word form is written as a metamorphic grammar terminal (prefixed by a special symbol, say, a #, to distinguish it from nonterminals). For example, the set of rules for the word przyjaciela (a friend) may be as follows:

PRZYJACIELA(GEN,SING,MASCPERS,3) == #PRZYJACIELA

PRZYJACIELA(ACC,SING,MASCPERS,3) == #PRZYJACIELA

This is how the syntactic preprocessing is simulated.

Beneath I shall give the list of non-elementary syntactic units which occur at the left sides of global replacement rules. The list must not be regarded as complete or definitive, because the set of rules made up so far ought to be verified and then perhaps modified in order to mirror more adequately the characteristics of the chosen subset of Polish. The verification would be carried out with some particular text corpus.

The list of non-elementary syntactic units is the following:

1) Sentence

2) Subject

3) Predicate
4) Noun phrases (four degress of complexity)
5) Verb phrases (u.s.)
6) Infinitive phrases (u.s.)
7) Adjective phrases (three degress of complexity)
8) Adverb phrases (u.s.)
9) Numeral phrases (u.s.)
10) Conjunctive construction (such as "a także", "jak również" - "also", "as well as")
11) Verbal construction (cf 5)
12) Verb with requirements, a separate unit for each of these situations: no requirement, noun required, preposition plus noun required, two nouns required, noun and preposition plus non required, subordinate clause required; this list can be amplified in the future.
13) An undetermined so far number of subordinate clauses, such as those connected with "że" ("that") or "który" ("which", "who").
14) Negation NIE, realized as the word "nie" or as an empty word.
15) Noun with attributes (introduced mainly for technical reasons).
16) Adjective with modifiers (u.s.)

The list will be probably expanded as a result of the verification mentioned above. Punctuation will be also taken into account, as in the initial outline it is not considered at all.

Syntactic analysis or synthesis of a sentence is activated by means of a special PROLOG command SYN with two parameters. The first parameter is an axiom of the metamorphic grammar (SENTENCE in our case), the second is the sentence put down as a concatenated list of consecutive words and punctuation marks. For purely technical reasons each syntactic unit will have an additional parameter used to transmit succesive approximations of a parsing tree produced during analysis. The same parameter will indicate the parsing tree of a sentence to be produced during synthesis. The tree will be transmitted as a term.

In the case of analysis the initial value of tree parameter of SENTENCE should be a free variable; the final value would then be a parsing tree. In the case of synthesis the second parameter of SYN command, initially a free variable, would eventually receive the sentence representation as a result.

The information connected with a node of a parsing tree may be as complicated as necessary. The term corresponding to the node may have any number of parameters. The daughter nodes (which are terms themselves) must be among them; one can also choose, for instance, to place in the node an information concerning some match of the daughter nodes, such as name and value of a matching syntactic category.

I shall present below a sample term which corresponds to a parsing tree of the sentence: "Syn mojej siostry i córka przyjaciela wczoraj znaleźli piłkę i zabrali ją do domu" ("The son of my sister and the friend's daughter found a ball yesterday and took it home"). For the sake of clarity I have simplified the term by omitting less significant stages of analysis; for instance, I have neglected all single-unit phrases (such as "single-noun phrase", cf 3), because they are not important in this example. I have also removed from the nodes almost all syntactic categories. The remaining categories appear as first parameters of the suitable nodes; other parameters are the daughter nodes (or the word forms in case of the nodes that describe elementary units).

The names of nodes have the following meanings:

SNP = series of noun phrases, NP = noun phrase, NP1T = trimmed single--noun phrase ;

SVP, VP, VP1T = as above for verbs;

ADJP, ADJP1T = similarly for adjectives;

VCON = verbal construction, VRN = verb requiring noun, VRNPR = verb requiring noun and preposition (plus noun).

MASP means masculin-personal, MASI - masculin-inanimate; another names are, hopefully, self-explanatory.

Four subterms (denoted ① - ④) have been taken out of the term so that it would be easier to read it. The items corresponding to daughter nodes have been succesively indented. The word forms have been underlined.

```
SENTENCE(SUBJECT(PL,
                 SNP(NOM,PL,MASP,
                     ①,
                     CONJ(I),
                     ② )),
         PREDICATE(PL,
                   SVP(PERS,MASP,PL,
                       ③ ,
                       CONJ(I),
                       ④ )) )
```

(1)

```
NP(NOM,SING,MASP,
   NP1T(NOM,SING,MASP,
        NOUN(NOM,SING,MASP,SYN),
      SNP(GEN,SING,FEM,
          NP(GEN,SING,FEM,
             NP1T(GEN,SING,FEM,
                  ADJP(GEN,SING,FEM,
                       ADJP1T(GEN,SING,FEM,
                              ADJPRON(GEN,SING,FEM,MOJEJ))),
                       NOUN(GEN,SING,FEM,SIOSTRY)) )))))
```

(2)

```
NP(NOM,SING,FEM,
   NP1T(NOM,SING,FEM,
        NOUN(NOM,SING,FEM,CÓRKA),
        SNP(GEN,SING,MASP,
            NP(GEN,SING,MASP,
               NP1T(GEN,SING,MASP,
                    NOUN(GEN,SING,MASP,PRZYJACIELA)) )) ))
```

(3)

```
VP(PERS,MASP,PL,3,
   MODIFIER(
               ADVERB(WCZORAJ)),
   VP1T(PERS,MASP,PL,3,
        VCON(PERS,MASP,PL,3,
             VRN(PERS,MASP,PL,3,ACC,
                 VERBPERS(MASP,PL,3,ACC,ZNALEŹLI),
                 SNP(ACC,SING,FEM,
                     NP(ACC,SING,FEM,
                        NP1T(ACC,SING,FEM,
                             NOUN(ACC,SING,FEM,PIŁKE)))) ))))
```

(4)

```
VP(PERS,MASP,PL,3,
   VP1T(PERS,MASP,PL,3,
        VCON(PERS,MASP,PL,3,
             VRNPR(PERS,MASP,PL,3,ACC,
                   VERBPERS(MASP,PL,3,ACC,ZABRALI),
                    SNP(ACC,SING,FEM,
                        NP(ACC,SING,FEM,
                           NP1T(ACC,SING,FEM,
                                SUBSPRON(ACC,SING,FEM,JA)))),
                   PREP(GEN,DO),
                   SNP(GEN,SING,MASI,
                       NP(GEN,SING,MASI,
                          NP1T(GEN,SING,MASI,
                               NOUN(GEN,SING,MASI,DOMU)))) ))))
```

The structure of the sentence revealed during analysis is roughly represented by this term. It can also be shown (in a simplified manner) in the following parenthesized form:

((((syn)(mojej siostry))(i)((córka)(przyjaciela)))

(((wczoraj)((znaleźli)(piłkę)))(i)((zabrali)(ją)(do domu))))

7. Conclusion

Automatic processing of Polish syntax reached only the preliminary phase of investigation. The task of this phase consists in disclosing problems and in indicating the course of further research. The syntax definition must be verified, corrected and improved. The set of rules must be then expanded to cover some richer subsets of the language; it seems that the restrictions as to word order and continuity of phrases would be dropped first. Well structured dictionary accompanied by a reasonably organized lookup should make syntactic preprocessing more efficient and flexible than in the current version.

The research should be carried on in two interacting directions. First, it is necessary to study Polish syntax, especially from the point of view of computer applications. Next, looking for even more sophisticated programming tools is essential to implement more powerful syntax processing systems. The results achieved in both directions will probably allow better insight into problems which arise during the work at automatic processing of natural language texts.

References

(Battani,Meloni 1975) G.Battani, H.Meloni, "Mise en oeuvre des contraintes phonologiques, syntaxiques et semantiques dans un systeme de comprehension automatique de la parole". G.I.A., Université d'Aix-Marseille, June 1975.

(Bień et al. 1973) J.St.Bień, W.Łukaszewicz, S.Szpakowicz, "Wprowadzenie do systemu MARYSIA". Reports of the Warsaw University Computation Centre, No 39, 1973.

(Bień et al. 1973a) J.St.Bień, W.Łukaszewicz, S.Szpakowicz, "Opis systemu MARYSIA. I. Zasady pisania scenariusza i scenopisu". Reports of the Warsaw University Computation Centre, No 41, 1973.

(Bień et al. 1973b) J.St.Bień, W.Łukaszewicz, S.Szpakowicz, "Opis systemu MARYSIA. II. Wprowadzanie haseł do systemu". Reports of the Warsaw University Computation Centre, No 42, 1973.

(Bień et al. 1974) J.St.Bień, W.Łukaszewicz, S.Szpakowicz, "Opis systemu MARYSIA. III. Tworzenie części gramatycznych słowników systemu". Reports of the Warsaw University Computation Centre,No 43, 1974.

(Colmerauer 1975) A.Colmerauer, "Les grammaires de metamorphose". G.I.A., Université d'Aix-Marseille, November 1975. (Also in this volume.)

(Doroszewski 1958) W.Doroszewski (ed.),"Słownik Języka Polskiego", vol. I-XI. Warszawa 1958-1969.

(Kowalski 1973) R.Kowalski, "Predicate calculus as programming language". D.C.L. Memo 70, University of Edinburgh, 1973.

(Kowalski 1974) R.Kowalski, "Logic for problem solving". D.C.L. Memo 75, University of Edinburgh, 1974.

(Kowalski, Kuehner 1971) R.Kowalski, D.Kuehner, "Linear resolution with selection function". Artificial Intelligence 2, 1971, pp.227-260.

(Łukaszewicz, Szpakowicz 1973) W.Łukaszewicz, S.Szpakowicz, "Stan prac nad systemem MARYSIA". In: "Zastosowanie maszyn matematycznych do badań nad językiem naturalnym". Wydawnictwa UW 1973, pp. 34-41.

(Łukaszewicz, Szpakowicz 1974) W.Łukaszewicz, S.Szpakowicz, "Charakterystyka systemu MARYSIA". In: "Systemy wyszukiwania informacji", PWN 1974, pp. 181-186.

(Łukaszewicz, Szpakowicz 1976) W.Lukaszewicz, S.Szpakowicz, "System konwersacyjny MARYSIA". In: "Zastosowanie maszyn matematycznych do badań nad językiem naturalnym II", Wydawnictwa UW 1976, pp. 127-137.

(Misz 1967) H.Misz, "Opis grup syntaktycznych dzisiejszej polszczyzny pisanej". Bydgoszcz 1967.

(Misz, Szupryczyńska 1971) H.Misz, M.Szupryczyńska, "Nad zagadnieniem deskryptorów dla niewspółrzędnych grup syntaktycznych dzisiejszej polszczyzny pisanej". In: "Problemy składni polskiej", Warszawa 1971.

(Roussel 1975) Ph.Roussel," PROLOG, manuel de reference et d'utilisation". G.I.A., Université d'Aix-Marseille, September 1975.

(Saloni 1974) Z.Saloni, "Klasyfikacja gramatyczna leksemów polskich". "Język Polski" LIV (1974), vol. 1, pp. 3-13, vol. 2, pp. 93-101.

(Saloni 1976) Z.Saloni, "Cechy składniowe polskiego czasownika". Wrocław 1976.

(Saloni 1976a) Z.Saloni, "Kategoria rodzaju we współczesnym języku polskim". In: "Kategorie gramatyczne grup imiennych w języku polskim", Wrocław 1976.

(Tokarski 1973) J.Tokarski, "Fleksja polska". Warszawa 1973.

Vol. 49: Interactive Systems. Proceedings 1976. Edited by A. Blaser and C. Hackl. VI, 380 pages. 1976.

Vol. 50: A. C. Hartmann, A Concurrent Pascal Compiler for Minicomputers. VI, 119 pages. 1977.

Vol. 51: B. S. Garbow, Matrix Eigensystem Routines – Eispack Guide Extension. VIII, 343 pages. 1977.

Vol. 52: Automata, Languages and Programming. Fourth Colloquium, University of Turku, July 1977. Edited by A. Salomaa and M. Steinby. X, 569 pages. 1977.

Vol. 53: Mathematical Foundations of Computer Science. Proceedings 1977. Edited by J. Gruska. XII, 608 pages. 1977.

Vol. 54: Design and Implementation of Programming Languages. Proceedings 1976. Edited by J. H. Williams and D. A. Fisher. X, 496 pages. 1977.

Vol. 55: A. Gerbier, Mes premières constructions de programmes. XII, 256 pages. 1977.

Vol. 56: Fundamentals of Computation Theory. Proceedings 1977. Edited by M. Karpiński. XII, 542 pages. 1977.

Vol. 57: Portability of Numerical Software. Proceedings 1976. Edited by W. Cowell. VIII, 539 pages. 1977.

Vol. 58: M. J. O'Donnell, Computing in Systems Described by Equations. XIV, 111 pages. 1977.

Vol. 59: E. Hill, Jr., A Comparative Study of Very Large Data Bases. X, 140 pages. 1978.

Vol. 60: Operating Systems, An Advanced Course. Edited by R. Bayer, R. M. Graham, and G. Seegmüller. X, 593 pages. 1978.

Vol. 61: The Vienna Development Method: The Meta-Language. Edited by D. Bjørner and C. B. Jones. XVIII, 382 pages. 1978.

Vol. 62: Automata, Languages and Programming. Proceedings 1978. Edited by G. Ausiello and C. Böhm. VIII, 508 pages. 1978.

Vol. 63: Natural Language Communication with Computers. Edited by Leonard Bolc. VI, 292 pages. 1978.